Politics in Familiar Contexts: Projecting Politics Through Popular Media

Communication: The Human Context

Politics in Familiar Contexts: Projecting Politics Through Popular Media

Robert L. Savage and Dan Nimmo, Editors

 ABLEX PUBLISHING CORPORATION
NORWOOD, NEW JERSEY

mah

Library of Congress Cataloging-in-Publication Data

Politics in familiar contexts: projecting politics through popular media / Robert L. Savage and Dan Nimmo, editors.
    p.   cm. — (Communication, the human context)
    Bibliography: p.
    Includes index.
    ISBN 0-89391-508-4
    1. Mass media—Political aspects.   I. Savage, Robert L.
II. Nimmo, Dan D.   III. Series.
P95.8.P65 1989
302.23—dc20   89–14901
                                    CIP

Ablex Publishing Corporation
355 Chestnut Street
Norwood, New Jersey 07648

6-14-91

Contents

The Contributors

S. Elizabeth Bird has taught in anthropology, folklore, and mass communication. Recent publications have appeared in *Communication Yearbook 10, Journalism Educator,* and *Folklore.* She is currently an Independent Scholar affiliated with the Institute of Women's Studies at the University of Minnesota–Duluth and conducting research for a book on American weekly tabloid newspapers from a cultural studies perspective.

Jeremy G. Butler is associate professor of broadcast and film communication at the University of Alabama. He has contributed recent articles on television soap opera and film melodrama to *Cinema Journal* and *Jump Cut,* and has written on *Miami Vice* for the *Journal of Popular Film and Television.*

Katherine Hale is assistant professor of communication at Oklahoma Baptist University. Her teaching and research interests include mass and political communication, publishing several articles in the latter field.

Michael R. Hemphill is associate professor of speech communication at the University of Arkansas at Little Rock. His teaching and research interests focus on organizational communication and technology, publishing in communication journals.

Lynda Lee Kaid is professor of communication at the University of Oklahoma. She is editor of *Political Communication Review.* As well as publishing articles in a number of communication and social science journals, she has co-authored or co-edited several books on political communication.

Tom Konda is assistant professor of political science at the State University of New York at Plattsburgh. He has published in such journals as *Social Science Quarterly* and *Journal of Politics,* and is at present writing the first history of political advertising.

Edward Larkey is assistant professor of German in the Department of Modern Languages and Linguistics at the University of Maryland—Baltimore County. His research deals with popular music and youth culture in the German-speaking world and he is currently preparing a monograph on youth and popular music in the German Democratic Republic.

Michael W. Mansfield is associate professor of political science at Baylor University. He co-edited *Drama in Life: The Uses of Communication in Society* and *Government and the News Media: Comparative Dimensions* and has contributed articles on political communication and research methodology to several books and journals.

Steven M. Neuse is associate professor of political science and director of the M.P.A. Program at the University of Arkansas. He has published widely in public administration and political science journals. Currently, he is working on a biography of David Lilienthal but retains an avid interest in the political implications of detective and spy thrillers.

Dan Nimmo is professor of communication at the University of Oklahoma. Among his books in political communication are *Newsgathering in Washington, The Political Persuaders, Popular Images of Politics, Political Communication and Public Opinion in America, Subliminal Politics, Handbook of Political Communication,* and *New Perspectives on Political Advertising.* He was editor of *Communication Yearbook 3* and 4.

Jimmie N. Rogers is professor and chair of the Department of Communication at the University of Arkansas. He authored *The Country Music Message: All about Lovin' and Livin',* and has otherwise published and lectured widely on the content of country lyrics.

Robert L. Savage is professor of political science at the University of Arkansas. He co-authored *Candidates and Their Images* and has written extensively on political communication and political culture with his work appearing in political science, communication, economics, and sociology publications.

Lee Sigelman is dean of the faculty of social and behavioral sciences and professor of political science at the University of Arizona. He formerly served as director of the political science program at the National Science Foundation. He has published widely in political science, public administration, sociology, and social psychology, but his central research interests lie in the areas of mass communication, public opinion, and political culture.

Larry David Smith is assistant professor of speech communication at Purdue University. His teaching and research interests focus on rhetorical theory and political communication.

Stephen A. Smith is associate professor of communication at the University of Arkansas, where he teaches courses in political communication and freedom of speech. He is the author of *Myth, Media, and the Southern Mind* and numerous articles in communication and popular culture journals.

Raymond Sprague is assistant professor of music and director of choirs at the University of New Orleans. Although his specialty is choral literature, he is concerned with the communicative powers of all styles and genres of music, and he has written and lectured extensively on the social significance of popular music.

David L. Swanson is associate professor of speech communication at the University of Illinois. His research and teaching focus on the social and political effects of public communication. His work on this subject has appeared in *Human Communication Research, Quarterly Journal of Speech, Communication Monographs, Communication Research, Communication Yearbook, Journal of Broadcasting & Electronic Media,* and *Handbook of Political Communication.* He is co-author of *The Nature of Human Communication.*

Kathleen J. Turner is associate professor of communication at Tulane University. Her research and teaching interests include political communication and popular culture. She is the author of *Lyndon Johnson's Dual War: Vietnam and the Press,* as well as articles in communication journals.

Anne Johnston Wadsworth is assistant professor of radio, television and motion pictures at the University of North Carolina. She is co-author of *Political Campaign Communication,* and has written on children and mass media, political communication literature, and content analysis. Her recent research has focused on the "political style" of candidates as presented through political advertising.

1

Imagination, Politics, and Popular Media: A Thematic Introduction

Robert L. Savage
Department of Political Science,
University of Arkansas

Dan Nimmo
Political Communication Center,
University of Oklahoma

Since at least the age of Platonic proscriptions of poets, playwrights, and musicians, there have been a host of questions raised about the sometimes complementary, sometimes conflicting—but always provocative—roles that popular entertainers and the media they use play in politics. In the contemporary era it is particularly appropriate to raise anew many of those questions. For these are indeed propitious times to examine the relationship between politics and popular communication. For example, the man who served as president of the United States for most of this decade was not only a former sportscaster, then Hollywood actor, but during his incumbency almost seemed to seize any opportunity to quote a one-liner from sports or movies to communicate his message. "I forgot to duck," he uttered from his hospital bed after an assassination attempt. "Go ahead, make my day," he liked to taunt congressional opponents. [1]

But there are other signs that these are the times of popular cultural political expression. Politicians rush to publish autobiographies, not so much to increase citizen understanding or even enhance their own political fortunes, but to exploit a potential best seller that will fatten their wallets and yield them celebrity status. [2] Or, politicians

---

[1] And Clint Eastwood, who first delivered this line on the silver screen, has served a term as mayor in the California city where he resides.

[2] Some may argue that autobiographies are a genre of history, thus rationalistic discourse and not popular communication. Autobiographies of politicians, like those of popular entertainers, almost invariably have a Horatio Alger formula in their narration, however, suggesting that their readers may be as interested in entertainment, if not more so, as enlightenment.

become popular media stars themselves—for example, Vice-president George Bush films an episode of "Miami Vice"; Speaker of the House Tip O'Neill appears on "Cheers"; or presidential candidate Jesse Jackson is host to "Saturday Night Live." So not only do actors become politicians, politicians become actors. So blurred is the line between popular entertainment and politics that even the Soviet Union gets into the act, publicly reacting to such Red-bashing films as *Rambo* and *Rocky IV*.

In the past, when questions of the political role of popular communication have been raised, however, research on the political character and pertinence of the popular media and their messages has been diffuse, unsystematic, often impressionistic, and focused largely upon presumed or hypothesized audience effects. The political relevance of popular media content has been addressed, to be sure, but largely in isolation. That is to say, there are more or less "invisible colleges" of scholars who have focused on politics and film, music and politics, politics and literature, and the like. There have also been the theoretical schools, for example, Frankfurt and Chicago, that address popular media more generally and more abstractly. These times, however, suggest that an effort to pull together many of these diffuse strains is desirable.

Accordingly, the essays collected here represent an initial step toward providing such a focal point. The collection seeks to make the case that popular media play important roles in politics, to present some alternative ways of approaching research in popular political communication, conceptually and methodologically, and to provide a set of exemplary studies of several popular media that are relevant to the communication of political values.

In focusing upon the politically relevant content of the popular media, we do not intend to impugn research directed at the audience. To the contrary, audiences are at least implicitly conceptualized through these essays. The process of communication is, after all, transactional in character. Whatever meanings lie in the messages transmitted through popular media ultimately depend upon those who attend to the media. Yet, those meanings depend upon the messages as much as the receivers.

POLITICAL MESSAGES AND POPULAR COMMUNICATION

The diffuse character of research on politics through the popular media derives in part from an unfortunate interpretation of the functions of mass media initially formulated by Harold Lasswell (1948). He posited the four functions of information, identification, socialization, and entertainment. The last of these functions, entertainment, was largely dismissed at the time. More importantly, Lasswell failed to establish that communication generally labeled as entertainment serves any or all of the other three functions at any given point in time. Indeed, to the extent that popular media transmit messages regarding potential value conflicts (including their obscuration), their entertainment packages are continually serving the identification and socialization functions as well. That is, popular or entertaining media constantly send messages that tell us who we are—or ought to be—within the context of the larger community and what values and institutions we should adhere to as members of that community.

The often noted prevalence of white middle-class families on American television sitcoms throughout the 1950s and 1960s is a classic example of such popularly mediated politics. In essence, this genre of popular television identified Americans not only as white and middle-class—indeed, most often as WASPs—but usually as members of a male-headed household in which the father was a professional or businessman, the mother a housewife, and the children (two or three) earnestly, if not always diligently, trying to cope with school. These sitcoms assuredly did not reflect the experiences of most Americans, but they provided ready role models for what Americans ought to be. Moreover, the sitcoms cast in high relief the values, such as good citizenship, and the institutions, such as public schools, worthy of support.

That such examples are common in popular media has been a prime basis for the argument that popular media generally ignore the reality of social conflict, giving rise to such concepts as media *hegemony* reflecting a *dominant ideology*. Such arguments point to the structure of the media but also indicate something of the audience as well, notably its *suggestibility* but also the likelihood of a resulting *alienation*. Distinctions drawn between elite (high) versus popular (low, mass, folk) culture or arts contributed further to such conceptualizations. Paradoxically, elitists could criticize popular media decision makers for not providing ennobling entertainment while suggesting that the larger audience was incapable of ingesting a richer diet of the arts. In any event, all these notions contributed to a *monistic* characterization of the popular media, most often stressing the role of economics and consumption in creating and sustaining mass communication systems in developed nations. Thus, the intentions of the producers of popularly mediated messages really made no difference. Whether they intended to support the dominant ideology or not, their productions were necessarily directed toward the lowest common denominator so as to gain continued or more frequent outlets through mass channels of communication.

Protest might emerge periodically under such a hegemonic system but its impact would almost certainly be limited to fringe elements in society. Formal censorship by government would not often be invoked because the largest part of the media structure would continue to follow the dominant ideology, drowning out any potentially subversive messages.

Other analysts have pointed to the diverse character of popular media. There are many different media, and within each, there are various possibilities for alternative messages. In turn, this fragmented media structure reaches out to an audience equally fragmented, that is, there are many audiences. This *pluralistic* image of popular media points to the need for emerging consensus in the face of greater group identification and the "us-versus-them" attitude associated with it. Yet, the economic need of media industries pushes them toward defining audience segments, very often through processes of social portrayal. Thus, the group may come to identify itself more through this media connection than through interpersonal processes of group membership and interaction. Indeed, the marketing research and production capabilities are now so sophisticated that groups may be created that have no interpersonal or organizational bases in the first place. The "yuppie" is one of the latest and more pervasive examples of such group identification, existing only through mediated audience segmentation and social portrayal.

The seeming explosion of "countercultures" in Western societies during the 1960s has become the standard source of exemplary materials for this pluralistic vision of popular media. The subcultures and alternate lifes-tyles that appeared to multiply so rapidly during that decade certainly invigorated champions of existing media systems. Technological changes producing greater capacities for self-selection of audience segments, that is, subcultures, have added even more appeal to this pluralistic image.

Those who view the popular media from a more monistic perspective, however, are more likely to fix upon the political significance of those media. This tendency follows from their premise that the media disregard other value alternatives present in society. By contrast, the more pluralistic vision assumes, perhaps all too easily, that conflicting values can find outlets through the popular media. Moreover, when those conflicts do not surface, politics can simply be ignored or disavowed, which is to say that the proper business of the popular media is to provide "pure entertainment." Both perspectives, however, often overlook the multiplicity of meanings that the audience may take from any given message directed toward it.

POPULARLY COMMUNICATED POLITICS AND THE PUBLIC IMAGINATION

Scholars, media critics, and media producers often share the tendency to view audience reception of popularly communicated messages in terms of some singular interpretation that all members of the audience are expected to hold in common. Ironically, for any given communication, the scholar, the critic, and the producer may disagree as to its "true" message for the audience. That in itself should suggest *polysemy*, a multiplicity of meanings, embedded in popular communications and recognized in the *decoding* activities of the audience. That actual meanings are the product of more or less idiosyncratic transactions between individual audience members and mediated messages might suggest a large degree of futility for research into the content, politically relevant or otherwise, of popular media.

On the other hand, both content and audience studies indicate that such a pessimistic outlook is unwarranted. Much is known about the parameters of semantic decoding. One example is the role of *myth* in political communication, popularly mediated or not (McGee, 1985; Nimmo & Combs, 1980). Some societal myths are more primordial than others; some myths offer a wider range of variants. Still, sensitivity to the prevalent myths of a given society with an ear for subcultural variations aids in understanding the more likely meanings drawn from particular communications.

Moreover, a number of useful theoretical perspectives on meaning systems and symbolism are available for analytical purposes. Some pertinent examples include dramatism (Burke, 1945; Combs & Mansfield, 1976), fantasy (Bormann, 1972; Cragan & Shields, 1980), and narration (Fisher, 1987). As all of these are used to some extent in one or more of the essays that follow, we shall not explore them further here.

Whatever the particularistic responses of individual audience members, the popular media remain a window case revealing the folklore, proverbial wisdom, and myths prevalent in society. These mythic elements reflect, among other things, the dominant values, concerns, and yes, even groups in society. The potential, and sometimes actual, conflicts that are the very essence of political action are thus everywhere transmitted through tales told and retold (re-presentations). Assuredly, there are greater stories and lesser stories, more stirring dramas and boring dramas. Moreover, these re-presentations are sometimes more direct in their political implications, more often not. Nevertheless, the images conjured up and projected by the media help to shape and reshape the images held by the audience. In other words, the public imagination is in part the imaginary experiences afforded by the popular media. Since those imaginary experiences seek to tell us, among other things, who we are, who others are (and are not), how we can resolve our differences (or ignore them) through preferred procedures and directions, and why some differences ought to be resolved in a particular way and other differences in still other ways, the popular media also reflect much of the political imagination in a society. In all communities, then, our understanding of politics will be enhanced by whatever extent we know the public imagination through the popular media.

COMING ATTRACTIONS

The following essays are explorations into the parameters of that public imagination so familiar to us and yet, as political communication, often so opaque. With the exception of the opening essay in this volume, each explores selected themes addressed in this Introduction as they apply to one popular medium or genre thereof.

However, the volume's first essay, by David Swanson, is more encompassing in intent and scope. It provides a succinct, yet thorough, examination of the major theoretical orientations shaping research into popularly mediated politics. In this effort Swanson systematically fashions the ties binding the themes noted in this Introduction and clarifies the conflicts that underlie their usage among differing schools of thought. The effort does not seek a comprehensive synthesis of the various strains of scholarly analysis but nonetheless lays the groundwork for a redirection of energies toward more fruitful cooperative efforts.

Dan Nimmo explores the distinctions to be drawn among elite, mass, and popular communications, emphasizing the utilitarian or instrumental character associated traditionally with the latter. He finds this distinction of value in examining popular magazines, especially in reviewing the various approaches to research of magazine content. Indeed, the methodological typology he offers here is likely to have utility for other popular media as well.

Katherine Hale and Michael Mansfield analyze the content of televised commercials, uncovering a number of American political values presented through them as symbolic themes. Such a finding is hardly surprising, given that media commentators and critics have recently remarked much upon this. Hale and Mansfield, however, bring a politically sensitive acumen to their analysis that reveals the phenomenon as much more pervasive than has been generally recognized. Moreover, they point to the problems for future political discourse that may arise from the tendency for trivialization of human conflicts and their resolution as reflected in contemporary advertising.

In a more specific application, Tom Konda and Lee Sigelman address the potential of commercial advertising for intervening in the electoral process. After providing an overview of earlier efforts of commercial advertisers to foster particular policy orientations in the body politic, they focus upon the more disturbing tendency, emerging just prior to the American presidential election of 1980, for some advertisers to reflect a partisan bias. Their analysis of a large number of magazine and newspaper ads run by several major corporations demonstrate that policy positions presented in these ads coincided with the positioning on issues of candidates, particularly Ronald Reagan and the Democratic contenders, during the campaign.

A more general treatment of popular cinema as a medium of political expression is offered by Robert Savage. Following an eiconic perspective, introduced seriously by Boulding (1956), Savage explores the imagistic content of film, pointing to the re-presenting of political myths and tales, suggesting that critics misunderstand the likely political impact when they insist that movies should exhibit veridicality with actual political experiences and institutions. He illuminates particularly pertinent examples of political cinema from the genre and social portrayal approaches to film study.

The thesis that popular media reflect a dominant ideology is examined by Jeremy Butler with particular application to American television soap operas. Assuredly, he finds some merit in the thesis, inasmuch as soap operas reflect certain traditional value assumptions associated with the middle class, especially the importance of family leading to, as he says, "the politics of monogamy and romance." Butler probes deeper, however, and finds a number of disconcerting themes underlying the narrative action of the soaps. His thematic analysis strongly points to structured polysemy in soap opera texts where viewers are able to negotiate meanings, at least within certain limits, rather than be subdued by the dominant ideology.

A more recent television genre, the musical video, is treated by Anne Wadsworth and Lynda Kaid. They utilize a rigorous content analysis to search for prominent political themes and images in a large sample of videos broadcast by MTV. They find a relatively small number of videos having explicit political themes or images; most of these fall into one or another of four general categories: political oppression, war, world peace, and American values. Wadsworth and Kaid speculate that a "collective dream" is represented in the concatenation of these themes.

Ironically, perhaps, this collective dream projected by 1980s music videos is similar to what many analysts have pointed to as the message of the protest music of the 1960s. A re-examination of that musical era is appropriately provided here by Raymond Sprague and Kathleen Turner. Although their thematic analysis of lyrical content does not significantly depart from earlier studies, the authors provide students of political communication with an innovative and provocative effort at relating the role of *music* in combination with lyrics augmenting the affective impact of political messages. Sprague and Turner ultimately and legitimately point to a pessimistic closure of 1960s protest music late in that decade; yet that message seemingly lives on in the recent synthesis of music and television.

Another form of popular music—country—has also drawn considerable attention for its supposed political message reflecting political and social values largely contrary to those reflected by rock music. Stephen Smith and Jimmie Rogers, however, present a content analysis of country song hits of more than two decades that clearly undermines the widely held supposition that this music is basically supportive of values associated with contemporary American political conservativism. In particular, they examine country lyrics for messages regarding race relations, law and order, and economics, finding that the genre more nearly reflects an essentially anarchistic political philosophy, or libertarianism, in current American political parlance.

More recently, American conservative partisans have attempted to appropriate at least some rock musicians to their cause, not least among these, the premier icon of contemporary rock music, Bruce Springsteen. Michael Hemphill and Larry Smith find no more support for this than the claim of conservatism in country lyrics. Using analytical tools derived from Burke's (1945) "representative anecdote," they reveal in the lyrics of Springsteen, an elegy exhibiting three phases: dreaming, reckoning, lamenting. Springsteen's message more or less continually focuses on the value of hope, but his rhetoric supports no specific political vista; his is a more particularistic image underpinning the individual aspirations of working Americans.

Whatever the efforts of American politicians to adapt particular popular media genres or performers to their causes and despite spo-

radic policy discussions focusing on such things as violence in television and morality in song lyrics, the content of popular media messages has not received sustained formal attention from the government in the United States. As Edward Larkey shows, that is not
necessarily the case in other nations. He recounts the evolution of public policy on rock music by the Communist regime in East Germany
over the past three decades. He finds that this evolution has occurred
in four stages, coinciding with broader, interpretive concepts of the nature of art and culture as they relate to national purposes. Larkey's essay addresses a number of concerns that have their parallels in nations
outside the Communist bloc, most notably cultural imperialism flow-
ing from the United States and Western Europe and the related connection between economic resources and the production values of popular media content. Moreover, while he focuses on the German
Democratic Republic, there is an implicit recognition that governmental activity in the field of popular media may be more than simply a
matter of censorship interfering with basic freedoms of the media or
the citizenry. There are economic concerns and questions of community identity as well that may prompt governmental action.

Also offering a perspective upon popularly mediated politics within
Communist nations is Steven Neuse. He examines one of the more
widely read literary genres of the modern world, espionage and detective fiction, as it has developed in the Soviet Union and Eastern
Europe. Viewing the Soviet Union, from a time of proscription to the
present promotion of such books, he paints a bleak picture from the
standpoint of literary censorship. Nevertheless, it is a compelling
study of governmental control of a popular medium directing it toward state purposes. The genre has evolved somewhat differently in
some other Communist nations, a tale we will leave for him.

Finally, Elizabeth Bird ventures into the likely interface between
mass-mediated popular entertainment and interpersonal storytelling.
Assuredly, the empirical focus of her study is a mass medium: American tabloids. Yet, she shows how the tabloids are ultimately an extension of urban folktales and graffiti. The substantive focus of her essay, the life, death, and yes, afterlife of John F. Kennedy, provides an
all-the-more compelling case for the intertextuality of political
communication.

A CONCLUDING POSTSCRIPT IN ADVANCE

The editors, as such, will not intrude again. Instead, we make some
postscriptual comments in advance precisely to suggest the open-

ness of the adventure undertaken here. This volume brings together a reasonably representative sample of works necessarily sharing only one premise: that popular culture and its media of transmission ought to be taken seriously as purveyors of politically relevant messages. It is because we feel that this subfield of political communication studies is at still a very early stage of development that we have avoided imposing rigorous conceptual and methodological strictures upon the contributors to this volume. We extend the same openness to its readers by not imposing such strictures ex post facto in this introduction.

Nevertheless, certain notions do mark this volume throughout, chiefly a very broad conception of what politics is. Politics is value-laden activity marked by human conflict, actual or potential. Consequently, politics is also marked by human efforts to cooperate so as to reach resolution of those conflicts. Popular media weave the reality and the myths of such human activities into tales to be told and re-told, dramas to be enacted and re-enacted, songs to be sung and sung again. To be sure, these playful re-presentations through the popular media are not mirror images of reality, political or otherwise. Yet, in telling us something of who we have been, who we are, and who we may yet be, the popular media necessarily communicate as much about human beings as *homo politicus* as they do about us as *homo ludens* (Huizinga, 1955).

REFERENCES

Bormann, E. G. (1972). Fantasy and rhetorical vision: The rhetorical criticism of social reality. *Quarterly Journal of Speech, 58,* 396–407.

Boulding, K. E. (1956). *The image: Knowledge in life and society.* Ann Arbor: University of Michigan Press.

Burke, K. (1945). *A grammar of motives.* Englewood Cliffs, NJ: Prentice–Hall.

Combs, J. E., & Mansfield, M. W. (Eds.). (1976). *Drama in life.* New York: Hastings House.

Cragan, J. F., & Shields, D. C. (Eds.). *Applied communication research: A dramatistic approach.* Prospect Height's IL: Waveland Press.

Fisher, W. R. (1987). *Human communication as narration: Toward a philosophy of reason, value, and action.* Columbia: University of South Carolina.

Huizinga, J. (1955). *Homo ludens: A study of the play element in culture.* Boston: Beacon Press.

Lasswell, H. D. (1948). The structure and function of communication in society. In L. Bryson (Ed.), *The communication of ideas* (pp. 37–51). New York: Institute for Social and Religious Studies.

McGee, M. C. (1985). 1984: Some issues in the rhetorical study of political communication. In K. R. Sanders, L. L. Kaid, & D. Nimmo (Eds.), *Political communication yearbook 1984* (pp. 155–182). Carbondale; Southern Illinois University Press.

Nimmo, D., & Combs, J. (1980). *Subliminal politics: Myths and mythmakers in America.* Englewood Cliffs, NJ: Prentice–Hall.

2

Popular Art as Political Communication

David L. Swanson
Department of Speech Communication,
University of Illinois

> Shall we just carelessly allow children to hear any casual tales which
> may be devised by casual persons, and to receive into their minds ideas
> for the most part the very opposite of those which we should wish them
> to have when they are grown up?. . . . Then the first thing will be to
> establish a censorship of the writers of fiction, and let the censors re-
> ceive any tale of fiction which is good, and reject the bad; and we will
> desire mothers and nurses to tell their children the authorised ones
> only. Let them fashion the mind with such tales.
>
> Plato, *Republic,* II, 377

The idea that popular literature has social and political consequences is ancient. It reverberates in familiar forms through two mil-
lennia of cultural history: the church's proscriptions of secular literature; the storytellers' efforts to arouse their hearers through tales of
injustice and martyrdom; the crusades of divines against vulgar en-
tertainments; the zeal of censors in every age. Throughout the last
hundred years, however, and especially in our own century, the
sweep and power of popular art have increased steadily, propelled by
the invention of mass media of communication, the mass audience,
and mass culture. In the process, what we mean by "popular art" has
been transformed, as have ancient ideas about its relationship to politics and social life. Today, some argue that popular art creates the
context within which social and political life occurs. Others are moved
to write scholarly books on the subject. And, everyone has an opinion—often held with fervor—about whether the social and political
consequences of popular art are good or bad.

This chapter reviews and comments upon some of the best thinking and research concerning contemporary popular art as political

communication in the broadest sense. The scope of the subject is vast, too vast for a single chapter. Necessarily, what follows is focused rather narrowly. The universe of popular art is constricted by a preoccupation with mass media entertainment. Insofar as possible, care is taken to disentangle popular art from mass media per se, though knowledgeable readers will recognize the difficulties of such an effort. Of the many interesting and provocative ways of thinking about possible consequences of contemporary popular art, only those which are concerned with broadly "political" consequences, attempt to say something about popular art as communication, and have most influenced scholarly study of our subject, are examined, and only selectively. Although these limits are confining, a reasonably comprehensive discussion—and, it is hoped, useful analysis—can be crafted within their compass.

THE HISTORICAL CONTEXT OF THINKING ABOUT POPULAR ART AS POLITICAL COMMUNICATION

Current thinking about the social and political consequences of popular art reflects a particular historical context. To understand current views best, it is necessary to recognize the circumstances out of which they arose and by which they have been shaped. While thinking about popular art's social and political aspects has an ancient lineage, we are interested here in the more immediate context of technological, intellectual, and social developments related to the creation and evolution of mass media and mass entertainment in the late 19th and early 20th centuries, especially in the United States. Of these developments, three were most important in shaping thinking about our subject: (1) intellectual responses to the transition from agrarian to urban, industrial society; (2) the ways in which succeeding new mass media created their audiences; and, (3) economic and political forces which led to viewing the content of mass media as a powerful and manipulative social force.

Urban Life and the Mass Society

Modern society was invented in the latter half of the 19th century and the early years of the 20th century. At the beginning of this period, the United States and the nations of Europe were largely agrarian societies. Most people lived on farms or in the small villages that were the centers of rural social and economic life. There were no means of rapid, mass transport of goods, persons, or information. Village life was inward-looking, dominated by commitments to place, to kin, to neighbors, and to the point of view and folk wisdom that had built up over time to constitute the local culture. Although the inexorable advance of technology and industrialization had already begun, life in the 1850s was, for most, lived within self-sufficient communities where the pace of change was slow, information about distant persons, places, and events was scarce, tradition held sway, and one was both supported and constrained by bonds to people and place that had been acquired at birth.

In the industrializing nations, the world of 1900 was almost unrecognizable from the world of 1850. By the turn of the century, many of the elements of modern life could be discerned. The accumulating results of technology had made possible industrialization, comparatively economical and rapid transportation of people and materials, the early stages of the mechanization of agriculture, the speedy transfer of information between distant points, and a host of other developments. Perhaps the most conspicuous result of these developments, and the one which best shows their interrelation, was the growth of large, modern cities. Industrialization required cities as sites of centralized production and distribution of manufactured goods. Economical mass transportation systems made possible the movement of manufactured goods to distant markets and the migration to the cities of workers needed to staff the factories. By reducing the proportion of the population that could be employed on farms, the mechanization of agriculture created a growing pool of labor for industry, a pool that swelled dramatically with the increasing number of immigrants arriving in the United States. New systems of communication, including the "wireless telegraph," allowed the rapid transfer of information needed to develop and sustain the large manufacturing, mercantile, and financial organizations which are the foundation of an industrialized economy.

Prior to 1850, London and Paris were the only cities in the world boasting populations of 1 million or more. By 1900, fourteen such metropolises existed, of which three were in the United States: New York, Philadelphia, and Chicago. Agrarian society was giving way to urban society and industrial cities, the confusing, complicated, interlinked, voracious metropolises that were ingesting more and more raw materials and workers and producing increasing amounts of manufactured goods.

The lumbering transition from agrarian to urban society eventually came to affect the ordinary person's life in profound ways. No longer would persons be so bound by place; society was becoming increasingly mobile. No longer would life be lived with a small, homogeneous social universe; the factory and urban neighborhood threw together persons who often had little in common and frequently were separated by language barriers. No longer would so many lives be consumed by the dawn-to-dusk labor of the farmer for subsistence; urban life brought with it, ultimately, the workday, the institutionalization of leisure time, and a growing middle class (although, of course, the early period of industrialization merely transferred the struggle for subsistence from farm to factory and, for many, made the struggle even more difficult with unsafe working conditions, exploitation of child labor, and the like). Where preindustrial community life was characterized by common experience, shared values built up over time, and strong bonds to kin and neighbors, urban life was typified by differences between coworkers and city dwellers in experience and values and by anonymity. In the transition from farmer to wage earner, from local to cosmopolitan, a new kind of society was emerging.

The "great society" was a term commonly used to refer to the new social order and way of living. Herbert Spencer and the Social Darwinists saw at work in the great society the same forces of coherence and differentiation which produced evolution in the biological world: Society was growing while becoming more complex; its parts were becoming increasingly differentiated and heterogeneous yet more integrated and interdependent. The "great society" was seen as a natural and inevitable advance over its less complex predecessor. This view had considerable influence. It led to the belief that the "natural forces" at work in the great society, such as market demand and capitalistic competition, should be free of restraint so that they could continue to produce evolution and progress.

Other observers thought of the great society not as an intricate, evolving social organism but rather as a new way of life experienced by ordinary persons living in the cities. In searching for the thread that would unravel and make understandable the complexity of the great society, these thinkers focused on the epoxy of social organization—the relationships that bind persons together. They concluded that, in the industrial city, a new kind of social relationship had arisen as the cornerstone of social and political life.

In an 1887 treatise, *Gemeinschaft und Gesellschaft*, Ferdinand Tönnies (1887/1957) proposed a formulation that, for many, seemed to capture what was new about social bonds in the great society. Tönnies contrasted industrial society (the Gesellschaft) to a romanticized conception of preindustrial community life (the Gemeinschaft) by describing the essential forms of social relationships upon which each is founded. The Gemeinschaft rests upon relationships in which "people are strongly bound to one another through tradition, through kinship, through friendship, or because of some other socially cohesive factor" (DeFleur & Ball–Rokeach, 1982, p. 151). That is, relationships in the Gemeinschaft are based more on who persons are as individuals and what they share than on persons' roles in society or what services they can provide. Thus, social relationships in the community are perhaps most closely approximated in the peasant family and small village.

In the Gesellschaft, in contrast, social relationships take the form of a contract. Persons take the role of parties who agree to exchange values—buyer and seller, employer and employee, landlord and tenant, and so on—each seeking to maximize his or her individual gain. Although Tönnies's descriptions were abstract portraits of opposing forms of social organization, not empirical analyses of the "great society" and its preindustrial predecessor, this conception of the contract-based Gesellschaft seemed to many to provide a useful way of understanding some of the more important features of the new urban social life.

Writing just before the turn of the century, Emile Durkheim (1893/1964) modified and elaborated on Tönnies's views, giving attention to the psychological consequences of the contractual relationships which characterize industrial, urban life. One such consequence, he thought, is anomie, an extreme sense of individual isolation and alienation resulting from the loss of traditional social bonds to others.

Alienation played an important role in what came to be called "mass society theory," a view built on the work of Tönnies, Durkheim, and others. According to mass society theorists, industrialization and technology had transformed the folk—the peasantry—into the mass: alienated, rootless, inward-looking city dwellers. Of special importance in understanding the influence of mass communication, persons in mass society, being removed from nexus of information, values, and culture which was the agrarian community, were suspected of being highly susceptible to the influence and manipulation of those who might endeavor to mold the masses' beliefs and actions. That is, members of the mass society were thought to be suggestible.

Belief in the suggestibility of mass society was reinforced by some early studies of the psychology and behavior of crowds and mobs. In an influential study, Gustave LeBon (1897) contended that being a member of a crowd made one suggestible, gullible, and irrational. Under the stimulation of a crowd, thought LeBon, rational persons may find themselves caught up in violent and brutal acts. The connection between crowd psychology and the mass society was made by Edward Alsworth Ross in the first American textbook on social psychology (1908). According to Ross, city life produced neurasthenia, a nervous exhaustion that was the particular affliction of urban dwellers. Living in the mass society exposed increasing numbers of persons to the conditions of overcrowding and overstimulation, impairing reason and producing heightened suggestibility.

At the turn of the 20th century, then, it was widely (though not universally) believed that among the products of the mass society was a public more gullible and credulous than before, a public that could be manipulated by skillful leaders. When the mass media of communication came into existence, it was this gullible public that many imagined to be their audience.

The Mass Media and the Creation of the Mass Audience

The decades bracketing the turn of the 20th century saw not only the emergence of the mass society but also the development of the mass media of communication. Some have argued that the mass media made possible the mass society (e.g., Turner & Killian, 1972, p. 112). Certainly mass communication made a return to isolated community life impossible, for the mass media conquered the forces of time and distance that had dominated agrarian life, localized culture, and encouraged diversity. Thus, it is not surprising thus most analyses of the mass society gave special prominence to the vast reservoir of information and entertainment that the new mass media ultimately made available to virtually everyone.

Many of the archetypes of popular art antedate the development of mass media. For example, Adorno (1957) marks the English novels published around the beginning of the 18th century, particularly the works of Defoe and Richardson, as "the beginning of an approach to literary production that consciously created, served, and finally controlled a 'market'" (p. 475). But, the advent of entertainment marketed to the masses awaited the development of modern mass media. Seen in historical perspective, that development occurred very quickly indeed.

The first real mass medium to develop was the mass-circulation newspaper. Before the 1830s, newspapers were geared to relatively elite audiences who could afford their comparatively high cost and had special interests in the matters of politics and commerce that were emphasized in the newspapers of the time. The model of a mass-circulation newspaper is generally attributed to Benjamin Day who, in 1833, sought to interest the general public by featuring in his New York Sun stories offering human interest, sensationalism, and humor, all for a penny per copy. However, it was not until after the Civil War, partly through developments in printing technology and the cheap manufacture of paper, that the mass press became a reality. Newspapers reached out to more and more potential readers with an expanding array of features—including comics, photographs, melodramatic coverage of crimes and disasters, and reform crusades—and circulation rose until, in 1900, it reached roughly one per American household. One consequence of the success of the mass press was to divide the audience for newspapers into the working classes, who "flocked to the Yellow Press," and elites, "which turned to such respectable papers as the New York Times and scorned the common man and his flamboyant press" (Kreiling, 1984, p. 39; see also Schudson, 1978).

Magazines followed a similar course. Magazines were published in the United States for more than a century before the Civil War but, like most of the newspapers of the same period, were aimed at social elites and those with special interests. It was not until shortly before the turn of the 20th century that mass circulation national magazines were born, boasting one million subscribers or more. The success of mass magazines was achieved by following the path carved out by newspapers, capitalizing on the appeal of human interest and providing entertainment and inspiration.

As the 20th century began, the first mass medium that was in no way limited to a literate audience appeared: the motion picture. Edison showed "movies" to the American public for the first time in 1896. A decade later there were 1,000 "nickelodeons" in operation, storefront theaters where films were shown to the public for a nickel. By 1910 there were 10,000 nickelodeons and, in 1930, following the introduction of sound in films, an average of 90 million persons per week went to the movies in the United States. The spectacular popularity of films followed the lead of the print mass media: movies sought less to enlighten than to attract the widest possible audience; comedy and melodrama were the order of the day.

As the pre-eminent medium of mass entertainment, movies attracted just the sort of audience mass society theorists had envisioned. A study of attendance in New York theaters in 1911 conducted by Russell Sage estimated that 72% of the movie-goers were members of the working class (Czitrom, 1982, p. 48). The presence in the audiences of large numbers of immigrants and children led to concern about the potential of this powerful entertainment medium to corrupt its viewers. The Chicago Tribune reported in 1907, for example, that the Juvenile Jewish Protection League "is the latest organization to declare war against the demoralizing influence of the 5-cent theaters . . . [which] minister to the lowest passions of childhood. . . . . The average 5-cent theater does not have a single thing to commend it. Its influence is wholly vicious" (quoted in Belting, 1986).

The themes of phenomenal growth and creating a mass audience by providing popular entertainment also dominate radio's development as a mass medium. The first transmission of the human voice by "wireless telephony" in 1906 was followed by nearly two decades of striking technical advances in the transmission and reception of radio signals, of public fascination with the novelty of being able to hear in one's home sounds from distant places, and disagreement and confusion about for what purposes and by whom radio was to be used. The chaos began to sort itself out when, in 1922, advertisers were first persuaded to purchase radio air time. It quickly became clear that radio stations could be self-sustaining, even profitable businesses as a result of the sale of advertising time. Unlike Britain, where radio broadcasting and programming were sustained by government-imposed license fees on each radio receiver, American radio developed as a privately owned commercial medium.

The rapid growth of radio on its way to becoming a mass medium is best illustrated by the proliferation of receiving sets in use in the United States through the 1920s and 1930s. Sixty thousand radio sets were in use at the beginning of 1922; 3 years later, by the end of 1925, the figure had climbed to nearly 3 million; in 1926, to almost 6 million; doubling to almost 12 million by 1930; nearly doubling again by 1935. By the end of the 1930s, radio permeated America, and nearly four-fifths of the world's receivers were in the United States.

The success of radio resulted initially from its novelty. The public soon lost its fascination with the ability to receive signals, however, and the content of programming then became important. Radio's real success came from its development into a medium of mass entertainment. Radio's standard fare became not information or education but rather music, variety programs, comedy, and drama (including the new phenomenon, the soap opera). In 1940, for example, 12% of the evening network radio schedule was devoted to news and comment, while 18% was devoted to variety programs, 25% to music programs, and 23% to dramas (Czitrom, 1982, p. 84).

Contemplating the radio audience and the programming they were receiving in 1948, Siepmann voiced the same concerns that earlier had surfaced with respect to the early movie-going audience: "Radio listening increases as you descend the socio-economic scale; the poorer, the less educated a man is, the more he listens to the radio. Second, serious listening decreases as you descend the socio-economic scale. Third, radio is the preferred medium of the most suggestible" (Siepmann, 1948, p. 178).

Although we have not discussed the development of those media, such as phonograph recordings and the inexpensive, mass-produced novel, which reached comparatively smaller audiences, our look at the evolution of largest-scale media demonstrates the essential themes. The development of mass media occurred simultaneously with what were thought to be profound changes in the character of social (as well as economic, cultural, and political) life. These changes seemed to produce for the new media a vast potential audience that was highly susceptible to being influenced. The media quickly succeeded in building large audiences by reaching out to segments of society that had not attended to earlier, more elite media. The primary means by which this was accomplished was the purveying of mass entertainment and the infusion into news of the melodramatic qualities of entertainment. Judged by the traditional standards of literate culture, the new popular art found in mass media was of low quality and suspected by many of exerting a strong and unhealthy influence on its audiences. In Albig's (1939) words, "great masses of people now experience a buzzing confusion of newspaper, motion-picture and radio stimuli, which provide vicarious experience that sometimes satisfyingly titillates, thrills and emotionalizes, but again frightens and makes uneasy" (p. 51). To those who were alarmed by the new media, it was not merely that mass communication existed, but that it existed within the mass society, reaching disproportionately persons who, removed from community life, might be least able to see through false claims, values, and ideologies.

The Association of Mass Media with Strategic Mass Manipulation

The belief that communication can mold opinions antedated mass media by centuries, of course. What mass communication introduced was the ability to disseminate ideas and experiences rapidly to virtually the entire population, thereby magnifying enormously the potential for social influence. Early in their histories, the mass media became associated in the public's mind with systematic and sometimes covert attempts to influence popular belief and action. The general presumption that mass media were highly successful in these influence attempts solidified the conception of the media as a vehicle of unprecedented social power.

That the mass media might be sources of great influence as well as of entertainment was perhaps most visibly brought to the public's attention by commercial advertising. Prior to the development of mass media, newspapers and magazines derived their income chiefly from the sale of comparatively expensive subscriptions. Mass-circulation newspapers and magazines, and radio, in contrast, succeeded in part because they provided their product at little or no cost to audience members and derived most of their income from advertising.

Since, in the American commercial media system, advertising and mass media have been interdependent, it is not surprising that the growth of advertising mirrored the growth of the mass media. Following the establishment in the 1890s of advertising agencies, which purchased space in newspapers and magazines and sold it to advertisers, along with assistance in creating advertisements, advertising grew steadily as a standard part of the content of most mass media. By 1909, newspapers were receiving a total of $149 million from the sale of advertising space, and magazines received $54 million. Yet between 1918 and 1923, *Printer's Ink,* a major trade journal of the developing advertising industry, was still devoting more articles to trying to convince companies that they should advertise than to discussions of merchandising and advertising techniques (Ewen, 1976). During the 1920s, media advertising experienced spectacular growth, becoming entrenched in something like its present position of prominence. By 1929, the volume of print advertising had more than quintupled in two decades, to nearly $800 million annually in newspapers and $320 million in magazines (Rorty, 1934).

Aiding the growth of advertising during the latter half of the 1920s was the rapid development of commercial radio. In just one year, radio's income from the sale of advertising time increased 24-fold, from $200,000 in 1926 to $4,820,000 in 1927. By 1929, radio's receipts from advertising were estimated to be at least $75 million (Rorty, 1934). By the end of the 1920s, the mass media's audiences were inundated by commercial advertising.

As the growth of advertising suggests, advertising was widely thought to be very effective in stimulating consumption. Consumption was increasing, and persons involved in advertising were quick to take credit, describing advertising as " 'business insurance' for profitable and efficient distribution" of consumer goods (Ewen, 1976, pp. 32–33). Advertising came to be regarded as essential to the nation's economy. Speaking to the American Association of Advertising Agencies in 1926, President Calvin Coolidge applauded the role of advertising in creating and directing "the enormous capacity for consumption of all kinds of commodities which characterizes our country" (quoted in Ewen, 1976, p. 41).

While advertising was increasing in volume and becoming more visible to the public, its content was changing. Before 1910, as Buckley (1982) explains,

> The dominant attitude among advertisers was that one considered consumers to be motivated by reason or "common sense." Advertisements were designed to educate or inform the public about the usefulness of a given product. Only a small minority of advertisers argued that efforts should be made to persuade and to create desires for new products.

Following 1910, "the accent on persuasion rather than information came to dominance within the advertising industry" (p. 213). Persuasion typically took the form of appealing to what were thought to be universal human instincts in order to stimulate sales of products. Hence, advertisers sought to create fears and stimulate desires in the media audience.

The combination of advertising's rapid growth, its apparent success, and the "growing tendency to regard advertising not as information for a rational consumer but as a method of persuading a nonrational public" (Buckley, 1982, p. 213) appeared to confirm the worries of those who believed the mass media might become powerful instruments for manipulating the mass audience.

The association of manipulation with mass communication was strengthened by the apparent success of another kind of systematic attempt to influence mass audiences, the propaganda campaigns of World War I. The term propaganda dates from Pope Gregory XV's creation in 1622 of a college of cardinals (the *Sacra Congregatio Christiano Nomini Propaganda*) charged with spreading or propagating the Christian faith *(de propaganda fide)*. There was little general interest or serious writing on the subject of propaganda, however, until the aftermath of the Great War. Then, a flurry of exposés, commentaries, and (often self-serving) memoirs by key participants revealed to the public that the belligerent governments had conducted massive propaganda campaigns during the war that were directed not only at enemy forces and populations but also, and more importantly, at their own citizens. In one of the volumes that pioneered serious attempts to study propaganda, Harold Lasswell (1927) explained,

> International war propaganda rose to such amazing dimensions in the last war, because the communization of warfare necessitated the mobilization of the civilian mind. No government could hope to win without a

united nation behind it, and no government could have a united nation
behind it unless it controlled the minds of its people. (p. 10)

The "war of ideas on ideas" (p. 12) was fought through "the management of opinions and attitudes by the direct manipulation of social suggestion" (p. 9). Concretely, the effort took such forms as sup-
plying newspapers with manufactured stories of enemy atrocities,
false information about the progress of the war on the battlefield and
at home, and messages designed to intensify patriotism and willingness to make sacrifices for the war effort. Eventually, official propaganda campaigns encompassed all media of communication, as in
the United States where "carefully designed propaganda messages
engulfed the nation in news stories, pictures, films, phonograph records, speeches, books, sermons, posters, wireless signals, rumors,
billboard advertisements, and handbills" (DeFleur & Ball–Rokeach,
p. 159). The enlistment of popular art in the war effort presaged the
more elaborate campaigns of World War II, in which the more fully
developed industries of mass entertainment "went to war" on a broad
front ranging from feature films to magazine fiction.

The effect of postwar revelations of official propaganda was widespread disillusionment and growing concern about the power of
mass communication in all its forms. As Lasswell wrote in 1927:

> A word has appeared, which has come to have an ominous clang in
> many minds—Propaganda. We live among more people than ever, who
> are puzzled, uneasy, or vexed at the unknown cunning which seems to
> have duped and degraded them. It is often an object of vituperation,
> and therefore, of interest, discussion and, finally, of study. (p. 2)

Worry about the power of mass media to shape public opinion was
expressed by Walter Lippmann (1922) who, in a highly influential discussion of the subject, called attention to the public's increasing reliance on mass media for information about the world and to the con-
sequent ability of the media, through news and popular
entertainment, to shape public knowledge in ways that were unhealthy for a democratic society—appealing to stereotypes, wishful
thinking, cultural myths, and so on.

Together, the new "psychological" media advertising and the apparently effective "suggestion techniques" of government propagan-
dists seemed to infuse mass media, including mass entertainment,
with a frightening power to manipulate, bringing to an end a process
which had begun with the suggestible public created by the mass society and continued with the dramatic success of new mass media

which created vast audiences by purveying entertainment. It was in this historical setting that systematic study of our subject, popular art as political communication, began.

POPULAR ART, CRITICAL THEORY, AND THE CONFLICT MODEL OF SOCIETY

Since the rise of mass media and mass entertainment was part of a series of interconnected, radical changes in social, economic, and political life, it is not surprising that, in some ways, thinking about the particular significance of popular art in mass media reflects more general conceptions of the nature of modern society. Two such conceptions are sometimes invoked to clarify the broad foundations and familial relationships seen in current views of our subject. These conceptions are, on the one hand, a model of society that is built on conflict and the struggle for power and benefits of opposing interests and, on the other hand, a model of society that is built on pluralism and a search for consensus. These are recognizable as frankly political theories, the former based primarily on Marxism and the latter a statement of liberal democratic theory.

Each of the two conceptions of society and politics may be seen as related to several different, valuable ways of understanding popular art as political communication. We shall use the two opposing political theories as devices for organizing these views of popular art in order to clarify relationships among the differing views. In doing so, we do not mean to minimize the importance of the disagreements which separate current views. Keeping in mind the respective political theories will help ensure that, in tracing the particular paths which current thinking has taken, we do not forget to notice the larger implications of these views. We shall begin with conceptions of our subject which have been framed by a conflict-centered understanding of how society works, reserving until later those conceptions which have grown out of a liberal or pluralistic view of society.

Mass Society Theory and the Frankfurt School

One of the earliest systematic assessments of the social impact of mass communication, and one which focused especially on popular art or the entertainment content of mass media, was the critical theory offered by members of the Institute for Social Research which was founded in 1923 at the University of Frankfurt, the "Frankfurt

School." Recruited chiefly from the ranks of radical intellectuals in the Weimar Republic, this group was a center for Marxist scholarship which set for itself the task of "keeping the critical light of Marxism burning during the 'dark years' which its members saw ahead" (Bennett, 1982, p. 42). When Hitler assumed power in 1933, the group moved to New York City, where it was affiliated with Columbia University, returning to Germany after the war in 1949. Among its most prominent members were Theodor Adorno, Leo Lowenthal, Max Horkheimer, and Herbert Marcuse.

Their efforts to understand the social upheavals they had witnessed in Europe led the members of the Frankfurt group to draw together in a distinctive way several different social theories. Their interest in Marxism led the Frankfurt theorists to seek an explanation for why the Russian revolution had not been exported to Western Europe. Their mass society theory provided an account of how, in industrial society, persons had been wrenched from the fabric of authentic social life and made rootless, alienated, and suggestible. The new mass media seemed to be a means by which the forces of entrenched economic and political power in industrial society were able to control the masses and to deflect their attention from the objective conditions of their existence.

A key feature of the Frankfurt School was their turning away from purely economic Marxist analysis to focus on the relation of culture to social life in modern society (see Jay, 1972, 1973; Streeter, 1984). In their view, "modern media have become technological instruments extending political and economic domination into the cultural sphere, debasing art and regimenting individual consciousness" (Czitrom, 1982, p. 144). Their concern with questions of cultural value, with the quality and consequences of media-based mass culture, was given special urgency by their experience in American exile. As Adorno recalls in a memoir, "I still remember the shock that a housemaid, an emigrant like ourselves, gave me during our first days in New York when she, the daughter of a so-called good home, explained: 'People in my town used to go to the symphony, now they go to Radio City.' In no way did I want to be like her. Even if I had wanted to, I wouldn't have been capable of it" (1969, p. 338).

The Frankfurt theorists believed that, in preindustrial society, traditional high culture had performed the social function of critique, opening space for oppositional voices. Traditional folk art, they thought, expressed the genuine conditions and concerns of the common people. With the new mass media came mass culture, an ersatz form that served the interests of the controlling classes and gained the acquiesence of the masses. Lowenthal, for example, distinguished between popular culture and genuine art as the difference "between spurious gratification and a genuine experience as a step to greater individual fulfillment" (1957, p. 51). In their analyses of particular forms of media entertainment and mass culture, such as Adorno's studies of music (e.g., 1941a, 1941b), members of the Frankfurt School argued their general thesis:

> The decline of the individual in the mechanized working processes of modern civilization brings about the emergence of mass culture, which replaces folk art or "high" art. A product of popular culture has none of the features of genuine art, but in all its media popular culture proves to have its own genuine characteristics: standardization, stereotypy, conservatism, mendacity, manipulated consumer goods. . . . all media are estranged from values and offer nothing but entertainment and distraction . . . they expedite flight from an unbearable reality. Whatever revolutionary tendencies show a timid head, they are mitigated and cut short by a false fulfillment of wish dreams, like wealth, adventure, passionate love, power, and sensationalism in general.
>
> (Lowenthal, 1957, p. 55)

Popular art in mass media stood indicted on two counts: (1) It ill-served its audience by fracturing the natural relation of consciousness and objective conditions, making the masses insensible of their actual circumstances and subject to the control of entrenched power; (2) By threatening eventually to drive authentic high culture and folk art out of existence as it consumed more and more of the audience and imposed bureaucratic structures on the creation of art (see Macdonald, 1957), it bade to close the oppositional spaces that had been provided in traditional society.

The Frankfurt School's analysis and condemnation of mass culture influenced in several ways the views of others who subsequently considered this subject. The Frankfurt analysis defined an extreme critical position that was widely argued during the postwar debate over mass culture and, more broadly, mass society in America. Dwight Macdonald argued stridently this position on mass culture in popular forums; David Riesman's popularized diagnoses of postwar American society were, in some respects, indebted to these views. Within the study of popular communication, the Frankfurt School's most important contribution probably was turning Marxism to a focus on the relationship of culture and social life, a focus that led to a generation of critical work based on the concept of ideology.

The influence of the Frankfurt group was limited, however, by their philosophical negativity. They rejected the more orthodox Marxist conception of theory as having its natural *telos* in action in favor of a passive position of transcendence. "Theory's purpose was not to change the world but to oppose to the world its powers of negation," a position from which theory was "deprived of any means whereby it might connect with reality in order to change it" (Bennett, 1982, 9. 46). Thus, they could offer no solution to the problems they exposed. Moreover, the mass society theory on which the Frankfurt School relied was manifestly unable to account for how social change could ever occur (see Bell, 1960, p. 38).

Popular Art and the Study of Ideology

The Frankfurt theorists had described the power of mass culture as residing in the view of individual and social life which the media presented to their audiences, a view which they thought constituted an ideology. The notion of ideology was taken from Marx. Although disputes about what Marx meant by ideology are complex and legion, most agree that the term calls attention to the relationship of signifying systems or forms of consciousness (Marx's examples include legal, political, religious, aesthetic, and philosophical forms) to actual material conditions and that the term implies some degree of distortion or misrepresentation of actual conditions (see Bennett, 1982, p. 47; Woollacott, 1982, p. 104). Marx also portrayed ideology as having relative autonomy in addition to its grounding in society's economic structures.

The suggestion, as in the Frankfurt School's critical theory, that mass media and mass entertainment operate as a social force by purveying ideology to their mass audience, made the study of ideology central to understanding the content and influence of media. Some theorists, such as Georg Lukács (1971), offered an economic-determinist view of consciousness and ideological forms as completely determined by persons' location within society's economic formation, thereby denying to ideology any independent influence in social processes. It was Althusser's view of ideology (1970/1971) that was of major importance in making this concept useful to students and critics of popular art. He proposed that ideology be understood not as completely determined by material conditions but rather as having an independent existence, under the control of the state, which predates a given individual's awareness and structures consciousness. In this view, ideology is, on the one hand, a set of ideas and form of understanding which rationalize and justify the economic and social order existing in society and, on the other hand, the concrete practices embodied in the institutions—such as churches, the schools, the family, and, especially, the mass media—which propound and reinforce these ideas. In capitalist society, as Bennett (1982) explains,

Individuals must be reconciled both to the class structure and to the class positions within it which they occupy. They must be induced to "live" their exploitation and oppression in such a way that they do not experience or represent to themselves their position as one in which they are exploited and oppressed. (p. 52)

This delusion of the working class is accomplished through the ideas and practices of ideology (for an example of the direct application of this view in the study of popular art, see Dorfman & Mattelart, 1971/ 1975).

The mass media and mass entertainment play crucial roles as ideological state apparatuses in Althusser's view, being themselves a key part of the concrete practices through which capitalist ideology, "a representation of the imaginary relationship of individuals with the real conditions of their existence" (Curran et al., 1982, p. 24), is given form and effectiveness. Based on this and similar understandings of ideology and the role of mass media, contemporary critics have analyzed popular art in the media in order to uncover the ideology which is presented and to demonstrate how the existing social order is affirmed through that ideology. They have argued, for example, that by portraying conflict as the result of individuals' pathologies, the genre of crime dramas on American television reinforces approval of regulative and even repressive state agencies (Requena, 1981). They have examined the ideological content of individual programs finding, as in Schwictenberg's (1987) study of *The Love Boat,* a structure which, "under the guise of personal transformation, operates to ensure, enforce, and perpetuate commodity-relations based on the structure of the nuclear family" (p. 138). And, they have looked to how entire media operate as ideological apparatuses (e.g., Corcoran, 1984). Such criticism has focused on what Jameson (1981, p. 219) terms a "negative hermeneutic" function, "demystifying the instrumental function of cultural texts in the perpetuation and reproduction of a given power structure" (Corcoran, 1984, p. 142).

More recently, the view of ideology presented in mass media as monolithic and imposed upon audiences has been questioned.

The Althusserian ideological approach . . . quickly reached the limits of theoretical articulation of the problem of the *"audience."* This formulation provided only a general abstract conception of the figure of the

audience as "subject," one common to all social institutions and specific to none, one that sustained a theory of totalizing ideological discourse. Nowhere did Althusser provide a place for the audience's differ-
ential positions and readings according to different levels or instances
of social position or practice.

(Browne, 1987, p. 586)

"Despite generations of life under the hegemony of capitalism," observed Fiske (1986, p. 392),

> There is still a wide range of social groups and subcultures with differ-
> ent senses of their own identity, of their relations to each other and to
> the centers of power. This diversity shows no signs of being homoge-
> nized into the unthinking mass so feared by members of the Frankfurt
> School, and, in a different way, by the ideological critics of the late
> 1970s.

If so, then "Ideology . . . is not monolithically imposed on a mallea-
ble subject"; rather, "individual television viewers . . . tend to process
television images according to their life situations (of which social
class is a determinant factor)" (Kellner, 1987, p. 483).

Recognition that the ideological content which critics discovered in
a message might be interpreted and responded to in different ways
by different members of the audience led to a decisive turn in much
of the contemporary critical scholarship that is concerned with popular art as political communication. From different points of view,
many of those who work in this tradition have sought to extend their
frameworks by including conceptions of how audience members interpret the ideology (or ideologies) found in popular art. In doing so,
they have not turned away from the larger project of understanding
and maintaining an oppositional stance to the ideological role of media in perpetuating the existing social order, but they have evolved
what might be described as a more sophisticated conception of how
media exert their ideological influence.

As will be seen in what follows, one way of conceiving the origins
and limits on audience members' interpretations of the ideological
content of messages has proved to be especially influential. This conception is derived from Parkin's (1972) treatment of class structures
as the basis of meaning systems. Parkin describes three "ideal types"
of ideological frameworks, which formed the basis of Hall's (1973,
1980) analysis of contrasting modes through which audience members, depending on their location in the class structure, interpret media messages. Fiske and Hartley's (1978, p. 104) description of these

three modes of audience interpretation or decoding is especially clear:

1. *The dominant system* . . . presents . . . the "official" version of class relations. It promotes endorsement of the existing inequality, and leads to a response among members of the subordinate class that can be described either as *deferential* [deferring to "the way things are"], or as *aspirational* [aspiring to "an individual share of the available rewards"].
2. *The subordinate system* . . . defines a moral framework . . . whereby the *framework* of the reward structure is accepted [and] all that is at issue is the share to be had by various communities or groups [as in the collective bargaining of trade unionism]. It promotes *accommodative* or *negotiated* responses to inequality.
3. *The radical system* is class-conscious . . . in that it rejects the frameworks by which one class achieves a dominant position, and so it promotes an *oppositional* response to inequality.

By opening room for alternative interpretations by audiences, the possibility of change is created. The critic's task shifts from revealing "ideology" to revealing "dominant ideology" or the "preferred meaning" inscribed in media texts and the way media texts may support a range of different interpretations.

Before leaving ideological criticism, it is important to note that this sort of work continues unabated and that its thrust additionally is being carried forward with concepts such as hegemony, developed by Gramsci (1971) as a more expansive and less monolithic and deterministic way of conceiving how media art exercises its conservative influence on audiences (see, e.g., Gitlin, 1987).

Structuralism and Semiotics

Contemporary structuralist and semiotic studies of popular art as political communication draw on a variety of theoretical views including, perhaps principally, Saussure's (1915/1974) linguistic analysis, Barthes's (1968, 1973) semiotic analysis, Lévi-Strauss's (1958/1972) structural anthropology, and Lacan's (1966/1977) psychoanalytic analysis. While there is great diversity in these studies, we may say generally that they regard language as a system of signs whose significance or meaning is determined by the internal arrangement of the system. In turn, language becomes a model for understanding social life, which also is conceived in terms of its structure, patterns, and relations. In this way, language or symbolic activity takes on a privileged role and study turns to the close analysis of the structure and internal organization of texts, especially the texts of popular art—television programs, literary works, films, and so on.

Texts are granted a large measure of autonomy (hence bear a complex relation to material reality) and are regarded as self-contained meaning systems which consist of signs and codes arranged in multi-layered oppositions, juxtapositions, and linkages. Latent content often is probed through the psychoanalytic elements within structuralism/semiotics. In this respect, such studies sometimes are similar to the psychological and psychoanalytic tradition in film studies (the paradigmatic examples include Kracauer, 1947, and Wolfenstein & Leites, 1950), which endeavor to go beyond showing how films reflect their culture by linking films to "deep and persistent patterns in the collective unconscious of a society or historical era" (Czitrom, 1982, p. 139). Myths are objects of special interest in many of these studies as they locate particularly powerful structures within codes of meaning. "Myth transforms the temporal common sense of ideology into the sacred realm of cultural prehistory and thus of eternal truth," writes Himmelstein (1984, p. 4). "It defuses at the outset any oppositional ideology that attempts to emerge to show the world of social relations as it really is." Gomery (1987), for instance, explains the popularity of the made-for-television movie, Brian's Song, by claiming that the film "reconstituted a potent mix of popular mythic material" to address contemporary concerns about race relations, women's roles, and big business (pp. 211–212) within the framework of the dominant ideology.

While structuralist and semiotic studies generally continue the project of ideological criticism by showing, through detailed internal analysis of linguistic structures, how ideology is reproduced in mass art, a particular theme of some recent work is the polysemy of popular art. That is, a prerequisite to a work of entertainment's being successful in modern society is thought to be constructing the work in a way that allows differing, even oppositional interpretations or decodings of the work to be constructed by different segments of the mass audience. As Fiske (1986, p. 391) argues in his analysis of television, because "the television audience is composed of a wide variety of groups or subcultures," then

> In order to be popular a television program must be polysemic so that different subcultures can find in it different meanings that correspond to their differing social relations. The dominant ideology is structured

into the text as into the social system, but the structure of both text and society allows space for resistance and negotiation.

Hence, studies examine the spaces opened up for contrasting interpretations within media texts including dominant, oppositional, and negotiated interpretations while still stressing the limits on interpretation created within texts and within society by class relations. The role of mass media entertainment as purveyor of the dominant ideology is preserved, but in a more sophisticated conception that allows room for discordant audience interpretations of media content. (For an elaboration of one form of this view, see Fiske & Hartley's [1978] notion of the "bardic function" of television.)

As the role of media and media entertainment comes to be seen as providing room for the expression of contradictions while maintaining the dominant ideology, its powerful, conservative social force is enhanced. As Gitlin (1987) explains in another context,

> The hegemonic system itself amplifies legitimated forms of opposition . . . by domesticating opposition, absorbing it into forms compatible with the core ideological structure. . . . This hegemonic core [that happiness, or liberty, or equality, or fraternity can be affirmed through the existing private commodity forms] is what remains essentially unchanged and unchallenged in television entertainment, at the same time the inner tensions persist and are even magnified. (pp. 526, 529)

Thus, the essential views and liberationist impulse within Marxist critical theory are maintained, but a more dynamic (and probably more useful) understanding of the ideological significance of mass entertainment is employed.

Studies of the Political Economy of the Media

An important contemporary strain of critical scholarship involves a revival of the base/superstructure grounding of ideology. Believing that contemporary Marxist cultural theory has erred by placing economic analysis at the periphery of its framework, those who study the political economy of the mass media and its products, including mass entertainment, insist that matters of media ownership, control, and markets are fundamental to any understanding of the ideological, social, and political operation of mass communication.

In an extreme form, which Grossberg (1984, p. 398) has labeled "economism," this view "looks behind the messages to see the mode of economic forces and relations, the systems of production and distribution. Consumption is monolithically determined by production, and hence both cultural texts and decodings are epiphenomenal products of the economic base.'" Hence, the autonomy of ideology as cultural production may be denied altogether (as in Smythe, 1977).

Some autonomy may be preserved for ideology and its operation in popular art better understood through a nondeterministic political economy of mass communication, however. Murdock and Golding (1979), for example, show how, over time, market forces impinging on mass media tend to exclude all but the most commercially successful materials and that this process "systematically excludes those voices lacking economic power or resources" (p. 37). The expression of oppositional views is muted and, even in successful media, a powerful preference for familiar, legitimated content is created. Murdock and Golding wish to avoid an economic-determinist view of the production and consumption of culture, but they insist that questions of media control, ownership, and production are prior to a useful understanding of "audiences within a class perspective" (p. 20).

The political economic viewpoint can yield important insights concerning particular types of media entertainment. For example, Shore (1983, cited in Grossberg, 1984), shows how control of a large share of world record production and distribution by six companies illuminates aspects of the ideological operation of records as an entertainment medium. Applied to television entertainment, explains Browne (1987, p. 598),

> The specific project of a political economy of the television megatext is to analyze the history and form of the schedule by linking the world of television entertainment and the world of work within the general mechanisms of the circulation of capital and commodity in Western industrialized societies . . . elaborating a framework that links the statements of social and psychical value specific to programs . . . and of particular audiences, to the processes of the general economy.

Cultural Studies of Mass Media

Cultural approaches to the study of mass media and popular art take several forms, of which perhaps the best known is the viewpoint that has evolved among persons associated with the University of Birmingham's Centre for Contemporary Cultural Studies, referred to more broadly as "British Cultural Studies." As this viewpoint has been exported to the United States and attracted more adherents who bring to it their own commitments and interests, it naturally has evolved and fragmented somewhat. But, it remains the most useful reference point for defining the cultural studies view of our subject.

Cultural studies incorporates elements of all the approaches to Marxist critical analysis of mass entertainment which we have examined. It is concerned with the social and political significance of media entertainment and conceives of that significance as exerted, largely, through ideology. It privileges language in social experience and examines, among other things, the signifying structures found in media texts, seeking their ideological significance. It is sensible of the political economy of media industries, and seeks to locate them within the general social and economic formation in society. All of this implies that cultural studies are a broad viewpoint. Perhaps what most distinguishes this approach, however, is its interest in understanding cultural production within the context of lived experience in modern society. Cultural studies are particularly interested in the nature of subjective experience, the roles and forms of ideology in experience, and the relation of experience to class and economic structures (see Streeter, 1984).

Study of subcultures (Hall & Jefferson, 1976) led to the notion of style as a means by which members of a subculture represent and symbolically resolve contradictions experienced in everyday life. As part of this process, subcultures appropriate cultural practices into their own constructed representations. This idea led to interest in the relation of class and subcultural locations to the decoding of media texts. In "Encoding/Decoding," Hall (1980) used Parkin's (1972) conception of dominant, negotiated, and oppositional ideological codes to understand how, through processes of interpretation or decoding, groups might appropriate within their own representations media content which legitimates dominant codes. Hall's claim was that dominant codes constitute the "preferred" meanings inscribed in media messages, but that language is necessarily open to divergent interpretations, thus allowing appropriation, even oppositional interpretations, by subcultural groups. What was needed was

> An approach which links differential interpretations back to the socioeconomic structure of society, showing how members of different groups and classes, sharing different "culture codes," will interpret a given message differently, not just at the personal, idiosyncratic level, but in a way "systematically related" to their socio-economic position.
>
> (Morley, 1980, pp. 14–15)

A two-part study which is often cited as defining the cultural studies approach concerned the British television program, *Nationwide*. In the first study, Brunsdon and Morley (1978), using semiotic analysis, revealed the codes by which the text endeavored to guide its interpretation by viewers and, in the process, to construct symbolically the identity of the viewers. In the second study, Morley (1980) interviewed groups of *Nationwide* viewers who were taken to represent differing subcultural formations (e.g., white male bank managers taking an in-service training course, white male apprentice electricians, Black women in a commercial studies curriculum) in order to discover how they interpreted the program. He found little relation between the program's preferred meaning and the interpretations made by audience members. Moreover, those interpretations were not directly correlated with social position: Groups sharing a common class position made conflicting interpretations; those higher in the class strata were more likely than others to make oppositional interpretations, and so on. The result was to underscore the difficulties with present conceptions of encoding and decoding, at least in this tradition of research, and to suggest that the relationship between audience members' interpretations of media messages and society's social and economic structures is more complex than had been anticipated.

In his most recent work, Morley (1986) has interviewed London couples to investigate the uses they make of television viewing. This work preserves an interest in the relation of class structures to interpretation but narrows the focus to smaller social units while at the same time broadening interest beyond interpretation to include use. A similar approach was taken by Radway (1984, 1985), who interviewed women readers of romance novels in order to determine how such novels are understood and used, relying on feminist theory, among other things, which may be considered a close relative of critical theory. In research of this sort, the cultural studies approach is coming to grips more directly with the role of culture and media in subjective, lived experience.

Summary

Emerging from the varied studies of popular art as political communication based on a conflict model of society is a picture of media, particularly of media entertainment content, as a powerful political force which reinforces dominant values, norms, and ideology. From this viewpoint, perhaps the most pernicious aspect of the dominant ideology found in popular media is its ability to appropriate and co-opt oppositional views, thus delegitimating genuine opposition and reducing it to mere style. However, critics have begun to acknowl-

edge that the ideology presented in the media's cultural texts is neither monolithic nor imposed upon the audience. Instead, recent work
has found, both within particular messages and across the entire content of popular media, materials that can support a variety of audience interpretations, even oppositional decodings. The process by
which media content is understood by audiences, in turn, has come
to be viewed as a more active and creative endeavor than early
thought about ideology imagined. Work in the cultural studies approach, especially, has stressed the ability of various segments of the
audience to appropriate media content within representational systems of their own construction that respond to their particular experience and position within society.

At present, the central question with which most strains of work
are grappling is how to understand better the process of interpretation or, in the language of this view, the relationship of encoding and
decoding. The move to acknowledging the existence of differing
codes in which audience members may interpret media content prob-
lematized the bases of interpretation. Interpretations are not seen as
completely individual and idiosyncratic, but their relation to social
and economic structures is clearly quite complex. The effort to preserve the bases of audience interpretations in society's social and
economic formations while still making room for divergent interpretive practices is leading critical researchers to probe how persons regard media content through such techniques as interviews and focus
groups. To many who work in the critical Marxist tradition, this style
of work is producing some of the most interesting and valuable research under way at present.

POPULAR ART, SYMBOLIST THEORY, SOCIAL SCIENCE, AND THE LIBERAL/PLURALIST MODEL OF SOCIETY

Set against the metaphors of conflict and struggle with which critical
researchers describe modern society and the role of popular art is a
quite different conception that relates, if loosely, a second group of
valuable and diverse scholarly traditions concerning our subject. At
base, this conception sees in modern society not so much dominance
and oppression as a search for shared understanding and consensus.
While differences of class and power are real and lead to differences
in circumstance, outlook, and aspiration, the focus here is on ways
by which persons and groups may understand each others' viewpoints and interests and, thereby, develop a consensus that responds

to diversity within a framework that seeks the common good. This is, of course, the ideal of the pluralist society in liberal democratic theory. It was born in the Enlightenment and developed especially in English liberal political thought and the writings of such figures as Locke and Mill.

In most cases, the views of popular art as political communication which are discussed in this section are not the products of scholars who have thought of themselves as explicitly pursuing a political agenda. Unlike the liberationist politics of critical researchers, these views have a more indirect, sometimes even problematic, relationship to any general political or social theory. Grouping these approaches together is an organizational convenience that clarifies their general thrust and exposes important family relationships, but the price of this convenience, perhaps even more than with Marxist critical scholarship, is papering over importance differences and, in some cases, implying a political agenda that the researchers themselves might be surprised to hear.

Communication and the Great Community

From the 1890s through the 1920s there developed at the University of Chicago an analysis of the role and prospect of mass communication that in some ways was a counterpoint to the Frankfurt School and mass society theory. This analysis was the work of Mead, Dewey, Park, and others, who framed what we commonly refer to as the "Chicago School of Social Thought." As the Frankfurt School prefigured the initial contours of critical studies of popular art, so the Chicago School serves as a point of departure for understanding some of the essential ideas that have informed what we might call liberal/pluralist conceptions of popular art and mass media. For this reason, it is necessary to sketch briefly some of the seminal ideas about communication that were developed at Chicago.

Mead's (e.g., 1934) social psychology placed language at the center of human life. The distinctively human qualities of mind, he thought, come to exist through social interaction. Interaction takes the form of exchanging with others significant symbols—words or gestures that evoke the same responses in those who use them. Because of the shared nature of significant symbols, their exchange in social interaction allows persons to develop the capacity for role taking, placing themselves in the other's point of view. In turn, grasping the other person's point of view allows foresight, the ability to anticipate the other's actions and responses. Language, thus, is the medium through which the essential human qualities of empathy and foresight are made possible.

Dewey (e.g., 1927) applied and extended Mead's analysis to the role of mass media in society. Dewey's conception of the ideal model of society was a community built on the sharing of experiences, interests, and control. Following Mead, he saw communication as the process which made possible the understanding of others' viewpoints and development of common perspectives that were the marks of ideal society. Like the mass society theorists, Dewey believed the complexity of industrial society and the interposition of its associated institutions had led to social fragmentation and confusion. The problem of modern democracy, he thought, was how to create a means whereby the free and unsuppressed communication necessary to achieving shared understanding and common opinion could be achieved. Dewey's solution was twofold: (1) A better understanding of the complex forces at work in industrial society through systematic inquiry; and, (2) A system of communication through which the resultant understanding could be made available to all members of the public. In this way, a far-flung public could gain control over its circumstances, develop shared and informed opinions, and regain democracy in the industrial age. The mass media thus were placed at the center of the political process as a vehicle through which the great society might be transformed into the great community.

These views created an optimistic prospect for contemporary democracy based on the pivotal role of mass communication. "From this standpoint, the differences among people appear to be remediable matters of misunderstanding and ignorance rather than fundamental differences of interest or value," notes Kreiling (1984, p. 41). Such a view "makes the means of social change a task of moral education and contributes to the faith in such agencies of education and persuasion as schools and communications media." Dewey's thought was of great importance in shaping American education, of course. His conception was elaborated as the basis of a new approach to journalism by Park (e.g., 1940); reverberated in the rejection of mass society theory by postwar American sociologists such as Daniel Bell (e.g., 1960); framed, along with the views of other members of the Chicago School, part of the context within which social-scientific American communication research began; and helped direct attention to study of symbols in human understanding and social life, as we see below. Along the way, Dewey offered perhaps the clearest statement of the liberal/pluralist conception of media's role in modern society.

Symbolist Theory and Popular Art

Art played an important role in Dewey's understanding of communication and human experience. If the distinctively human qualities of understanding and expression are their symbolic dimension, and if art is the paradigm case of purely symbolic expression, he thought, then art held the key to understanding much about individuals and society (see Dewey, 1922, 1934). The ideas of Dewey and Mead were important in shaping the later development of what we might term "symbolist theory," a diffuse group of conceptions that focus on the symbolic dimensions of human experience. These conceptions have been formulated and applied in a variety of disciplines, including political science (e.g., Edelman, 1964), sociology (e.g., Goffman, 1956/1959), and philosophy (e.g., Cassirer, 1944), and their diversity cannot be captured here. In general, however, they begin with the belief that

> Man lives in a symbolic universe. Language, myth, art, and religion are parts of this universe. They are the varied threads which weave the symbolic net, the tangled web of human experience. . . . No longer can man confront reality immediately; he cannot see it, as it were, face to face. . . . He has so enveloped himself in linguistic forms . . . that he cannot see or know anything except by the interposition of this artificial medium.
>
> (Cassirer, 1944, p. 25)

Through study of the use of linguistic and symbolic forms, symbolists seek to uncover the nature of experience. Material reality, they stress, comes to be known only through the symbolic forms in which it is apprehended. Art as a symbolic form has received special attention from symbolists, following Dewey, most often because it has been thought to encapsulate many elements of human perception, understanding, expression, and motivation. Not surprisingly, then, symbolist views have generated substantial scholarship concerned with popular art in the mass media.

A symbolist theory that has been especially useful in understanding popular art as political communication was offered by Kenneth Burke (e.g., 1962, 1966). Burke's far-ranging conception of language, experience, and social processes cannot be presented here, but we can note a few of his ideas that are germane to our subject. The aim of Burke's analysis was to show language to be the medium through which disagreement and difference may be overcome and common understanding created. Differences in viewpoints and interests necessarily are produced by hierarchical social order, he thought. But differences can be transcended through language as persons come use the resources of language to create shared experiences, motives, and purposes. The form of all human experience, for Burke, is dramatic. Everyday events are understood by seeing within them plots, conflicts, actors performing roles, and dramatic resolutions. Art thus plays a vital role in defining the shape of human understanding and is the prototype for experience itself. The basic processes that make society possible, in this analysis, are not coercion and oppression but communication and persuasion.

Hugh Duncan (1962, 1968) elaborated Burke's ideas in a detailed analysis of popular art's social functions. He argued that drama and comedy, as forms of understanding as well as forms of art, are essential to the functioning of society. Drama—in society's histories, rituals, and popular literature—gains acceptance at all levels of society of the transcendent social principles that are thought to justify the social order and to describe its ideals. Comedy performs the crucial tasks of subjecting the social order to the scrutiny of reason in order to point out where change is needed and of easing the strain on individuals of adjusting to society's demands by providing an arena in which disrepect and doubt may be voiced. In his writings, Duncan used this conception to illuminate the ameliorative social function of great comics such as Bob Hope and W. C. Fields and describe the consequences of social dramas enacted at public celebrations.

The particular symbolist theory that is exemplified by Burke and Duncan is dramaturgical in nature; that is, it conceives of human understanding and experience in dramatic terms (for a general presentation of dramaturgical theory, see Combs & Mansfield, 1976). This view has proved to be a powerful one for understanding the social and political consequences of popular art, and it has spawned several different critical approaches. Rhetorical critics have analyzed the construction of symbolic experience in dramatic form offered in popular films and television series (e.g., Frentz & Rushing, 1978; Medhurst, 1978; see especially Medhurst & Benson, 1984) in order to discover how popular art represents motives, dramatizes and resolves conflicts, and interprets social life. Rushing and Frentz (1980), for example, show how the popular film, *The Deer Hunter*, presents a construction of war as a complex aesthetic ritual of initiation which unites opposing aspects of human character, while Chesebro (1987) identifies several different conceptions of the nature of social problems and practical solutions which define the symbolic structures and logics underpinning some common formulas used in television series.

Fantasy theme analysis is an approach developed by rhetorical critics that elucidates with great clarity the dramatic constructions of experience offered in mass media (e.g., Bormann, 1972, 1973, 1977) This approach has been applied to the construction of personal relationships in popular magazines (Kidd, 1975) as well as to popular movies, sports, and other forms of popular art (e.g., Nimmo & Combs, 1983). An important feature of fantasy theme analysis is its interest in examining the relationship between dramatic constructions offered in media and the perceptions of the media audience; such constructions are traced from audiences to media and back again to show how dramatic forms structure everyday interaction was well as media content. A similar point has been made by Davis and Baran (1981) and Meyrowitz (1985), who have examined the relationship between television's construction of social interaction and Goffman's dramaturgical analysis of the forms of everyday interaction.

Traditional genre studies of the conventions by which crime shows, detective stories, Westerns, and the like construct symbolic reality also illustrate part of the impulse driving much dramaturgical criticial analysis (e.g., Cawelti, 1976). These studies, which are to be distinguished from the ideology-based structural analyses discussed earlier, seek to uncover formulary symbolic conventions that define particular forms of experience associated with genres of popular art. The familiar analysis of the symbolic structure of the Western movie, for example, depicts the hero as mediating between civilization and the wilderness and ultimately forced to take actions than bring about the end of the precivilization life. In this way, Westerns are seen as representing conflicts which inhere in life within society.

Symbolist-based studies of popular art, like critical studies in the Marxist tradition, offer close analysis of media texts. Where structuralists and semioticians seek to understand social life through analyzing self-contained texts, symbolists reverse the procedure, understanding texts through the symbolic dimension of lived experience. Symbolic understanding is regarded as "real," as the essential form of human thought and perception, not as a (more or less accurate) way of representing some material reality than can be known without the interposition of symbols. Unlike Marxist studies, the theoretical framework undergirding symbolist studies views popular art as a means of communication and persuasion whereby difference may be overcome and experience may be shared. Hence, popular art is seen as an arena in which conflict can be addressed and resolved symbolically; indeed, the capacity for symbolic resolution is often cited in these studies as a source of the wide appeal of popular art. In this way, symbolist analyses of the social influence of popular art fit squarely within the liberal/pluralist view of the role of media in society.

Studies of the Effects of Popular Art

Social-scientific studies of the effects of popular art on its audiences date back to the beginnings of social science in the opening decades of the 20th century. These studies have always been driven, in part, by public concern about possibly harmful consequences of mass entertainment on the beliefs, attitudes, and behavior of audience members, especially of children (see Wartella & Reeves, 1985). Furthermore, effects studies have always been based on a very wide range of different ideas about how communication works and what its role in society might be. The diversity of this work is so great that one may question any attempt at placing it on a conflict model of society-liberal/pluralist model of society continuum.

Effects studies are taken up at this point in our discussion for several reasons. As Delia (1987, pp. 30–37) has pointed out, the broader enterprise of communication science of which effects studies are a part was shaped early on by the thought and social agenda of the Chicago School. And, as a group, effects researchers have long been criticized (rightly or not) by critical scholars for the formers' alleged acceptance of the social and political aims of the media industry as defining the framework within which research is conducted (e.g., Brown, 1970; Golding & Murdock, 1978; Rowland, 1983). In general, effects studies do not begin by presuming media dominance, nor focus on ideological content as necessarily the most significant feature of media content, nor conceive of audiences as representing forms of consciousness defined by class structures.

As Delia (1987) and Wartella and Reeves (1985) have shown, effects research has always been characterized by great diversity in the viewpoints represented, questions asked, and methods employed rather than by a dominant paradigm or succession of paradigms. As a result, the research that has considered the social consequences of popular art organizes itself into a set of themes reflecting the kinds of questions that have been asked. One major theme centers around possible harmful effects of media entertainment on children. A major research effort, the Payne Fund studies, was launched in the early 1930s to examine the effects of movies on child audiences. These studies typified later work by bringing to bear a variety of theoretical ideas and research methods and by finding, in general, that movies'

effects were mediated by a variety of factors (the child's age, perceptions, predispositions, prior experiences, sex, parental influence, and
so on) such that a given film would affect different children in different ways (the summary volume of the Payne Fund studies is Charters,
1933). Similar findings have emerged from subsequent generations
of studies of the effects of media on children, although more recent
work, which incorporates more sophisticated ways of disentangling
the influence of individual and situational variables, has begun to
clarify the impact of media content. Several such studies have suggested a relationship between the direct viewing of violence and various indices of agression (e.g., Dominick & Greenberg, 1972). At the
same time, researchers have shown prosocial effects (e.g., increases
in children's desirable behaviors such as cooperation) to be associated with viewing prosocial media content (such as Stein & Friedrich's
1972 study concerning the television program, *Mr. Rogers' Neighborhood*). Concerning the consequences to children of viewing media
entertainment, it is clear that the processes which lead to effects are
mediated in complex ways by a host of variables.

The case with adults is similar. In general, research has endeavored to show that under some conditions certain kinds of content
may be associated with particular effects. The basic model for these
studies searches for a relationship between some social or political
element (e.g., a particular belief or attitude) in the content of an entertainment message and corresponding beliefs and attitudes held
by audience members. This model has been in place for several decades. In early trials, Thurstone and Peterson (cited in Fearing, 1947)
found an association between viewing the film *Birth of a Nation* and
an increase in negative attitudes toward Blacks, and Glock (1955)
found that feelings of anti-Semitism were reduced after subjects had
seen the movie, *Gentlemen's Agreement.*

In a recent example of this approach, Elliot and Schenck–Hamlin
(1979) found that viewing the film, *All the President's Men*, was associated with change in attitudes that seemed to be directly relevant to
the movie (i.e., increased political alienation but not a decrease in
interest in the political campaign, then under way; changes in opinions about the obligations of journalists that were mediated by viewers' political party preferences). Studying the consequences of viewing a similar media message (*Washington: Behind Closed Doors*, a
television "docudrama" also about the Watergate episode), Kaid,
Towers, and Myers (1981) found that feelings of political inefficacy
and political cynicism were not increased as a result of viewing. The
only effect found was an increase in negative feelings toward the

presidency, and that effect was not mediated by political party prefer-ence or other social and demographic factors.

Mediating factors figured prominently in Hur's (1978) study of the impact of the television "mini-series," *Roots,* on Black and white teen-agers. Hur observed that possible attitudinal effects of the program were mediated by viewers' pre-existing racial attitudes, with percep-tions of the hardships of slavery being felt mainly by viewers who already had what the researcher regarded as "liberal" general racial attitudes. Feldman and Sigelman (1985) found that the attitudinal im-pact of *The Day After,* a much-publicized television film about the aftermath of nuclear war in the United States, was limited largely to less-educated viewers who had not previously thought much about nuclear war, and noted that much of the overall impact of the pro-gram resulted not from viewing the television movie but from the journalistic attention that surrounded the program. Their summary accords with this line of research in general:

> It is simply too much to expect a television program [or, we might add, any other work of popular art] to transform people's fundamental social and political values. . . . Only when a program directly addresses a rela-tively narrow issue on which viewers lack highly structured attitudes does change seem at all likely.
>
> (Feldman & Sigelman, 1985, p. 559)

Effects researchers have also looked beyond the unusual instances of explicitly political content in popular art to examine the conse-quences of ordinary fare, such as popular television series. Here, too, the role of mediating factors has been stressed. In perhaps the best-known example, Surlin's (1976) review of research on the television series, *All In the Family,* noted that, despite the intended liberal ideol-ogy, the series was attracting and being enjoyed especially by high-prejudiced viewers who agreed with Archie Bunker. Dealing with less controversial content, however, more straightfoward effects have been found. Volgy and Schwarz (1980), for instance, found that view-ing medical series on television (all of which portrayed doctors and the health care system in a favorable light) was associated with posi-tive feelings toward doctors, and that viewing television series about minorities in which problems of bigotry and economic disadvantage were not portrayed was associated with decreased concern about ra-cial problems in society.

Space does not permit extended discussion of the large number of effects studies that have examined popular art in the media. The studies noted above display perhaps the most important characteristics of this work. Researchers have surveyed a wide range of content for its effects on audiences' attitudes and opinions and have produced results which underscore the many factors which limit the power of popular art. Effects researchers in general have not theorized media content in any way that would allow them to determine possible effects on audiences beyond gross consequences of the sort we have discussed, however, so the failure to find substantial effects with adult audiences must not be taken as denying the possibility that popular art might affect audiences in ways not yet considered. Social characteristics of audience members, especially those related to class, such as income and education, typically are included as a possible mediating variable in this research, and no strong or consistent picture of responses to popular art as class-based or class mediated has emerged. Instead, the most successful accounts of audience responses have been those which highlight individual differences, such as differences in attitudes, that are found within members of the same social groups.

Content Analysis

Content analysis in communication research dates back to the early study of propaganda and the work of Lasswell (e.g., 1938). Quantitative methods of content analysis were formalized during the 1950s through the efforts of persons such as Pool (1959) and have since been turned to many different purposes. We are interested here in how researchers have used content analysis to reveal something about the nature of popular art.

The best-known approach to analyzing the content of popular art using quantitative methods is incorporated within the cultivation analysis research program conducted by Gerbner and his coworkers (Gerbner & Gross, 1976a, 1976b; Gerbner et al., 1977; Gerbner, Gross, Jackson—Beeck, Jeffries—Fox, & Signorielli, 1978; Gerbner, Gross, Signorielli, Morgan, & Jackson—Beeck, 1979). The research program consists of two parts: (1) Quantitative analysis of certain features of the content of prime-time and weekend network television dramatic programs appearing in yearly samples of one week's programming; (2) An attempt to relate elements found within program content to beliefs and attitudes held by "heavy viewers" of television. In linking content to audiences, the cultivation strategy has assumed that television content offers a systematically distorted view of reality and that the more viewers are dependent upon television, the more likely viewers will be to accept television's distorted picture as a true portrait of reality.

The efforts of Gerbner and his associates to connect television content to viewers' perceptions of reality have come under damaging criticism on both theoretical and methodological grounds (see Gerbner, Gross, Morgan, & Signorielli, 1981a, 1981b; Hirsch, 1980, 1981a, 1981b; Newcomb, 1978). The details of this dispute need not concern us here. The effect has been to raise serious questions about the audience research portion of cultivation analysis. We are interested, however, in the content studies that have been conducted under the aegis of cultivation analysis. Such studies might be discussed at several different points within this narrative but are taken up here because of the increasingly close links between content analysis and effects studies (e.g., Surlin, 1976; Volgy & Schwarz, 1980).

A special interest of the Gerbner group, and one that reflects general public concern, is assaying the dimensions of violent content presented in television. They have found that an average of 8 out of 10 programs and 6 of 10 major characters in their samples are involved in violence in some way, with an average of 7½ episodes of violence per hour in prime time and almost 18 per hour in weekend daytime children's programs (Gerber, Gross, Signorielli, & Jackson–Beeck, 1979).

Television's presentation of social roles also has received detailed scrutiny from content analysts. Butsch and Glennon (1980) concluded from their analysis of television series centered in families and aired between 1947 and 1977 that there were striking differences in the presentation of middle-class and working-class families. The great majority of the series depicted middle-class family life (only 11 of more than 200 series concerned working-class families) and, in general, working-class families were shown to consist of husbands/fathers whose foolish actions caused problems that were solved by sensible wives/mothers while these roles were reversed in middle-class series. Roughly similar results were reported in Thomas and Callahan's (1982) study of prime-time series focused on family units in 1978–1980, where the consistent if infrequent portrayal of wealthy families (e.g., the Ewings of *Dallas*) suggested that money does not buy happiness or family solidarity.

Sex-related differences in the presentation of adult characters have been documented in television programming (e.g., Downing, 1974; Long & Simon, 1974; Tedesco, 1974) and popular fiction (e.g., Franzwa, 1974; Lazer & Dier, 1978), as well as other popular media. Generally, dramatic portrayals have been found to show women as more likely to be unemployed or housewives and more restricted to a narrow range of occupations than the facts of women's actual employment patterns would indicate.

While there is a host of content-analytic studies of popular art which have not been mentioned, the research described above illustrates some of the major characteristics of most such scholarship. Researchers have been drawn to investigating content across messages within media (such as presentations of family life in many different television series) rather than to examining the content of a single message, as is more often the case in general effects research. In selecting themes or aspects of content to inspect, analysts typically have focused on topics which seem to reflect important social concerns: the prevalence of violence, family structure, sex roles. Often, depictions noted in popular entertainment are compared with their corresponding occurrence in society to determine whether the depictions are accurate reflections of real life (in nearly every case, as in the examples described above, fictional portrayals are found to be inaccurate by this standard.)

As an approach to understanding the social and political significance of popular art, content analysis has two features that should be noted. First, their interest in comparing themes across many messages has allowed content analysts to offer a somewhat clearer picture of the socially and politically relevant elements offered in popular art as a whole than has been possible in general effects research. Second, this sort of research supports several different conclusions about the consequences of popular art. Popular art might be castigated, as many content analysts have done, for failing to offer accurate or realistic portrayals of contemporary life. At the same time, some have argued that to expect "accuracy" is to misunderstand the nature and significance of popular art. Fiske and Hartley (1978, p. 24) contend:

> Television does not represent the manifest actuality of our society, but rather reflects, symbolically, the structure of values and relationships beneath the surface. So the high proportion of middle-class occupations is not a distortion of social fact, but an accurate symbolic representation of the esteem with which a society like ours regards such positions and the people who hold them.

Hence, content analysis may be seen as reaching in one direction to general effects research by discovering broad social themes in content for which effects might be sought and reaching in another direction to symbolist studies which attempt to describe the symbolic construction of society which is offered in mass entertainment.

Uses and Gratifications Studies of Popular Art

The uses and gratifications framework defines a particular approach to understanding the process of mass communication. From the earliest studies, uses and gratifications researchers have been interested in the entertainment content of mass media (e.g., Herzog, 1944) as well as news and other forms of media messages. As with the other rubrics which organize this discussion, uses and gratifications refers to a range of quite different views that have evolved over time. However, the essential claims of the gratifications framework may be summarized as follows:

> In the uses and gratifications model, persons are described as motivated by psychological, social, and sociocultural influences to use mass media to accomplish particular ends, conceived as "gratifications." Empirical studies have discovered that gratifications take many forms, from learning information that can be instrumental in performing one's role as a citizen to consuming media fare in a relaxing ritual. Various aspects of a received message (i.e., attributes of the medium, genre of media content, or specific message or program) may provide gratifications. The particular gratifications experienced by audiences, though, are not thought to be controlled entirely by the message, genre, or medium. Instead, audience members exhibit some independence and diversity in linking gratifications to media messages as they creatively use mass communication to try to accomplish their desired ends. Media messages are seen as at least partly malleable, capable of being interpreted or taken in somewhat different ways by auditors who seek different gratifications from them. Concomitantly, the effects of messages are believed to be channeled to some extent by the gratification seeking that provides the interpretive context in which the messages are experienced by their audiences.
>
> (Swanson, 1987, p. 238)

The focus in uses and gratifications research generally has been on the motives persons identify as leading them to attend to a message or medium and on the ways those motives may influence or channel exposure to mass communication and the consequences of exposure. At the most general level, this research has shown that the fects on individuals of exposure to media are shaped by the motives—such as to acquire information, or to relax, or to enhance social interaction by viewing with others or discussing media content with others—which underlie the individuals' exposure, that a wide range of motivations lead persons to attend to mass media, and that media content is multifunctional, capable of being put to many different uses by members of the audience (for an assessment of the state of the art in gratifications research, see Rosengren, Wenner, & Palmgreen, 1985).

Gratifications researchers have examined forms of popular entertainment ranging from horoscope columns in newspapers and magazines (Weimann, 1982) to music videos (Rubin et al., 1986). Their findings have mirrored the results of gratifications studies of other types of media content. For example, a wide range of motives has been found to lead persons to watch television soap operas. Babrow (1987) recently reported 16 such motives, including diversion, arousal, learning, identity needs, emotional release, and social interaction (see also Lemish, 1985). Carveth and Alexander (1985) and Perse (1986) have shown that some effects of soap operas, such as influencing viewers' perceptions of social life in general, are influenced by the particular motives that lead persons to watch the programs. Strongest effects of the sort mentioned occur, within the total audience, in viewers who watch for entertainment that is also informative (as contrasted to viewers who watch for entertainment that is simply relaxing and diverting). In this way, gratifications research, like effects research, has stressed the role of individual differences in shaping the consequences to individuals of media entertainment and other messages.

Perhaps because of what it has had to say about the consequences of popular art, gratifications research has encountered strong objections from critical theorists of various stripes (e.g., Carey & Kreiling, 1974; Elliott, 1974; Morley, 1980). While a number of objections have been raised, two related criticisms are most germane to our interest here. First, it has been charged that gratifications research is conducted in a way that ensures its results will show popular art's consequences in a favorable light. Allegedly, this is so because gratifications researchers ask persons what motives media exposure satisfies and then investigate how this satisfaction occurs. But, it is claimed, people are likely to give researchers only socially desirable motives and, moreover, there may be motives and social or economic forces guiding exposure to media that people are not consciously aware of. In taking viewers' word at face value, researchers are being socially and politically naïve and producing an overly "psychologistic" explanation of audiences and effects. As a result, gratifications research is guaranteed to show that popular art provides satisfaction to socially desirable motives of its audience. Second, gratifications research has been faulted for lacking any theory of symbolic forms. Without an explicit theory of messages or texts, researchers must take viewers' word for what is found in popular art and are unable to examine directly how the messages work to structure experience or to explain why the features of a particular message lead to certain consequences.

Gratifications researchers have responded to these criticisms in two ways that are important to our subject here. On the one hand, they have directed more attention to discovering the social and other forces outside the individual that might influence a person's conscious motives for attending to popular entertainment (see Blumler, 1985). For example, Rubin (1985) has described the ways in which social needs and opportunities change from childhood through older adulthood and how these changes relate to uses of mass communication. Donohew, Palmgreen, and Rayburn (1987) have investigated the way four different common life-styles (each a particular combination of personality and social needs, self-perceptions, attitudes, and individual and social behaviors) lead to different motives for using media. Looking beyond the immediate social environment, Blumler, Gurevitch, and Katz (1985) have stressed the need to bring social structure into the gratifications framework. As they put it,

> We never meant to talk about abstracted individuals, but about people in social situations that give rise to their needs. The individual is part of a social structure, and his or her choices are less free and less random than a vulgar gratificationism would presume. (p. 260)

Second, gratifications researchers have acknowledged the need to bring into their framework the symbolic content of messages and propose to do so by studying the relationship between interpretive processes used by audiences in understanding messages and the symbolic content of the messages (Blumler et al., 1985; McQuail, 1984). Since, in the gratifications framework, individuals' motives are thought to guide their interpretation of messages, then proceeding in this way can link motives to the consequences of exposure through the interpretation of symbolic content. Some writers have recently begun to explore conceptions of interpretive processes and their relation to symbolic content that might provide a foundation for elaborating gratifications research in this direction (e.g., Swanson, 1987).

Summary

Emerging from the eclectic group of studies based (if loosely) on a liberal/pluralist model of society is a more cautious view of the social and political consequences of popular art than we saw earlier. Popular art is seen more as a symbolic than an explicitly political force in society. That is, the messages of media entertainment offer complex symbolic constructions of human experience which become appealing by representing and, sometimes, resolving anxiety and conflict, and by providing a range of satisfactions to their audiences. Media constructions do not directly nor accurately reflect contemporary society, so much as they mirror the values and aspirations that hold sway in society.

In understanding the power of popular art, liberal/pluralists begin by looking within the individual audience member and only later turn to broad social and economic forces that may impinge on individuals. They find great variation within the individual and these variations, more than great economic forces, seem to limit and channel the effects of popular art. Hence, popular art is conceived, ultimately, as offering complex messages which are filtered through individual differences to produce a similarly complex range of effects or consequences. In understanding this process, ideas of class and dominance are less useful than are ideas of difference, creativity, and independence.

POINTS OF CONTACT

Organizing scholarship about popular art as political communication around two quite different views of society in the way we have done raises several questions. Are these views incommensurable approaches to understanding popular art as a social and political force? Is assessing the influence of popular art a purely political exercise? Will the future of scholarship on the subject consist of parallel advances along these two tracks that never converge? These questions deserve to be addressed before closing our discussion.

Curran et al. (1982) have pointed out the extent to which some of the differences in these two views of media influence result from having asked different questions rather than from having arrived at different answers to the same questions. Concerning the effects of media portrayals of violence, for example, they note that British critical researchers have asked whether media content has reinforced public support for the forces of law and order. Researchers

> Have thus examined the impact of the mass media in situations where mediated communications are powerfully supported by other institutions such as the police, judiciary and schools, and sustained by already widely diffused attitudes favourable towards law enforcement agencies

and generally unfavourable towards groups like youth gangs, student radicals, trade union militants and football hooligans.

(Curran et al., 1982, p. 14)

Asking the question in this way has led to seeing media content as a powerful force that reinforces the dominant culture. In contrast, researchers in the liberal/pluralist tradition have posed the question in terms of whether media portrayals encourage violence in real life in a context in which violent behavior is "opposed to deeply engrained moral norms and . . . a network of social relationships and powerful institutions [that are] actively opposed to 'anti-social behavior' " (Curran et al., 1982, p. 14). Formulating the question in this way has led to seeing limits on the power of media content. While we should not push this point too far, it is fair to say that their different ways of framing the issue of popular art as political communication may exaggerate the differences between these two traditions.

Without minimizing differences that are real and substantial, we may note three points of contact between what the two traditions currently are saying about popular art as political communication. First, scholars in both traditions believe that popular art has important social and political consequences which occur at several levels. They believe that popular art can affect individuals' beliefs, attitudes, values, and perceptions of reality, that through the vehicle of popular art individuals experience conventional or "dominant" views of how society works, that popular art is on balance a conservative social force, though its messages contain diverse elements.

A second point of contact is that many scholars in both traditions have come to believe that, in order to understand the social and political significance of popular art, it is necessary to theorize about both audiences and media content. Early ideological studies employed a detailed theoretical conception of media content but saw no need for a parallel conception of audiences. More recently, critical scholars have acknowledged that different segments of the audience can interpret a given message in different ways and have begun to consider how the audience can be theorized in order to understand the origins of differing interpretive practices or codes. Similarly, effects studies and, until recently, uses and gratifications studies employed a fairly elaborate theory of audiences, stressing the attributes of individuals that channel and limit the effects of messages, but lacked any theoretical conception of the symbolic content of messages. Current theorizing is struggling with ways of conceptualizing messages so that the significant attributes of content can be identified and understood. At the most general level, then, the directions taken by theory in some of the domains of work within the two traditions may be seen as mirror images.

Finally, many scholars working in the two traditions agree that an important priority for the immediate future is to understand better how persons interpret the content of media messages. Critical scholars retain their commitment to approaching interpretive processes by looking first at broad social and economic structures, while effects and gratifications researchers remain committed to approaching interpretive structures through the individual audience member and moving to the broader social formation only as it presents itself in the experience of the individual. Starting from these different points, both efforts seem to have reached the level of the social group. In cultural studies, for example, the social group has been turned to in such forms as subcultures; in gratifications studies, for example, efforts are being made to push beyond individuals to observe the consequences of social groups on individuals' use of media. To be sure, subcultures are not the same as membership groups. Still, there seems to be movement toward a common reference point. And, both traditions seem to believe that audience members themselves are our best source of information in understanding interpretive processes. To continue the above examples, both cultural studies and gratifications researchers employ focus groups, interviews, and similar methods of collecting data from audience members in order to understand how media content is experienced and interpreted.

Plato believed that "when modes of music change, the fundamental laws of the State always change with them" (*Republic*, IV, 424). Critical theorists would perhaps invert the equation. Somewhere between these two views lies our best understanding of popular art as political communication.

REFERENCES

Adorno, T. W. (1941a). On popular music. *Studies in Philosophy and Social Science, 9*(1), 17–48.

Adorno, T. W. (1941b). The radio symphony. In P. F. Lazasrfeld & F. N. Stanton (Eds.), *Radio research, 1941* (pp. 110–139). New York: Duell, Sloan, & Pearce.

Adorno, T. W. (1957). Television and the patterns of mass culture. In B. Rosenberg & D. M. White (Eds.), *Mass culture: The popular arts in America* (pp. 474–488). New York: Free Press.

Adorno, T. W. (1969). Scientific experiences of a European scholar in America (D. Fleming, Trans.). In D. Fleming & B. Bailyn (Eds.), *The intellectual migration: Europe and America, 1930–1960* (pp. 338–370). Cambridge, MA: Harvard University Press.

Albig, W. (1939). *Public opinion.* New York: McGraw–Hill.

Althusser, L. (1971). *Lenin and philosophy and other essays* (B. Brewster, Trans.). London: New Left. (Original work published 1970)

Babrow, A. S. (1987). Student motives for watching soap operas. *Journal of Broadcasting & Electronic Media, 31,* 309–321.

Barthes, R. (1968). *Elements of semiology.* London: Cape.

Barthes, R. (1973). *Mythologies.* London: Paladin.

Bell, D. (1960). *The end of ideology.* New York: Free Press.

Belting, N. (1986, June 29). Illinois past: Movie violence created havoc in early 1900s. *News–Gazette,* p. C–2., Champaign–Urbana, IL.

Bennett, T. (1982). Theories of the media, theories of society. In M. Gurevitch, T. Bennett, J. Curran, & J. Woollacott (Eds.), *Culture, society and the media* (pp. 30–55). London: Methuen.

Blumler, J. G. (1985). The social character of media gratifications. In K. E. Rosengren, L. A. Wenner, & P. Palmgreen (Eds.), *Media gratifications research: Current perspectives* (pp. 41–60). Beverly Hills, CA: Sage.

Blumler, J. G., Gurevitch, M., & Katz, E. (1985). Reaching out: A future for gratifications research. In K. E. Rosengren, L. A. Wenner, & P. Palmgreen (Eds.), *Media gratifications research: Current perspectives* (pp. 255–274). Beverly Hills, CA: Sage.

Bormann, E. G. (1972). Fantasy and rhetorical vision: The rhetorical criticism of social reality. *Quarterly Journal of Speech, 58,* 396–407.

Bormann, E. G. (1973). The Eagleton affair: A fantasy theme analysis. *Quarterly Journal of Speech, 59,* 143–159.

Bormann, E. G. (1977). Fetching good out of evil: A rhetorical use of calamity. *Quarterly Journal of Speech, 63,* 130–139.

Brown, R. L. (1970). Approaches to the historical development of mass media studies. In J. Tunstall (Ed.), *Media sociology: A reader* (pp. 41–57). Urbana: University of Illinois Press.

Browne, N. (1987). The political economy of the television (super)text. In H. Newcomb (Ed.), *Television: The critical view* (4th ed., pp. 585–599). New York: Oxford University Press.

Brunsdon, C., & Morley, D. (1978). *Everyday television: "Nationwide."* London: British Film Institute.

Buckley, K. W. (1982). The selling of a psychologist: John Broadus Watson and the application of behavioral techniques to advertising. *Journal of the History of the Behavioral Sciences, 18,* 207–221.

Burke, K. (1962). *A grammar of motives and a rhetoric of motives.* New York: World Publishing.

Burke, K. (1966). *Language as symbolic action.* Berkeley: University of California Press.

Butsch, R., & Glennon, L. M. (1980). Families on TV: Where was the working class? *Televisions, 7*(2/3), 11–12.

Carey, J. W., & Kreiling, A. L. (1974). Popular culture and uses and gratifications: Notes toward an accommodation. In J. G. Blumler & E. Katz (Eds.), *The uses of mass communications: Current perspectives on gratifications research* (pp. 225–248). Beverly Hills, CA: Sage.

Carveth, R., & Alexander, A. (1985). Soap opera viewing motivations and the cultivation process. *Journal of Broadcasting & Electronic Media, 29,* 259–273.

Cassirer, E. (1944). *Essay on man.* New Haven, CT: Yale University Press.

Cawelti, J. G. (1976). *Adventure, mystery, and romance.* Chicago: University of Chicago Press.

Charters, W. W. (1933). *Motion pictures and youth.* New York: Macmillan.

Chesebro, J. W. (1987). Communication, values, and popular television series—A four-year assessment. In H. Newcomb (Ed.), *Television: The critical view* (4th ed., pp. 17–51). New York: Oxford University Press.

Combs, J. E., & Mansfield, M. W. (Eds.). (1976). *Drama in life: The uses of communication in society.* New York: Hastings House.

Corcoran, F. (1984). Television as ideological apparatus: The power and the pleasure. *Critical Studies in Mass Communication, 1,* 131–145.

Curran, J., Gurevitch, M., & Woollacott, J. (1982). The study of the media: Theoretical approaches. In M. Gurevitch, T. Bennett, J. Curran, & J. Woollacott (Eds.), *Culture, society and the media* (pp. 11–29). London: Methuen.

Czitrom, D. J. (1982). *Media and the American mind: From Morse to McLuhan.* Chapel Hill: University of North Carolina Press.

Davis, D. K., & Baran, S. J. (1981). *Mass communication and everyday life: A perspective on theory and effects.* Belmont, CA: Wadsworth.

DeFleur, M. L., & Ball–Rokeach, S. (1982). *Theories of mass communication* (4th ed.). New York: Longman.

Delia, J. G. (1987). Communication research: A history. In C. R. Berger & S. H. Chaffee (Eds.), *Handbook of communication science* (p. 20–98). Newbury Park, CA: Sage.

Dewey, J. (1922). *Experience and nature.* New York: Norton.

Dewey, J. (1927). *The public and its problems.* New York: Holt, Rinehart, & Winston.

Dewey, J. (1934). *Art as experience.* New York: Minton, Balch.

Dominick, J. R., & Greenberg, B. S. (1972). Attitudes toward violence: The interaction of television exposure, family attitudes, and social class. In G. A. Comstock & E. A. Rubinstein (Eds.), *Television and social behavior: Vol. 1. Television and adolescent aggressiveness* (pp. 314–335). Washington, DC: U.S. Government Printing Office.

Donohew, L., Palmgreen, P., & Rayburn, J. D., II. (1987). Social and psychological origins of media use: A lifestyle analysis. *Journal of Broadcasting & Electronic Media, 31,* 255–278.

Dorfman, A., & Mattelart, A. (1975). *How to read Donald Duck: Imperialist ideology in the Disney comic* (D. Kunzle, Trans.). New York: International General. (Original work published 1971)

Downing, M. (1974). Heroine of the daytime serial. *Journal of Communication, 24*(2), 130–137.

Duncan, H. D. (1962). *Communication and social order.* New York: Bedminster Press.

Duncan, H. D. (1968). *Symbols in society.* New York: Oxford University Press.

Durkheim, E. (1964). *The division of labor in society* (G. Simpson, Trans.). New York: Free Press. (Original work published 1893)

Edelman, M. (1964). *The symbolic uses of politics.* Urbana: University of Illinois Press.

Elliott, P. (1974). Uses and gratifications research: A critique and a sociological alternative. In J. G. Blumler & E. Katz (Eds.), *The uses of mass communications: Current perspectives on gratifications research* (pp. 249–268). Beverly Hills, CA: Sage.

Elliott, W. R., & Schenck–Hamlin, W. J. (1979). Film, politics and the press: The influence of "All the President's Men." *Journalism Quarterly, 56,* 546–553.

Ewen, S. (1976). *Captains of consciousness: Advertising and the social roots of the consumer culture.* New York: McGraw–Hill.

Fearing, F. (1974). Influence of movies on attitudes and behavior. *Annals of the American Academy of Politcal and Social Science, 254,* 70–79.

Feldman, S., & Sigelman, L. (1985). The political impact of prime-time television: "The Day After." *Journal of Politics, 47,* 556–578.

Fiske, J. (1986). Television: Polysemy and popularity. *Critical Studies in Mass Communication, 3,* 391–408.

Fiske, J., & Hartley, J. (1978). *Reading television.* London: Methuen.

Franzwa, H. H. (1974). Working women in fact and fiction. *Journal of Communication, 24*(2), 104–109.

Frentz, T. S., & Rushing, J. H. (1978). The rhetoric of "Rocky": Part two. *Western Journal of Speech Communication, 42,* 231–240.

Gerbner, G., & Gross, L. (1976a). Living with television: The violence profile. *Journal of Communication, 26*(2), 173–199.

Gerbner, G., & Gross, L. (1976b). The scary world of TV's heavy viewer. *Psychology Today, 9*(11), 41–45, 89.

Gerbner, G., Gross, L., Eleey, M. F., Jackson–Beeck, M., Jeffries–Fox, S., & Signorielli, N. (1977). TV violence profile No. 8: Highlights. *Journal of Communication, 27*(3), 171–180.

Gerbner, G., Gross, L., Jackson–Beeck, Jeffries–Fox, S., & Signorielli, N. (1978).

Cultural indicators: Violence profile No. 9. *Journal of Communication, 28*(3), 176–206.

Gerbner, G., Gross, L., Morgan, M., & Signorielli, N. (1981a). A curious journey into the scary world of Paul Hirsch. *Communication Research, 8,* 39–72.

Gerbner, G., Gross, L., Morgan, M., & Signorielli, N. (1981b). Final reply to Hirsch. *Communication Research, 8,* 259–280.

Gerbner, G., Gross, L., Signorielli, N., Morgan, M., & Jackson–Beeck, M. (1979). The demonstration of power: Violence profile No. 10. *Journal of Communication, 29*(3), 177–196.

Gitlin, T. (1987). Prime time ideology: The hegemonic process in television entertainment. In H. Newcomb (Ed.), *Television: The critical view* (4th ed., pp. 507–532). New York: Oxford University Press.

Glock, C. Y. (1955). Some applications of the panel method to the study of change. In P. Lazarsfeld & M. Rosenberg (Eds.), *The language of social research* (pp. 242–244). New York: Free Press.

Goffman, E. (1959). *The presentation of self in everyday life.* Garden City, NY: Doubleday Anchor. (Original work published 1956)

Golding, P., & Murdock, G. (1978). Theories of communication and theories of society. *Communication Research, 5,* 339–356.

Gomery, D. (1987). *Brian's Song:* Television, Hollywood, and the evolution of the movie made for television. In H. Newcomb (Ed.), *Television: The critical view* (4th ed., pp. 197–220). New York: Oxford University Press.

Gramsci, A. (1971). In (Q. Hoare & G. N. Smith (Eds.), *Selections from the prison notebooks.* New York: International Publishers.

Grossberg, L. (1984). Strategies of Marxist cultural interpretation. *Critical Studies in Mass Communication, 1,* 392–421.

Hall, S. (1973). *Encoding and decoding in the television discourse* (Occasional Papers, No. 7). Birmingham, England: Centre for Contemporary Cultural Studies.

Hall, S. (1980). Encoding/decoding. In S. Hall, D. Hobson, A. Lowe, & P. Willis (Eds.), *Culture, media, language* (pp. 128–138). Hutchinson.

Hall, S., & Jefferson, T. (Eds.). (1976). *Resistance through rituals.* London: Hutchinson.

Herzog, H. (1944). What do we really know about daytime serial listeners? In P. F. Lazarsfeld & F. N. Stanton (Eds.), *Radio research 1942–1943* (pp. 3–33). New York: Duell, Sloan, & Pearce.

Himmelstein, H. (1984). *Television myth and the American mind.* New York: Praeger.

Hirsch, P. M. (1980). The "scary world" of the nonviewer and other anomalies: A reanalysis of Gerbner et al.'s findings on cultivation analysis, part I. *Communication Research, 7,* 403–456.

Hirsch, P. M. (1981a). On not learning from one's own mistakes: A reanalysis of Gerbner et al.'s findings on cultivation analysis, part II. *Communication Research, 8,* 3–37.

Hirsch, P. M. (1981b). Distinguishing good speculation from bad theory: Rejoinder to Gerbner et al. *Communication Research, 8,* 73–95.

Hur, K. K. (1978). Impact of "Roots" on black and white teenagers *Journal of Broadcasting, 22,* 289–298.

Jameson, F. (1981). *The political unconscious.* Ithaca, NY: Cornell University Press.

Jay, M. (1972). The Frankfurt School in exile. *Perspectives in American History, 6,* 339–385.

Jay, M. (1973). *The dialectical imagination: A history of the Frankfurt School and the Institute of Social Research, 1923–1950.* Boston: Little, Brown.

Kaid, L. L., Towers, W. M., & Myers, S. L. (1981). Television docudrama and political cynicism: A study of *Washington: Behind Closed Doors*. *Social Science Quarterly, 62,* 161–168.

Kellner, D. (1987). TV, ideology, and emancipatory popular culture. In H. Newcomb (Ed.), *Television: The critical view* (4th ed., pp. 471–503). New York: Oxford University Press.

Kidd, V. (1975). Happily ever after and other relationship styles: Advice on interpersonal relations in popular magazines, 1951–1973. *Quarterly Journal of Speech, 61,* 31–39.

Kracauer, S. (1947). *From Caligari to Hitler*. Princeton, NJ: Princeton University Press.

Kreiling, A. (1984). Television in American ideological hopes and fears. In W. D. Rowland, Jr. & B. Watkins (Eds.), *Interpreting television: Current research perspectives* (pp. 39–57). Beverly Hills, CA: Sage.

Lacan, J. (1977). *Ecrits: A selection* (A. Sheridan, Trans.). New York: International. (Original work published 1966)

Lasswell, H. D. (1927). *Propaganda technique in the world war*. New York: Knopf.

Lasswell, H. D. (1938). A provisional classification of symbol data. *Psychiatry, 1,* 197–204.

Lazer, C., & Dier, S. (1978). The labor force in fiction. *Journal of Communication, 28*(1), 174–182.

LeBon, G. (1897). *The mind of crowds*. London: Unwin.

Lemish, D. (1985). Soap opera viewing in college: A naturalistic inquiry. *Journal of Broadcasting & Electronic Media, 29,* 275–293.

Lévi-Strauss, C. (1972). *Structural anthropology* (C. Jacobson & B. G. Schoepf, Trans.). London: Penguin. (Original work published 1958)

Lippmann, W. (1922). *Public opinion*. New York: Harcourt Brace Jovanovich.

Long, M. L., & Simon, R. J. (1974). The roles and statuses of women on children and family TV programs. *Journalism Quarterly, 51,* 107–110.

Lowenthal, L. (1957). Historical perspectives of popular culture. In B. Rosenberg & D. M. White (Eds.), *Mass culture: The popular arts in America* (pp. 46–58). New York: Free Press.

Lukács, G. (1971). *History and class consciousness*. London: Merlin.

Macdonald, D. (1957). A theory of mass culture. In B. Rosenberg & D. M. White (Eds.), *Mass culture: The popular arts in America* (pp. 59–73). New York: Free Press.

McQuail, D. (1984). With the benefit of hindsight: Reflections on uses and gratifications research. *Critical Studies in Mass Communication, 1,* 177–193.

Mead, G. H. (1934). *Mind, self, and society*. Chicago: University of Chicago Press.

Medhurst, M. J. (1978). Image and ambiguity: A rhetorical approach to *The Exorcist*. *Southern Speech Communication Journal, 44,* 73–92.

Medhurst, M. J., & Benson, T. W. (Eds.). (1984). *Rhetorical dimensions in media: A critical casebook*. Dubuque, IA: Kendall/Hunt.

Meyrowitz, J. (1985). *No sense of place: The impact of electronic media on social behavior.* New York: Oxford University Press.

Morley, D. (1980). *The "Nationwide" audience: Structure and decoding.* London: British Film Institute.

Morley, D. (1986). *Family television: Cultural power and domestic leisure.* London: Comedia.

Murdock, G., & Golding, P. (1979). Capitalism, communication and class relations. In J. Curran, M. Gurevitch, & J. Woollacott (Eds.), *Mass communication and society* (pp. 12–43). Beverly Hills, CA: Sage.

Newcomb, H. (1978). Assessing the violence profile studies of Gerbner and Gross: A humanistic critique and suggestion. *Communication Research, 5,* 264–282.

Nimmo, D., & Combs, J. E. (1983). *Mediated political realities.* New York: Longman.

Park, R. F. (1940). News as a form of knowledge: A chapter in the sociology of knowledge. *Journal of Sociology, 45,* 669–686.

Parkin, F. (1972). *Class inequality and political order.* London: Paladin.

Perse, E. M. (1986). Soap opera viewing patterns of college students and cultivation. *Journal of Broadcasting & Electronic Media, 30,* 175–193.

Pool, I. de Sola. (Ed.). (1959). *Trends in content analysis.* Urbana: University of Illinois Press.

Radway, J. (1984). *Reading the romance: Women, patriarchy, and popular literature.* Chapel Hill: University of North Carolina Press.

Radway, J. (1985). Interpretive communities and variable literacies: The functions of romance reading. In M. Gurevitch & M. R. Levy (Eds.), *Mass communication review yearbook* (Vol. 5, pp. 337–361). Beverly Hills, CA: Sage.

Requena, J. G. (1981). Narrativity/discursivity in the American television film. *Screen, 22,* 38–42.

Rorty, J. (1934). *Our master's voice: Advertising.* New York: John Day.

Rosengren, K. E., Wenner, L. A., & Palmgreen, P. (Eds.). (1985). *Media gratifications research: Current perspectives.* Beverly Hills, CA: Sage.

Ross, E. A. (1908). *Social psychology.* New York: Macmillan.

Rowland, W. D., Jr. (1983). *The politics of TV violence: Policy uses of communication research.* Beverly Hills, CA: Sage.

Rubin, A. M. (1985). Media gratifications through the life cycle. In K. E. Rosengren, L. A. Wenner, & P. Palmgreen (Eds.), *Media gratifications research: Current perspectives* (pp. 195–208). Beverly Hills, CA: Sage.

Rubin, R. B., Rubin, A. M., Perse, E. M., Armstrong, C., McHugh, M., & Faix, N. (1986). Media use and meaning of music video. *Journalism Quarterly, 63,* 353–359.

Rushing, J. H., & Frentz, T. S. (1980). "The Deer Hunter": Rhetoric of the warrior. *Quarterly Journal of Speech, 66,* 392–406.

Saussure, F. (1974). *Course in general linguistics.* London: Fontana. (Original work published 1915)

Schudson, M. (1978). *Discovering the news.* New York: Basic Books.

Schwichtenberg, C. (1987). *The Love Boat:* The packaging and selling of love, heterosexual romance, and family. In H. Newcomb (Ed.), *Television: The critical view* (4th ed., pp. 126–140). New York: Oxford University Press.

Siepmann, C. A. (1948). Radio. In L. Bryson (Ed.), *The communication of ideas* (pp. 177–196). New York: Harper.

Smythe, D. (1977). Communications: Blindspot of western Marxism. *Canadian Journal of Political and Social Theory, 1,* 1–27.

Stein, A. H., & Friedrich, L. K. (1972). Television content and young children's behavior. In J. P. Murray, E. A. Rubinstein, & G. A. Comstock (Eds.), *Television and social behavior: Vol. 2. Television and social learning* (pp. 202–317). Washington, DC: U.S. Government Printing Office.

Streeter, T. (1984). An alternative approach to television research: Developments in British cultural studies at Birmingham. In W. D. Rowland, Jr., & B. Watkins (Eds.), *Interpreting television: Current research perspectives* (pp. 74–97). Beverly Hills, CA: Sage.

Surlin, S. H. (1976). Five Years of "All in the Family": A Summary of Empirical Research Generated by the Program. *Mass Comm Review, 3*(3), 2–6.

Swanson, D. L. (1987). Gratification seeking, media exposure, and audience interpretations: Some directions for research. *Journal of Broadcasting & Electronic Media, 31,* 237–254.

Tedesco, N. S. (1974). Patterns in prime time. *Journal of Communication, 24*(2), 119–124.

Thomas, S., & Callahan, B. P. (1982). Allocating happiness: TV families and social class. *Journal of Communication, 32*(3), 184–190.

Tönnies, F. (1957). *Community and society* (C. P. Loomis, Trans. & Ed.). East Lansing: Michigan State University Press. (Original work published 1887)

Turner, R. H., & Killian, L. M. (1972). *Collective behavior* (2nd ed.). Englewood Cliffs, NJ: Prentice–Hall.

Volgy, T. J., & Schwarz, J. E. (1980). TV entertainment programming and sociopolitical attitudes. *Journalism Quarterly, 57,* 151–155.

Wartella, E., & Reeves, B. (1985). Historical trends in research on children and the media: 1900–1960. *Journal of Communication, 35*(2), 118–133.

Weimann, G. (1982). The prophecy that never fails: On the uses and gratifications of horoscope reading. *Sociological Inquiry, 52*(4), 274–290.

Wolfenstein, M., & Leites, N. (1950). *Movies: A psychological study.* Glencoe, IL: Free Press.

Woollacott, J. (1982). Messages and meanings. In M. Gurevitch, T. Bennett, J. Curran, & J. Woollacott (Eds.), *Culture, society and the media* (pp. 91–111). London: Methuen.

3
Popular Magazines, Popular Communication, and Politics

Dan Nimmo
Department of Communication
University of Oklahoma

He was writing more than a century and half ago, penning what was to be recognized later as a masterful commentary on the nature of American civilization. But what Alexis de Tocqueville said of the popular arts might as easily be written today:

> It would be a waste of my readers' time and of my own to explain how the general moderate standard of wealth, the absence of superfluidity, and the universal desire for comfort, with the constant efforts made by all to produce it, encourage a taste for the useful more than the love of beauty. Naturally, therefore, democratic peoples with all these characteristics cultivate those arts which help to make life comfortable rather than those which adorn it. They habitually put use before beauty, and they want beauty itself to be useful. (p. 465)

Of the modes of popular communication in the United States today few so aptly illustrate the durability of the accuracy of Tocqueville's observation than what is to be discussed here as "popular magazines." Although the modest contribution offered here to defining the field of popular communication will speak to the conceptual differences between mass and popular communication and review briefly current approaches and studies of popular magazines, its main thrust will be to exemplify a theme close to Tocqueville's heart. Namely, this note takes as its basic formulation a paradox to which Tocqueville alludes, sometimes directly, sometimes obliquely. It is that mass communication, or at least what is too often so labeled, is a key factor not in the massification of American society but in enhancing the pluralist character which Tocqueville found so pervasive in this new nation.

MASS VERSUS POPULAR COMMUNICATION: ARE THEY THE SAME?

There was interest in it well before World War II, but it was shortly after the end of that conflict that scholars raised serious questions about the deleterious impact of mass communication upon civilization as we seemed to know it. Impressed by the seeming success of mass propaganda in enabling the Nazis to control the German people (and the Soviet leadership to galvanize the Russians), "As a host of recent conferences, books and articles indicate, the role of radio, print and film in society has become a problem of interest and a source of concern to some." So wrote Paul Lazarsfeld and Robert Merton in a seminal assessment of the relationship of mass communication to popular taste in 1948 (p. 95). Lazarsfeld and Merton went on to account for why, as they phrased it, "the ubiquity of the mass media leads many to an almost magical belief in their enormous power." Chief among their reasons was "the possibility that the continuing assault of these media may lead to the unconditional surrender of critical faculties and an unthinking conformism," as well as constituting "a major avenue for the deterioration of esthetic tastes and popular cultural standards" (p. 97).

The fear that mass communication might produce the massification of popular taste was, of course, hardly reduced by the entrance of television as yet another medium of mass entertainment and propaganda. Indeed, empirical studies lent credence to the fear. For example, Wilensky (1964) contrasted the distribution of "high" and "mass" culture among a large-size probability sample of males in the Detroit metropolitan area. By high culture he referred to content created by or under the supervision of an elite operating within some aesthetic, literary, or scientific tradition and applying critical standards independent of those applied by the consumer of the product. Mass culture consisted of products manufactured solely for a mass market (much of television content, for example) characterized by standardization, not critical standards. By generous estimate only 19 of his 1,354 respondents could be designated "media purists," that is, those who insulated themselves from mass culture. Wilensky concluded with an interesting observation: "To be socially integrated in America is to accept propaganda, advertising, and speedy obsolescence in consumption." That squares well enough with the concern over massification of popular taste. Yet, he went on, "the fact is that those who fit the image of pluralist man in the pluralist society also fit the image of mass man in the mass society." Hence, "any accurate picture of the shape of modern society must accommodate these ambiguities" (p. 193).

Whether we are dealing with ambiguities, however, may well depend upon whether in defining the field of popular communication we equate it with mass communication. Oscar Handlin (1960) detected a worthwhile difference in the two phenomena. Handlin took account of three varieties of culture. There was, he said, "defined culture," that is, the capital "C" Culture defined by the elite. It parallels Wilensky's high culture in that its content conforms to specified traditions, standards, and canons. "Popular culture" Handlin believed to be different. Unlike defined culture, popular culture "retained a functional quality in the sense that it was closely related to the felt needs and familiar modes of expression of the people it served." Handlin noted, for example, "popular songs were to be danced to, vaudeville to be laughed at, and embroidery to be worn or to cover the table" (p. 327). Put in Tocqueville's language, use is put before beauty and beauty itself must be useful. Finally, Handlin wrote that "mass culture—or more properly speaking of the culture communicated through the mass media—has had a disturbing effect upon both popular and defined cultures" (p. 327). Being mass it does not carry the values of the defining elite (Wilensky's high vs. mass difference). But more importantly, mass culture is not an extension of past popular culture either. Why? Handlin gave four reasons, each of which fits the Tocqueville view: (1) Popular culture dealt with the concrete world intensely familiar to its audience; (2) It had a continuing relevance to the situation of the audience exposed to it; (3) It was closely tied to the traditions of those who consumed it; and (4) Popular culture had a strong emotional appeal. "Millions of people," wrote Handlin, "found in this culture a means of communication among themselves and the answers to certain significant questions that they were asking about the world about them" (p. 329).

As vehicles of mass culture, Handlin thought that "Television, the movies, and the mass-circulation magazines stand altogether apart from the older vehicles of both popular and defined culture" (p. 328). But he was writing a quarter of a century ago—before cable TV, movies aimed at segmented audiences, and specialized popular circulation magazines. To focus solely on magazines, is it possible to say that popular magazines are indeed popular, not mass, communication in the sense that Handlin makes the distinction? This is not the place to recount the history of the magazine in America, not is it necessary to do so. Let it suffice to say that many of the earliest of U. S. magazines served defined or high culture. Thus, for instance, short stories, poems, and scholarly essays comprised the pages of such periodicals as the original *Harper's* and *Atlantic* toward the end of the 19th century, as indeed they do today. Standards, not standardization, was the characterizing criterion. *McClure's* as a mass circulation magazine emerged toward the end of the century and heralded in an era that, in retrospect, was fairly brief. That era, which reached its zenith between 1950 and 1970, witnessed the publication of such mass priodicals as *Life, Look,* and the *Saturday Evening Post,* fare appealing to large, hetereogeneous audiences, delivering them to eager advertisers. But TV cut into mass circulation advertising revenue. Many mass magazines either ceased publication or were recast as more specialized magazines targeted for clearly defined smaller audience segments. At the same time the special interest magazine, which had been relatively common prior to the era of mass circulation publications, was born again. Today large circulation magazines continue, but the designation is not synonymous with mass, as is seen in *TV Guide's* special interest orientation in spite of a circulation of 20 million. Ninety percent of consumer magazines are directed at specialized audiences of less than one-half million.

As Snow (1983) indicates, there are more than 10,000 periodicals available—trade and consumer—serving ever-increasing special interest clienteles. "Therein," he says, "lies the most important characteristic of magazines today—they serve the interests of subcultures ranging from the esoteric to popular and general culture, and provide information and validation and provide identities associated with the subcultures" (p. 80). By examining the grammar, perspectives, and influence of magazines (something he does as well in considering newspapers, novels, radio, TV, and film) Snow suggests a characterizing set of features of magazines that comes strikingly close to those Handlin employs in speaking of popular culture. By grammar Snow refers to the patterned fashion used in a communication medium for presenting itself to audiences. Magazines, thus, typically employ attention-grabbing covers, with photographic or graphic emotional appeals, suitable to appropriate audiences and with emotional overtones. They place advertising in prominent, easily accessible places, organize content to meet readers' needs and habits (bold headlines, arresting photos, and other devices to attract the attention of either the serious "front-to-back" or thumbing "back-to-front" reader; they employ vocabularies consistent with special interest readerships. Perspectives encompass the value orientations of the magazine and its target readers—verbal and visual clues regarding what binds subculture members together as do-it-yourselfers, skiers, tennis addicts, gourmets, voyeurs, gardeners, and so forth. Finally, the magazine's influence depends in large degree upon what people do with what they read, namely getting involved actively in the subculture to which the periodical is addressed: "people come to rely upon magazines as references and even reference groups" (p. 96). In short, to employ once more Tocqueville's terminology, magazine beauty is useful. To return to Handlin, contemporary magazines—like the popular culture of old—deal with a concrete world familiar to audience members, are relevant to the everyday world of readers, appeal and enhance the utility-oriented traditions of targeted consumers, and have a strong emotional appeal in binding members to their reference groups.

APPROACHES TO STUDYING POPULAR MAGAZINES

To summarize the argument, one must say that to consider popular magazines as popular communication it is necessary to examine that medium from the viewpoint of popular, not defined or mass culture. The fact is that such a viewpoint is seldom apparent in studies of the genre. It is an oversimplification, but nonetheless a convenient one, to suggest four lines of inquiry that have stood out in examining magazines as media of communication.

The first has been essentially historical. Typical is the discussion one finds in Thomas Kando's 1975 textbook on leisure and popular culture. In a chapter entitled "Mass Culture: The Printed Media," Kando traces the growth of magazines from the earliest colonial almanacs, through the "large-scale magazine boom" of the mid-19th century (circulations of 40,000), to the mass circulation, then specialized era of the present. Major trends in readership, profiles of selected magazines (especially *Reader's Digest*), or the relative emphases on particular topics across time periods (e.g., Lowenthal's study of biographies in popular magazines) are variations on the theme of historical analysis; 1956).

Often blending with historical studies are those that emphasize taxonomic features, deriving a typology of magazines, then devoting descriptive accounts to each of the magazines of a particular type. For example, Ford (1969) categorizes magazines by manifest audience appeal: home and family magazines; juvenile-oriented publications; leisure-oriented; religious; company, industry, business, and labor journals; professional association periodicals; rural and agrarian. More analytical, and potentially more insightful in drawing comparisons across types, is Compaine's (1982) "Consumer Magazine

General–Special Interest Matrix" typology. Compaine describes two dimensions for classifying types of magazines. The first consists of the type of information that magazines provide. Two categories of information come into play: passive and active. The former is information intended for the reader's entertainment or general knowledge; the latter is information intended for specific use by the reader. Compaine cites the difference between an article on the life of Billie Jean King (passive) versus one on how to cure a tennis elbow (active). The second dimension involves the type of audience reached by the magazine: mass or limited. Employing the two categories for each of two dimensions Compaine derives a fourfold classification of magazines: (1) Passive, mass audience magazines—with a median circulation of 3 million—including *Reader's Digest, People,* and *Ladies Home Journal.* (2) Active, mass audience magazines with a median circulation of 1.8 million, including *Family Circle, Popular Mechanics,* and *Sports Afield.* (3) Passive, limited audience magazines, including *New Yorker, Ms., Rolling Stone, Modern Romance,* and others with a median circulation below one-half million; (4) Active, limited audience magazines with median circulations around 300,000, exemplified by *Golf Digest, Trains,* and *Car and Driver.* Note that regardless of the category, most consumer magazines emphasize a content of use over beauty. (Certainly the emphasis of *Cosmopolitan* is the very paradigm case of Tocqueville's view that Americans want "beauty itself to be useful.")

Another key focus in the study of American magazines has been upon the production side. Such matters as the economic and business aspects of publishing, the pros and cons of advertising, magazine management, readership studies and marketing management, editorial functions, and so forth, have all received due consideration, by way of either comparative or case studies. Drawing upon a variety of such studies Zuilen (1977) formulated what he designated the "life cycle of magazines," development, growth, maturity, saturation, and decline/death. He sought to explain the "decline and fall of the general interest mass audience magazines" in this country between 1946 and 1972. Zuilen, along with other researchers, cited the increased appeal of special interest magazines as one of the reasons for the final stage in the life-cycle of general audience magazines.

Standing apart from the approaches to studying popular magazines that emphasize manifest historical, social, and economic trends are those which place their stress on latent aspects of popular communication and attempt to demystify the content of the media in order to specify their covert roles in society. Ellen McCracken ably summarizes five of the "demystifying" approaches in a study of a single issue of *Cosmopolitan* (1982). It is useful to describe each of these, for they provide bridges toward what may be an even more promising path for exploring popular magazines as popular communication.

The first such approach is what McCracken labels "ideological" but might more accurately be designated as Schiller (1973) does when he writes of "packaged consciousness." Schiller argues that "America's media managers create, process, refine, and preside over the circulation of images and information which determine our beliefs and attitudes and, ultimately, behavior." When the messages they generate (Schiller says "deliberately" but the premise holds even without intent) "do not correspond to the realities of social existence," they "create a false sense of reality and produce a consciousness that cannot comprehend or wilfully rejects the actual conditions of life" (p. 1). Schiller goes on to demonstrate how such magazines as *TV Guide* and *National Geographic,* the former purporting to provide readers with "neutral" information and the latter offering a "nonideological" geographic survey, covertly reinforce the interests of a reigning, capitalist ideology. By the same token, McCracken purports to demystify a fashion feature in *Cosmopolitan,* claiming that the verbal text masks a view of Latin America that actually creates the "false consciousness" of an exotic continent sans social history or social problems. In a more informal fashion, and with different intent than Schiller or McCracken, Cowan, (1983) "digests" the *Reader's Digest* along lines similar to those of an ideological approach. And, to the degree that he derives from his informal content analysis of newsmagazines the "enduring values in the news" (ethnocentrism, altruistic democracy, responsible capitalism, small town pastoralism, individualism, and moderatism) Gans (1980, pp. 42–52) also is describing a packaged consciousness. Finally, those familiar with the work of Dorfman and Mattelart (1975) are aware of other examples of a packaged consciousness perspective in the analysis of popular communication.

Schiller's approach to the analysis of popular culture is intertwined with a second method of studying popular magazines as popular communication, namely, what McCracken calls the "infrastructural." Magazines may be published for fun and profit but the emphasis is clearly on the latter. Thus infrastructural studies have a twofold focus. One is on the corporate interests served through the publication of popular magazines; the second examines magazines as advertising vehicles designed to deliver consumers to sellers. Corporate and conglomerate structures, circulation data, advertising rates and linage, production costs, profits and losses, and so forth—all are observation points for infrastructural inquiries.

As Berger (1982) has since spelled out in considerable detail, a third of McCracken's approaches holds considerable promise for the analysis of the products of popular culture, especially popular magazines. Among other matters semiotic studies enable investigators to uncover the hidden myths in the content of popular magazines. For example, McCracken explores the mythology underlying advertising for Calvin Klein jeans, pleasures derived from sexual freedom, affluence, and beauty. Although not employing precisely the techniques of semiotic analysis, Goffman (1976) exposed the mythology of gender underlying more than 500 ads found in newspapers and popular magazines.

McCracken employs a fourth approach, specifically referred to as "feminist." Here the emphasis is upon how popular magazines "sell" (both through the verbal and visual content of articles and via advertising) female self-images. The tangible product, be it the magazine itself or the wares advertised within it, take second place to the self-image consistently portrayed by the magazine and its ads. In some cases, different magazines sell women different self-images. One need only to thumb through a current copy of *Cosmopolitan* and *Ms.* to detect this (although a more deeply rooted, semiotic-oriented analysis might reveal remarkable similarities). But, as McCallum's (1975) study of how females are portrayed in "True" magazines—*True Story, True Romance, True Confessions, True Experience, True Love,* and so forth—indicates the portrayal of the self-image of working-class women has precious little variation. The formula is consistent: working-class women are conflict-ridden. Husbands are unfaithful or die of heart attacks, alcoholism, and other maladies; pregnancies miscarry; children run away; economic woes mount. Yet, "however conflict-ridden the stories may be, the conflict is always resolved," writes McCallum, for "No True story ever has a genuinely unhappy ending" (p. 43). A new marriage, a new pregnancy, a new friend—each offers the prospect of rebirth and renewal. Hence, concludes McCallum, women's popular magazines of the "True" genre actually portray working-class women in a "world without conflict" in spite of it all.

Such a feminist approach to the study of the content of popular magazines is, of course, capable of broader applications. In effect, it is a social portrayal approach and there is no inherent reason to limit it to how the female self-image is portrayed. It could be applied to any social category of readers—male as well as female; Blacks, whites, Hispanics, and other groups; teen-agers, senior citizens, even yuppies. However applied, it leads to the question of how such self-images are received by audiences. Do readers "buy" into them, adopt them, and act them out? Such questions fall under the purview of a final approach suggested by McCracken, that of reception analysis, "perhaps the most important of the methodologies though one of the most neglected up to now" (p. 39). Too frequently receptionist analysis implies readership studies—how many people of what social category read what magazines for what superficial reasons. But there is something more implied.

TAKING POPULAR MAGAZINES (AND POPULAR COMMUNICATION) SERIOUSLY

Kreiling (1978) has argued that a great many students of popular culture have, in effect, dismissed the phemonena of their inquiries as without substance. Popular culture in such studies but reflects more deeply embedded social categories and structures: "Culture is reduced to a product of sociological forces and a mechanism that satisfies psychological needs." Instead of examining popular culture for its own sake, the "reflection" argument "imputes such things as needs, values, norms, and culture patterns to personalities and social structures and then takes them as explanations for cultural artifacts." Kreiling goes on to comment, correctly insofar as this discussion is concerned, "If sociologists are to say anything very penetrating about culture, they will have to treat it as an important realm in its own right instead of a derivative facade for unmasking to divulge the 'real' forces behind it" (p. 242).

As Kreiling suggests, a useful way to begin to take popular culture seriously is to make an effort "to grasp the meanings known and felt by populations within the human realities of their own experiential worlds and expressed in the symbolic forms of cultural materials" (p. 241). Without discounting the contributions made to the study of popular magazines as popular communication by analyses of packaged consciousness, infrastructure, semiotics, and social portrayals, one may still confess to a sense of disquietude, even disappointment. Each approach in its own fashion hints that the symbols that are the content of popular magazines reflect something more basic, more real—forces of capitalistic control, primal myths, prejudicial social stereotypes, and so forth. What is not clear is how those symbols operate within the lives of those who are Tocqueville's "democracy in America."

A conventional analysis of the symbols that comprise the content of popular magazines typically, as Kreiling recognizes with respect to conventional sociological analysis of popular culture, notes that they "express" deeper social forces. Thereby expressive symbols are reduced to "instrumental" symbols, symbols that say nothing in and of themselves but are tools for achieving goals that are more "real" or "tangible." But expressive symbols are not so easily dismissed, for they constitute "a dramatic enactment of people's hopes, fears, conceptions, and identities." They are meaningful for what they are, not for what they might produce in the way of tangible ends. To say they are not reducible to instrumental symbols, however, is not to say they are not useful. Indeed, they are that of which Tocqueville might have been writing when he said Americans want "beauty itself to be useful." Or, as Kreiling argues, "We need to learn to see the changing and fragmented expressive actions of contemporary life—fashion, leisure activities, popular culture—as expressive forms in which people enact patterns of sentiment, meaning, and identity" (pp. 246–247).

What form might such expressive enactments take? Many scholars concerned with that question as it pertains to the popular arts turn to the views of Kenneth Burke (Kimberling, 1982, is a leading example) for guidance. But a theorist more directly interested in popular culture per se than has been Burke—and who acknowledged his debt to Burke—who also provided considerable assistance in answering that question was Hugh Duncan (1962). This is not the place to summarize the detailed works of Duncan. Cuzzort and King (1980) offer a helpful precis. Rather, the focus here is upon a particular element in Duncan's work, that is, his concern with play (a notion elaborated in even greater detail later by Stephenson, 1967).

Reviewing the contributions of the sociologist Georg Simmel to the development of communication theory, Duncan takes note of Simmel's views of sociation. Sociation—reciprocal relationships among humans—has both form and content. Forms of sociation arise to satisfy needs, but once they do so many "free themselves from the practical needs which produced and sustained them" (Duncan, 1962, p. 21). They become autonomous and take on a life of their own. Employing Tocqueville's language, one might say that the popular arts start out having "uses" but in fulfilling them free themselves to achieve "beauty" as well. Duncan cites many examples of freed forms of sociation—science originated to solve practical problems and now is a value in itself. But, says Duncan, the "greatest example" of this is "play." Originated to serve practical needs—hunting for food, for example—such forms were "lifted out of the flux of life and freed of their inherent seriousness and gravity" (p. 21). Play became an autonomous activity enjoyed for itself, though it "draws its strength from its origin in life" which keeps it "permeated with life." Writes Duncan,

In play, individuals free themselves from all other ties. Play exists for its own sake and for the sake of the fascination which, in its liberation from other ties, is created by the game itself. Thus, while we are acting together in economic associations, religious societies, criminal associations, or art cliques we feel there is something more in our relatedness than economic, religious, criminal, or aesthetic activity. This is a feeling "of being sociated," of being together on a social basis. (p. 22)

Here, one suspects, lies the guidance for taking popular communication and popular magazines seriously as expressions and enactments of human meanings. For what popular magazines provide—which membership in formal organizations cannot—is that "feeling 'of being sociated,' of being together on a social basis." More is involved here than treating popular magazines as the focal objects of "reference" groups (as contrasted to interacting groups). The case is that the magazine creates and expresses the very identity and the very meaning of the sociated life, that is, the group. Hence, to take popular magazines seriously as popular communication is not to conduct "receptionist" analysis in the conventional mode of readership studies. One is better advised to turn to Stephenson's (1967) ludenic studies of news reading for direction. The question is not who reads *Cosmopolitan* with what effects but whether *Cosmopolitan* is *the* (sociation of) *Cosmopolitan* woman.

If one entertains the notion that the symbols that comprise the symbolic content of popular magazines are expressive forms in which people enact patterns of sentiment, meaning, and identity for their own sake, then it follows that an increasing number and variety of popular magazines are opportunities for and indicators of pluralized and diversified modes of enactments. In short, popular magazines—appealing as they do to vastly different segments of the overall market—express a growing number of "taste cultures." Not taste cultures as defined by Gans (1974), namely, as determined by class, education, social standing, and so forth, but as people creating, expressing, and enacting convergent meanings of life. Plural formulas, each specific to a specific genre of magazine (e.g., the "True" genre, the car genre, the upbeat genre, etc.) suggest plural interest cultures. Hence, popular magazines as popular communication create and reinforce interest cultures, thus possessing precisely the utility-beauty qualities among the popular arts of which Tocqueville wrote. As manifestations of popular communication magazines have fragmenting, pluralizing consequences consonant with popular media, not massifying consequences congruent with an allegedly awesome and, presumably to be feared, mass media.

REFERENCES

Berger, A. A. (1982). *Media analysis techniques.* Beverly Hills, CA: Sage.

Compaine, B. M. (1982). *The business of consumer magazines.* White Plains, NY: Knowledge Industry Publications.

Cowan, W. H. (1983, March 21). Digesting the "Digest". *Christianity and Crisis, 43,* 94–98.

Cuzzort, R. P., & King, E. W. (1980). Communication, art, and victims. In R. P. Cuzzort & E. W. King (Eds.), *Twentieth century social thought* (pp. 327–349). New York: Holt, Rinehart, & Winston.

Dorfman, A., & Mattelart, A. (1975). *How to read Donald Duck.* New York: International General.

Duncan, H. D. (1962). *Communication and social order.* New York: Oxford University Press.

Ford, J. L. C. (1969). *Magazines for millions: The story of specialized publications.* Carbondale: Southern Illinois University Press.

Gans, H. J. (1974). *Popular culture and high culture.* New York: Basic Books.

Gans, H. J. (1980). *Deciding what's news.* New York: Vintage.

Goffman, E. (1976). *Gender advertising.* New York: Harper Colophon.

Handlin, O. (1960, Spring). Comments on mass and popular culture. *Daedalus, 89,* 325–332.

Kando, T. M. (1975). *Leisure and popular culture in transition.* St. Louis: C. B. Mosby.

Kimberling, C. R. (1982). *Kenneth Burke's dramatism and popular arts.* Bowling Green, OH: Bowling Green University Popular Press.

Kreiling, A. (1978, July). Toward a cultural studies approach for the sociology of popular culture. *Communication Research 5,* 240–263.

Lowenthal, L. (1956). Biographies in popular magazines. In W. Petersen (Ed.), *American social patterns* (63–118). Garden City, NY: Doubleday.

McCallum, P. (1975, September). World without conflict: Magazines for working class women. *Canadian Forum, 55,* 42–44.

McCracken, E. (1982, Fall). Demystifying *Cosmopolitan:* Five critical methods. *Journal of Popular Culture, 16,* 30–42.

Lazarsfeld, P. F., & Merton, R. K. (1948). Mass communication, popular taste and organized social action. In L. Bryson (Ed.), *The communication of ideas* (pp. 95–118). New York: Harper.

Schiller, H. I. (1973). *The mind managers.* Boston: Beacon Press.

Snow, R. P. (1983). *Creating media culture.* Beverly Hills, CA: Sage.

Stephenson, W. (1967). *The play theory of mass communication.* Chicago: University of Chicago Press.

Tocqueville, A. de, (1969). *Democracy in America.* (J. P. Palmer, Trans.). Garden City, NY: Anchor.

Wilensky, H. (1964, April). Mass society and mass culture. *American Sociological Review, 29,* 173–197.

Zuilen, A. J. van (1977). *The life cycle of magazines.* Uithoorn, Netherlands: The Graduate Press.

4

Politics: Tastes Great or Less Filling

Katherine Hale
Department of Communication Arts,
Oklahoma Baptist University

Michael W. Mansfield
Department of Political Science,
Baylor University

An understanding of the nature of popular culture and specifically of the political nature of that culture is dependent upon an understanding of how we communicate and what we communicate through the various modes of discourse of a society. Root (1987) states that the artifacts of any culture are related to three major areas: entertainment, commerce, and information. The artifacts

> Will exemplify a society's interest in amusing itself, in providing goods and services for itself, and in informing itself about its activities, including events which are of interest and significance to its community and also ideas about itself and its members' relationship with other cultures and one another.
>
> (Root, p. 11)

These major areas of popular culture all communicate and often reflect specific values and ideas, say Root.

Commercial product advertising, an artifact relating primarily to the commerce of a culture, is a form of expression particularly reliant on the ability to evoke and invoke values, myths, assumptions, and so forth, to achieve that state of "identification" necessary to get consumers to buy their products. A study by Geis (1982) indicates that television advertising contains implications of unstated claims which may influence viewers more than direct claims, suggesting that those underlying themes are an important subject of analysis. It is reasonable to ask whether the values and concepts embodied and reflected in television advertising are political, since the values behind other popular modes of expression have been identified as political and latent, or subliminal.

Studies of the relationship of politics to entertainment and information categories of popular culture have identified political themes in a variety of popular culture phenomena, including movies, comic strips, news reports, election campaigns, folk heritage, Western myth, popular art, and so forth (Combs, 1984; Nimmo & Combs, 1983). Political themes have been found in comics, not only in such obviously political comic strips as "Doonesbury," but in those popular comics regularly read and collected by children and adults. Skidmore and Skidmore (1983) conclude that such comics are high in political content and that several specific themes can be identified across a number of comic labels and titles.

The popular media have demonstrated specific interest in the consideration of political themes in commercial advertising. A December, 1985 issue of *Newsweek* (Goldman, McAlevey, Doherty, McCormick, & Maier, 1985) argues that there is evidence from several forms of popular culture (including the "Rocky" and "Rambo" movies and related toys, clothes, etc.) of a re-emergence of "Russophobia." The rise of a cold war mentality can also be seen in such television commercials as a Wendy's hamburger ad featuring a Russian fashion show. Showing the same nondescript outfit (with comic change of accessories) for day, sport, and evening wear, the ad concludes that while some places offer no options, a person has choices at Wendy's.

In a 1985 episode of *NBC Nightly News,* Tom Brokaw discusses Soviet concerns with their portrayal in American media. Examples of negative portrayal in the NBC report include the Wendy's commercial described above, a comic commercial by Meister Brau set in "a foreign embassy in Washington, D.C." (obviously Russian), and the ABC mini-series "Amerika." Ted Koppel directs a similar discussion on *ABC's Nightline.*

A syndicated report in the *Arkansas Gazette* (McLaughlin, November 17, 1985) criticizes the popular use of jingoism to sell today's products. The article asserts that the philosophy of today's ad campaign managers is "If you want to sell it, baby, wrap a flag around it, paint it red, white, and blue, and people will throw greenbacks at it." But the positive side of patriotism, that is, pride in America, dependability, and belief in the goodness of the American people, is also evident in commercials, according to a *Dallas Morning News* (Lippert, 1986) report.

Both scholarly writing assessing political themes in popular culture and current media concerns with political themes in commercial advertising indicate a likelihood that television advertisements will contain both overt and latent political messages and themes. Our investigation of this topic is based on the research approach advocated by Glaser and Strauss (1967), which holds that all areas of data collection, classification, integration, and of theory construction be guided by emerging theory. This study's focus is not on organizing a mass of data but on organizing ideas that emerge from the data that can then be "re-fit" to the data throughout the research process.

Guiding the process of discovery, however, is a structure employed to identify that which is to be considered political. Following Arthur Bentley's advice (written in 1908), we have chosen in this study not to cut ourselves off from the materials we need by drawing arbitrary distinctions between political activity and other varieties of social activity. Instead, we chose to investigate "any phenomenon or set of phenomena belonging to the roughly recognized field of government" (Bentley, 1967, p. 199).

Among the competing definitions of politics is one that conceptualizes politics as "the activity of people collectively regulating their conduct under conditions of social conflict" (Nimmo, 1978). People are individuals who will invariably disagree, and when those disputes are addressed and resolved, that's politics. The communication involved in such conflict resolution is rhetorical, since, according to Burke (1950), rhetoric includes those symbolic resources which function to promote social cohesion and those which induce attitudes and/or actions. Since collective activity taken to regulate conduct under conditions of social conflict is activity which promotes social cohesion by inducing attitudes or actions, key concepts of both definitions are important in establishing a structure for examination of television commercials.

First, we must consider the introduction of conflict as a format for the discussion of a product. Do television commercials reflect the general conflict of humans and their resulting dilemmas? Is such conflict a significant format for advertisers? What forms of conflict are used, in what social context do they occur, and how is conflict used to sell the product?

Secondly, what activity is taken or prescribed to "regulate conduct" or to resolve the conflict? Under what circumstances is the use of the product the resolution of the conflict?

Thirdly, do television commercials reflect human attempts to achieve social cohesion collectively? Jean-Jacques Rousseau's *Social Contract*, a classic 1762 essay on political theory (1950), states that "man is born free, and everywhere he is in chains. Many a man believes himself the master of others, and yet he is a greater slave than they." Rousseau's argument is that justice and equality are matters of human relations, not of human beings in isolation, but in an association which defends and protects with the whole force of the community the person and property of everyone in the association. In this social contract humans are in harmony with nature and each other. One achieves civility by giving oneself to all, and in doing so gives oneself to nobody. Thus, by entering into the social contract, one frees oneself by gaining the equivalent of all that he or she loses, and more power to preserve what one has. This notion of contract suggests a principle of common will. This *volonté général* is not quantitative, but a qualitative will for a common good. In determining whether television commercials reflect or employ concepts relating to human efforts toward social cohesion, we will ask specifically if the commercials portray this general theme of social contract and its related tenets.

Finally, there are specific values which arise out of social cohesion in any given culture, and may therefore be expected to be called upon in rhetorical situations. For Americans, such matters as patriotism, chauvinism, the "Protestant work ethic," equality, expectations of progress, and so forth, represent the kinds of themes one might expect to see used as a basis for achieving the kind of identification necessary to affect attitudes toward a product. This analysis will look specifically, then, for recognizable American values employed in the ads.

The sample of television ads used was obtained by the generation of a list of "top 10" and "top 10 fringe" programs (based on Nielsen ratings) for the first 3 weeks in December, 1985. Choosing from this list 13 programs which remained consistently in or near the top 10 over the 3-week period, we taped commercials aired during those programs over a 2-week period. This sample provided representativeness of popular commercials, and we supplemented the sample to achieve diversity, including ads from several holiday specials and football bowl games (football games offer more commercials per half hour than do other types of programming). The result was 493 unduplicated commercials which comprise the sample upon which this study is based.

CONFLICT

Analysis of the sample revealed that television commercials reflect both substantive conflict representative of a general dilemma in dealing with life, and trivial, contrived conflict designed primarily to get attention, yet often "hitting home" in terms of its reflection of petty interpersonal rivalries.

The presence of commercials depicting people in social conflict situations is no more apparent than in the popular Miller Lite beer commercials. It is this series of commercials, so obviously based on conflict, that inspired the title of this chapter. The commercials don't just involve conflict, the premise of the ads are based on the creation of conflict by the advertiser. Each commercial centers around a group of celebrities, most of whom are retired sports celebrities, who are singing the praises of Miller Lite. Some of the group announce that they drink Lite beer because it "tastes great," the rest respond by shouting that Lite beer is "less filling." While both sides agree that Miller Lite is the best beer, they continue their conflict during commercial after commercial in this series. In addition to the obvious use of conflict in the Lite commercials, several categories of conflict were identified.

Conflict and change. Conflict related to change is a central theme for many of the commercials sampled. The conflict, which is basically over quality of life as it is affected by the old and the new, takes two opposite approaches. The first is an approach which equates change with progress, that says new is better than old. The second equates progress with modernization and a dehumanizing of people. It portrays adherence to tradition as evidence of refusal to compromise quality and personal treatment of people.

An example of the first approach, that which equates change with progress, is the GTE Sprint commercial entitled the "Changing of the Guard." The Sprint ad begins with black and white shots of familiar 1950s scenes, including shots of people watching the Ed Sullivan Show, Eisenhower's nomination, and a newspaper headlining his victory. Switching to color shots of the modern era, the voice-over points out that there has been a changing of the guard, and that the new generation knows that long-distance telecommunication is no longer a luxury, but a necessity. While the audience is expected to enjoy looking at where we've been, we are also expected to see that that time period is a luxury we can't afford, that we operate in a modern era and GTE is part of what we need to function in it. A second example of this same approach, IBM's "Jim Walsh's Dairy" commercial, focuses more strongly on the conflict in the way people feel about change. The ad depicts four oldtimers riding in a 1970s vintage automobile to visit their friend's dairy. While three of the four occupants of the car praise the success of the dairy resulting from change and innovations brought on by its association with IBM, the driver of the car makes disparaging remarks. Obviously in conflict with either Jim or the idea of change, the oldtimer finally comments about Jim, "It's no big deal making his job easier. It's the cows that do all the work." While we as the audience are intended to like the oldtimer, we are at the same time intended to find him ridiculous, and to identify with the other three occupants in the car—those who can recognize and appreciate progress, personified here in IBM.

The other side of the coin, however, is that progress leads to a loss of individuality in the name of modernity. The conflict comes in our wanting to hold on to our individualism in an era when bigger is better. A commercial typifying this category is an ad for Miller beer. The O'Reilly brothers, individuals fighting the big conglomerate, refused to sell their 70-year-old family-run bar. Instead, they told the corporation wanting to buy them out, "Go ahead and build your skyscraper around us." The bottom line in this ad is that it's nice to know "there's still a place where some things are not for sale, and where Miller's the beer." GMAC provides an additional example, dramatizing the impersonal nature of banks. This ad shows a meek little man trying to negotiate with an automated teller for a bank loan. The disastrous results are used to suggest that this man should go to GMAC, where they treat people like people.

The conflict resulting from change, then, is a fertile field for advertisers. By dramatizing the feelings of conflict that people feel when involved in what is essentially a tradeoff between the security of the traditional and the efficiency of the modern, advertisers can choose to enhance whichever side of the conflict best suits the characteristics of their product.

Conflict and class distinction. The struggle for elite status and the recognition of differences in status result in a kind of conflict which forms another major theme of television ads. While there are commercials based on the simplest version of this theme (e.g., this is the car, perfume, investment firm, etc., of the elite), none was found in this sample. There are several other variations of the theme, however.

First is the idea that status is reciprocally related to ambition, drive, competition, and excellence. This can be seen clearly in two Hilton Hotel commercials. Hilton notes in one ad that ambition is the fuel that drives business and that makes Hilton America's business address. A second ad says that it's competition that makes business go and that drives Hilton to be America's business address. Whichever it is that causes these results, Hilton is ambitious, competitive, and high status, like those ambitious, competitive, and high-status individuals who stay at their hotels.

A second variation, found primarily in the American Express commercials, is the idea that being elite isn't what it used to be, or at least, isn't enough to avoid conflict situations. Even men of distinction, such as Tom Landry and Mr. Morita (the president of Sony), may find themselves in conflict as a result of the failure of people to recognize their eliteness. The solution here is easy, however. Don't leave home without the American Express card.

Honda's "Dueling Banjos" ad is representative of commercials that attempt to cross class distinctions with their product. This ad depicts two men with violins, one in a tuxedo playing "Dueling Banjos" in a distinctive classical style, the other in Western wear playing the same song with a popular Western flare. The men play their versions one at a time, in a challenging manner. The voice-over explains that "it doesn't matter what kind of person you are, Honda has a car to fit your style, whether your tastes are simple (the camera pans to the man in Western clothes) or refined (camera goes to the man in the tuxedo)." There is, then, no need for the class distinction conflict, since this product is appropriate to all.

Finally, there is the ad that sets up the conflict of price versus quality. We as consumers want the quality of an elite product, but we prefer to pay the price of the common product. But with some products, the conflict is resolved, since the product offers the consumer high quality at a low price. Typical of this theme are two Meister Brau ads in which a central character has been assigned to procure the beer for the club in one commercial and the ship's crew in the other. In both instances, the crew and the club members discover that Meister Brau only tastes expensive, and that they've been cheated by the procurer who was making them pay a high price to get the high price taste.

The creation of conflict through class distinctions is a popular format for commercials. This kind of conflict provides versatility of approach to the advertiser, since he or she can have the product provide status, thus resolving the upward struggle, or can have the product be available and/or appropriate to all classes, thus resolving class competition.

Conflict arising from authority. Several commercials established conflict in the context of challenge of or rebellion against authority. While the right to question authority is a value held by many, that right conflicts with appreciation for the value of expert advice, opening the way for multiple conflict and conflict resolution possibilities. Three major variations of this theme emerged.

First is the idea that those who are supposedly inferior actually know more than the person in authority and therefore are in conflict with the authority figure. Kraft mayonnaise depicts a cooking class in which two little ladies prefer the Kraft brand to the mayonnaise preferred by the chef teaching the class. The conflict is established with the clashing preferences of students and teacher, then is resolved by the students convincing the teacher that Kraft mayonnaise really is best.

A second approach portrays the idea that people who don't listen to the advice of others are foolish. In Burger King's "Herb" commercials, Herb's parents try to explain why Herb has ignored their advice to try a Whopper. Herb has always been a misfit and apparently feels no conflict in not listening to everyone's recommendations, a fact which causes conflict for the parents. The resolution here is simply that we accept weirdness as an explanation for Herb's failure to heed good advice.

A third variation is that there is conflict present because there appears to be a rejection of authority, but the conflict is resolved because, in actuality, authority has been upheld. Subaru shows a father who is concerned that his son has purchased a sleek sports car instead of the Subaru that the father had recommended. It turns out that the son did buy a Subaru, so he has heeded his father's advice and pleased himself at the same time. The Subaru ad reflects some substantive conflict, that resulting from a perceived break with the family value of a son's respect for his father. The resolution, too, is more important than in the other commercials, since the traditional authority of the father has been upheld, as has the decision of the son and the relationship between the two.

Except for the Subaru commercial, all the commercials couched in the conflict resulting from a break with authority are humorous and treat the conflict and the resolution in a trivial manner. In this sample, it appears that the context of conflict arising from a break with authority is not something generally used for products requiring a somewhat serious ad treatment.

Rather than challenging authority, several commercials equate their product with a form of authority, that is, power. Power gives a person authority, enabling one to be influential in conflict resolution, or to avoid conflict because one is in a position of authority. Chevrolet Cavalier features Dan Marino holding a football, with a voice-over saying, "You don't get to the top by looking back. . . . You go for it." The ad continues, "Power, confidence, poise. . . . When you finally make your move, you're going to go all the way. Cavalier, for people who know exactly where they're going." A Wheaties commercial shows a water polo scene, emphasizing strength, power, and athletic ability, and tells viewers "Go tell yo' mama what the big boys eat."

Conflict and product competition. A kind of conflict frequently used is simple competition between products. In this approach, other products are denigrated in favor of the qualities of the product the ad was designed to promote. Two basic kinds of conflict come into play: conflict between the products competing for recognition as the best, and the conflict felt by the consumer trying to choose among so many alternatives. In addition, three basic formats were used: the anonymous competitor, direct confrontation with an identified competitor, and competition with a pseudocompetitor.

An example of the conflict felt by the consumer is the Dristan commercial in which a woman in a drugstore moves from one product to another, comparing ingredients. The competitor products are on the shelf, but are in the shadows and are not identified verbally. The woman doesn't want one product because it contains aspirin, another because it contains alcohol. She eventually picks up Dristan and says she wants that product because it provides "strong cold relief without ingredients you don't want." This ad also illustrates the anonymous competitor format, as does a Kentucky Fried Chicken ad which cautions that anonymous food purveyors who serve chicken may not be what "they're cracked up to be."

The second kind of conflict, conflict among the products vying for recognition as best is well illustrated in a Sinex commercial. George Kennedy points out that some nasal sprays have it and some don't. Aftron doesn't and Dristan doesn't. Only Sinex has "instant and complete relief." This ad also illustrates the format of direct confrontation with a named competitor.

The comparison format using the pseudocompetitor is illustrated by Contac, which compares Mom's chicken soup to their cold medicine. At the end of the commercial, Steve Landesberg tells Mom not to feel bad, because several other cold remedies (specifically identified at this point) couldn't beat Contac either.

The category of conflict established by product competition can employ a fairly straightforward approach in which one product is asserted to be better than another (like recent Pepsi taste test commercials), or it can use a more complex approach, playing on a variety of consumer needs to select the right product out of a confusing array of alternatives. The second approach might be expected to lend itself to more serious treatment of the product, while the first has more flexibility for either humorous or serious treatment.

CONFLICT RESOLUTION, SOCIAL COHESION, SOCIAL CONTRACT

While some of the commercials discussed above offer their product as the resolution of the conflicts created, others identify their product with those positive advantages gained through the social contract. People attempt to resolve conflict and achieve social cohesion, and the valued outcomes of those attempts are found to be a frequently used context for television commercials. Tenets of the social contract found as contexts for the commercials include harmony, civility, freedom of man, protection and defense, community, and family. These tenets overlap to a considerable degree, making it impossible to place commercials in discrete categories. While some commercials seem to emphasize a particular concept, others are based more broadly in the overall concept.

Overall theme. This political theme of social contract and its basic tenets of harmony, civility, and freedom of man is portrayed most cogently in a series of commercials produced for the Coors Beer Company of Golden, Colo., narrated by Mark Harmon. Coors's use of the social contract theme can best be seen in the ad entitled "taking your time," in which Harmon is seen fishing in a mountain stream. In these natural surroundings, Harmon tells us, "Patience—That's what struck me the most in learning about Coors beer, from the malting, to the brewing, aging, the whole process, they never hurry. It takes about twice as long to make Coors as it does any other major beer. Yeah, they do take their time, but you can taste the difference. . . ." Most of the time Harmon is delivering his lines he is looking out over the stream rather than at the camera. Other ads in the series are similar in theme. In one, Harmon is outdoors working with his wood tools, proclaiming that people loved Coors long before the "hype" and "hoopla." In another he is sitting in a barley field, explaining that while others buy their barley, Coors grows their own. Still another ad shows Harmon in an aging cooler explaining that Coors ages their beer longer than any other beer, and that's why if you want beer that is smooth and with spirit, "Coors is the one." As one communes with nature, the implication is that man is civilized, in harmony with nature, and freed from the rat race to take his time, sign the social contract, and buy Coors.

Harmony. While a serious use of the concept of harmony in the the Coors commercial illustrates the overall social contract theme, more trivial application is also used. McDonald's wants us to believe that they have achieved perfect harmony by inventing an unwieldy package that keeps the hot side hot and the cool side cool. The harmony theme is accentuated in the ad by the background song's lyrics, "hot beefy McD, cool crisp LT in perfect harmony."

Phillips 66 makes a direct claim that it brings humans into contact with their environment, because every time Phillips issues a performance report "they have made the environment cleaner."

Civility and protection. In some ads, the product provides that civility and/or protection that people need. Prudential portrays life as a jungle from which they can rescue us and our families. Themes of both civility and protection are incorporated into a Dodge Caravan commercial containing multiple political messages. The narrator states, "The traditional caravan journey was as unmerciful as the desert sun." But now, the "revolutionary" Caravan with its "civilized features" such as front-wheel drive "frees" people of their heavy burden, and "protects" them with a 5-year, 50,000-mile protection plan. It is interesting that front-wheel drive is a civilized feature and that there was a protection plan rather than a warranty. (Actually, the protection plan is a "limited warranty." During the discussion of the protection plan a disclaimer appears, stating that restrictions apply to the limited warranty and that it excludes leases, and the viewer should "see copy at your dealer.")

Man's freedom. This is a popular theme for commercials. Two basic contexts of the man's freedom theme were evident. The first one is that people have choices in life, and they should exercise their freedom to make those choices rather than allow someone or something else to choose for them. The second is that certain products provide a means of escape from the responsibilities of life.

In an excellent example of the first theme, AT&T has Cliff Robertson tell viewers, "you're going to be getting a piece of mail and you're going to be asked to make a choice. Don't throw it away. Don't give that right to someone else. . . . For 100 years we were there, and you can keep it that way be sending in your ballot. AT&T—the right choice." In this ad, the choice of which long-distance service a person will choose is characterized as the right of suffrage and is couched in terms of marking a ballot, as though the viewer were engaged in the American democratic process itself.

The same theme of freedom of choice is altered slightly in the next example. The Association of American Gynecologists and Obstetricians wants viewers to know that people have choices that they shouldn't allow circumstances of life to take away. Women have the freedom, says the ad, to be president, to go back to school, to control when they want to start a family. But "nothing changes intentions faster than an unintended pregnancy."

Freedom to escape responsibility is illustrated by a Ford Mustang commercial. Mustang allows people to "get out and get away." In this commercial a woman gets away by handing her briefcase and work papers to a male counterpart, jumping in her Mustang and speeding away.

Community will. A modification of Rousseau's concept of *volonté* *général,* provides the context for both Ford Taurus and State Farm Insurance. Both commercials emphasize that their company is responsive to the needs of the consumer. In advertising its new Taurus, Ford says it built a car for all of us who will not compromise. "Ford listened, Ford created Taurus for us." The jingle emphasizes this point by repeating the rhyme "Taurus for us." Similarly, State Farm claims to listen to the will of the community, at least, in this case, the community of women. "State Farm listens to women, so women talk to State Farm." The result is life insurance designed for women. As in the case of Ford, their product was created in response to the needs and stated will of the community. The people behind the products, therefore, are civilized people participating in the social contract and contributing to the community.

Equality. Two variations of the equality theme were identified, one focusing on equal treatment for everyone, the second on the broader aspects of inherent equality and brotherhood of peoples. The first theme appears in a Braniff commercial which emphasizes that with Braniff, all seats on their flights cost the same. There is, therefore, no difference in service and food among passengers. Everyone is equal on Braniff, the classless airline. The second theme is portrayed by Kodak. In this commercial, a little Caucasian girl leaves a Christmas present for an elderly Black friend. The impression is one of brotherly love, of seeing all people as valuable, and therefore as equal, regardless of race.

Family. The family theme is particularly political. In his discussion of political theory, Rousseau (1950) contends that "the most ancient of all societies, and the only one that is natural, is the family" (p. 9). The importance of family is evident in several commercials, including some of the American pride commercials discussed above and in some of the women's roles commercials described later in this chapter. It can best be seen as a major theme, however, in some of the AT&T commercials urging us to "reach out and touch someone." An example of an AT&T commercial specifically urging us to reach out and touch our families is the one in which a grandfather recites "t'was the night before Christmas" to his grandson over the phone. As the child falls asleep during the recitation, the mother reminds her father "it still works." The linking of a commercial product to those close feelings of family love and unity is recognized by advertisers as a very positive association.

Defense of the community. The social contract permits man to "defend and protect with the whole force of the community the person and property of every associate. . . ." (Rousseau, 1950, pp. 13–14). John Hancock assumes the role of protector by providing financial security, while State Farm, "like a good neighbor" (community) will protect your family. Your American Express card is "worth more than it can buy"; it provides security. (The security that it provides is that if you lose your card, you can get another one tomorrow.) A slightly different use of the concept is seen in the Sperry commercial in which Kirk Douglas assures us that "Sperry sets the standard for airline safety."

Those civil aspects of life gained through cooperative association with our fellow being seem to be very popular as a context for television advertising. The approach is either "use this product because you are a part of this civility (as in the AT&T commercial)," or "use this product to gain such civility (as in the Dodge Caravan commercial)." Interestingly, very few of the commercials in these settings use a humorous approach. A subtle humor is introduced in the McDonald's rollicky and light-hearted ad, but for the most part, the ad intent is for the audience to take them seriously. That's not to say, however, that they are not trivial in their application of the concepts (e.g., Dodge Caravan, American Express). The equating of security with fast replacement of a credit card, civility with having four-wheel drive, and freedom with the right to choose AT&T is probably not what Rousseau had in mind.

AMERICAN POLITICAL VALUES

A variety of themes that we have labeled American political values were evident in the commercials sampled. They include symbols of government authority and security, chauvinism, American pride, work ethic, family, and roles of women.

Symbols of government. The use of symbols representing the government in varying ways appeared in a large number of commercials. The ads can be loosely grouped according to the use of the symbols.

Some commercials use government symbols as spokespersons or sources of credibility for the product. For example, Delco dramatizes the maintenance-free feature of their batteries by having former Air Force test pilot Chuck Yeager compare the sophisticated aviation electronics of an Air Force jet fighter with the little green light on the Delco battery that lets us know it has water in it. Nabisco Better Cheddars are backed by the four Presidents enshrined on Mount Rushmore, and the State of Florida's Department of Citrus gives its seal of approval to Florida orange juice, so "orange you smart" to buy it? Ford tries to achieve credibility for it Aerostar design by associating it with the design of the space shuttle (this ad predates the Shuttle disaster). While no actual governmental spokesperson is used, the credibility of the space shuttle speaks for Aerostar.

Some commercials in this category use military symbols to imply protection and security. Kemper Insurance Company compares their homeowner's insurance with the insurance provided by the U.S. Cavalry to the frontier homeowner. The video shows a cavalry charge, but they're carrying the Kemper flag, implying that Kemper provides the same protection as the cavalry. Prudential shows a sheriff coming to the rescue of a damsel in distress. Without Prudential, we, like she, would be helpless.

The use of military symbols to link a product with self-pride is evident in two commercials. Old Spice allows us to stand tall like the drill sergeant in their ad, and Wrigley's Spearmint gum can give us the same spring it puts into the step of a young Naval officer.

A few commercials are obvious in their use of government symbols, but don't use them in any ways common to other commercials. Pepperidge Farm hails the "revolution" in croissant pizzas, and the "great American political tradition of 'passing the buck'" can lead to no one taking responsibility to turn the dishwasher on, which in turn necessitates the use of Sunlight dishwashing detergent.

Finally, the epitome of this kind of commercial is illustrated in an ad for Chrysler LeBaron. The $12,000 LeBaron is pitted against the $24,000 BMW 528E in a high-performance duel. The duel takes place on the deck of a U.S. aircraft carrier. The two cars race around the deck of the carrier, encircling a row of naval fighters, and, "in a crucial test, the LeBaron beat the legendary BMW." As the duel comes to a conclusion, the BMW narrowly avoids disaster by stopping inches from the end of the carrier. In the background a chorus of men begin humming the World War I anthem "Over There." The narrator states emphatically, "and we'll keep on beating BMW," with the chorus chiming in, "till it's over over there."

Chauvinism. This kind of political value, cited by the popular media and discussed earlier in this text, refers to a fanatical patriotism or an unreasonable devotion to country. This sentiment leads to the denigration of other nations in the name of loyalty to one's own country. This kind of zeal is obvious in several commercials. A commercial for Meister Brau shows a bureaucrat of a "foreign embassy in Washington, D.C." calling for his male secretary Vladimir and demanding to know the whereabouts of Comrade Petrenko. Vladimir explains that Petrenko is out buying "high-priced capitalist beer" (Meister Brau). The bureaucrat responds "nyet," and goes on to explain that Meister Brau only tastes expensive. The commercial then shows Comrade Petrenko enjoying the fruits of his fraud, like the characters of the other Meister Brau ads discussed earlier.

Continuing the chauvinistic theme the media found so intriguing is the Wendy's commercial satirizing Russian fashion as nondescript and unchanging. Miller beer aired a commercial featuring Russian immigrant comedian Smirnov sitting in a bar extolling the virtues of America (and of course, Miller beer's less filling, great taste). He explains that "in America you can always find a party. In Russia, the party always finds you."

During the time period in which commercials were being recorded for this story, the distributor of *Rocky IV* aired an ad announcing that by popular demand the picture was being released in additional theaters. The scenes used to promote the movie were scenes of confrontation between Rocky, the American, and Ivan Drago, the Russian fighter. The television ad for *Spies Like Us,* another contemporary film, used a scene where a man with a Cossack hat, a Russian accent, and a big knife threatens Chevy Chase. The man explains, "Every minute you don't tell us why you're here, I cut off a finger." Chevy replies, "Mine or yours?" The implication is that the Russian might just be dumb enough to cut off his own fingers.

American pride. Many commercials centered around a more positive aspect of patriotism, pride in America. Miller beer produced several commercials with this theme, and one of the best examples is the story of Barnaveld, Wis. The ad tells how a tornado practically destroyed the town the previous year, and outsiders believed the town was finished. But not the residents of this small town. They knew they could come back, and as a resident points out, "we have." A series of video montages of town residents pitching in, shaking hands, hugging each other, eating, and celebrating is accompanied by a descriptive song. The Miller commercial tells the story of the rebuilding of the town. The nationalistic pride in America and its people is evidenced in the text of the song: "A place where people have a sense of pride, that's what keeps them right here, where you count on your own, you call it your home, and Miller's the beer. Miller's made the American way, born and bred in the U.S.A. Just as proud as the people who are drinking it today, Miller's made the American way." This is a not very subtle attempt to say that Miller is the true American beer.

Chrysler waves the American flag as blatantly as did Miller. Chrysler's Plymouth Voyager ad announces, "the pride is back" with the advent of this "born in America car." But while Miller ties the product to America primarily through the lyrics of the accompanying jingle, the Voyager ad makes the connection through visual symbols. The

Chrysler logo, a modern star design, is pictured in the color blue on an animated background of waving red and white stripes. In the video montage which follows, a father and son share a saddle while the father teaches the son the art of roping, a hard hat raises his fist in prideful celebration, an American Indian is shown close up, followed by American landscapes, including both urban and rural scenes. A man of Polynesian ancestry is shown holding his newborn, followed by a small Indian girl dancing, followed by a Puerto Rican boy, followed by a waving Lee Iaccoca, himself of immigrant ancestry, and a picture of the Statue of Liberty (this ad predates Iaccoca's celebrated problems with the Liberty restoration project). The commercial ends with the Chrysler logo on the red and white stripes background with the lyrics "the pride is back, born in America" being sung in the background.

Cutlass Sierra promoters changed the lyrics of a folk song from "Hello, America, how are you? Don't you know me, I'm your native son" to "Hello, America, how are you? Don't you know me, I'm your native car." Car manufacturers evidently like tying their products in with the American theme, probably a not-so-subtle admonition for all of us to buy American in the face of foreign car imports.

Other commercials use the theme of the American way. A CBS ad boasts that evening in America is typified by families getting together and turning to Dan Rather, a traditon that "keeps America on top of the world." A cause and a consequence of American pride is American achievement, quality, and uniqueness. The United States Army helps us become "all that we can be," the Marines want "a few good men," and the armed forces are "not a company but your country."

American work ethic. Elements of the American work ethic can certainly be seen in some of the American pride commercials described above. But a few commercials use the "work hard" concept more overtly. Budweiser commercials salute the American worker, and the accompanying video montage focuses mainly on blue-collar workers. These are the people who "make America work—this Bud's for you." Recognition of the work ethic with a slight challenge in it can be seen in an ad for the *Wall Street Journal.* The commercial reminds us that the American dream takes more than hard work and luck. It also takes a vision of what tomorrow holds. And the *Wall Street Journal,* of course, brings America that vision. But so does Dean Witter, who recognizes that "you're working hard to make your dreams come true," and their company wants "to dream them with you." So "no matter what you do or who you are, Dean Witter will help you plan your investment like no one else, because you're like no one else."

Women's roles. The way women are portrayed in this set of commercials seems to us a reflection of an array of political values relating to the role of women in society. Ads ranged from stereotypical to traditional to contemporary in their characterization of women in dramatic portrayals of their products.

Mercury Sable produced a stereotypical ad that appears, at first glance, to be contemporary. A sophisticated woman executive is shown sitting at the head of an empty table in a corporate meeting room. The scenes are interspersed with a male playing racquet ball. The jingle seems to emphasize the woman's acumen when it says, "get ready, here I come, I'm on my way," but it soon becomes apparent that the new shape of the car is being compared with the shapely female executive and the athletic male. The ad ends with the comment, "Mercury Sable, the shape you want to be in." A Finesse hair conditioner commercial stereotypes in a different way, showing a beautiful and demure woman receiving flowers and looking charming and feminine. She uses Finesse, "the conditioner you control with time," and the ad visually hints that perhaps her finesse extends to control of the men in her life.

An ad that completely reverses the stereotypical "women as sex object" approach is the Coors Silver Bullet commercial. In it, a woman sits on a bar stool, fantasizing about a chance of meeting a "hunk." She then looks over her shoulder to discover that a very attractive man has just sat down on the bar stool next to her. In this ad, the man is viewed as the sex object.

Several ads portray women in contemporary roles of responsibility and expanded opportunity. Two Hewlett-Packard commercials show a woman in the middle of several men coming up with the solution to a client's puzzling problem. State Farm twice featured women agents in their commercials. Oil of Olay shows a woman finishing a 10K race, another receiving a university degree, and another playing with her baby. In song these women say to us, "It's my turn to see what I can see . . . I hope you'll understand, this time's just for me." These women seem to be establishing their own identity and independence, a reflection of current changes in society.

Other commercials emphasize the dependence of others on women, primarily in a traditional context. In these ads, women assume roles of significant others and authority figures, but always in those areas where tradition would expect women to be in authority. Sudafed gives a mother relief in 22 minutes, since she does not have time to slow down and needs to accomplish her important tasks of the day. Downy fabric has a young camper writing his mother, not his father, to explain he misses home. Mom writes back, informing him he only misses Downy, not his home and Mom.

In two ads, the male is pictured as inept in the absence of the experienced woman. A father of a small son relates a tale of woe in which he bought a shampoo other than Johnson's No Tears shampoo. He washed his son's hair with it, got shampoo in the child's eyes, and felt very guilty. All of this happened because his wife wasn't there. Another father shows the same ineptitude in a commercial in which he washes the dishes in the dishwasher on the energy cycle. His daughter explains that if you're going to use the energy cycle, you've got to use Cascade.

The variety of portrayals of women in these ads is reflective of the range of perspectives of the American audience on the role of women in society. While no particular portrayal can be identified through this study as dominant, it is obvious that advertisers are aware of stereotypical, traditional, and contemporary views of women and are willing to adapt those concepts as backgrounds for appropriate products.

CONCLUSION

The examination of television commercials in this study indicates that politics pervades popular commercials in America. With few exceptions, the commercials we viewed were found to embody concepts of conflict, conflict resolution, identification with elements of the social contract, and/or specific political cultural values.

The relationship of these television commercials to politics is complex. Certainly aspects of people's physical and emotional conflicts as they deal with nature and with other people are present. But what we see are the commercial world's interpretations of that conflict and of the resulting dilemma in the context of the advertiser's reality. As a result, while there are manifestations of conflict related to serious and perhaps accepted universal human conflict and dilemma (i.e., quality of life, societal change, individualism, humanity, security, etc.), much of the creation of conflict is based on the trivial. The triviality is, in a sense, inherent to the process, since broad, generic concepts are being applied and interpreted through specific (trivial) situations. More important to our analysis is the more traditional interpretation of the trivial, that is, lacking depth or seriousness. Thus, the "general conflict" as reflected through many ads is a kind of superficial conflict brought about by such conditions as too much choice among products, multiple reasons for liking a product, and clashing product preferences among people in relationship to each other.

Even when conflicts emerge out of more substantive contexts, their personification and resolution are trivialized. The substantive conflict of humanity when pitted against modernization is personified in an ad where a family-owned bar is surrounded by a skyscraper, and the resolution of the conflict introduced by such confrontation is to drink Miller beer.

Similarly, the attempt by advertisers to link their products with those positive advantages gained through the social contract represent trivial applications of the concepts of civility. In our sample, this is illustrated when harmony with nature is equated with drinking Coors beer, civility is represented by four-wheel drive, and community will boils down to market research for the creation of Ford Taurus.

In the group of commercials identified as political primarily by virtue of their reflection of American political cultural values, there appears to be a dichotomy of trivialization. On the one hand are commercials associated with chauvinism, which continue to treat conflict as trivial, such as the Wendy's commercials based on the conflict between the United States and Russia. In a world in which these two superpowers are locked in a struggle over nuclear disarmament, this commercial portrays the conflict as one of fashion and food, with the United States, of course, providing choice both in fashion and in hamburgers. On the other hand there are the commercials which deal with, in a more serious vein, American values such as pride, hard work, and so forth. But the commercial world manages to trivialize those substantive values by associating them with the commercial product. Hence, the pride in America in the spirit that rebuilds a Midwest town destroyed by a tornado is equated with Miller beer, as if that rare combination of hops and barley instills in Americans the will, the community, the determination, the harmony, to rebuild not only the town of Barnaveld, Wis., but the character of America.

In a world of sundry definitions of politics, we chose to characterize politics as the activity of people in consort negotiating resolutions of disputes. If this definition is an accurate or fair assessment of political activity, then the trivializing by commercials of conflict and its subsequent resolution, or lack of it, may have meaningful implications.

First, it has been argued that while Americans are socially mature, they are political adolescents. The meaning of that interpretation is that the American people are wise when it comes to social understanding, but are immature when it comes to political understanding. The American public is increasingly reliant on television for information about political affairs, the situational and technological constraints inherent to television and the television industry make it difficult to portray variety and complexity, and the rank and file public have been found to be only moderately informed, even in election years. With these facts comes the speculation that there has been a reduction in the quality of political discourse among Americans (Manheim, 1976). If there is any support for such characterizations of the American public, the trivializing of political activity as evidenced in the commercials we have discussed may contribute to this political immaturity. Certainly the naïvete of the portrayal of conflict in television commercials would contribute little to the development of better political understanding among viewers.

Secondly, the trivializing of conflict creates a problem in that if conflict is not serious, then the need to resolve it is not serious. Politics, by definition, is the engagement of people in the process of resolving conflicts, and in that process there is sometimes agreement to disagree. But in the world of television commercials, people are not encouraged to be tolerant of the views of other, but rather choose up sides to make a choice between "tastes great" or "less filling." While the real world of politics accepts diversity and encourages some tolerance of different versions of reality in order to preserve social cooperation, politics as trivia encourages divisiveness and disunity through its failure to treat conflict and its resolution seriously.

Finally, while this study supports the contention that there are latent political values in popular television advertising, findings suggest that the way in which these values are presented may be more than subtly reaffirmed, or restated, or altered political myths. Instead, they may create political myths that by the nature of popular commercials as a mode of expression are less psychologically, socially, or politically functional than studies of popular culture have previously suggested.

REFERENCES

Bentley, A. (1967). *The process of government.* Cambridge, MA: Belknap Press.

Burke, K. (1950). *A rhetoric of motives.* Englewood Cliffs, NJ: Prentice–Hall.

Combs, J. E. (1984). *Politics and popular culture.* Bowling Green, OH: Bowling Green University Popular Press.

Gailey, P. (1985, February 1). On heroes and "sleaze." *New York Times,* sec. 10, p. 1.

Geis, M. L. (1982). *The language of television advertising.* New York: Academic Press.

Glaser, B. G. (1978). *Theoretical sensitivity.* Mill Valley, CA: Sociology Press.

Glaser, B. G., & Strauss, A. L. (1967). *The discovery of grounded theory.* Chicago: Aldine.

Goldman, P., McAlevey, P., Doherty, S., McCormick, J., & Maier, F. (1985, December 23). Rocky and Rambo. *Newsweek*, 58–62.

Key, W. B. (1974). *Subliminal seduction.* New York: New American Library.

Libbert, B. (1986, January 20). Chevy ads speak softly, carry a strong message. *Dallas Morning News*, p. 5–E.

Manheim, J. B. (1976). Can democracy survive television? *Journal of Communication, 26,* 84–90.

McLaughlin, M. (1985, November 17). I lift my lamp beside the golden ad. *Arkansas Gazette.*

Nimmo, D. (1978). *Political communication and public opinion in America.* Santa Monica, CA: Goodyear.

Root, R. L. (1987). *The rhetorics of popular cultures: Advertising advocacy, and entertainment.* New York: Greenwood Press.

Rousseau, J.–J. (1950). *The social contract and discourses* (G. D. H. Cole, Trans.). New York: E. P. Dutton.

Skidmore, M. J., & Skidmore, J. (1983). Political themes in contemporary comic books. *Journal of Popular Culture, 17*(1), 83–90.

5

Ad-Versarial Politics: Business, Political Advertising, and the 1980 Election

Tom Konda
Department of Political Science,
State University of New York at
Plattsburgh,

Lee Sigelman
Office of the Dean,
College of Arts and Sciences
University of Arizona

The widespread use of sophisticated modern advertising techniques by candidates for public office, first analyzed by Stanley Kelley Jr. (1956) and later chronicled in Joe McGinniss's (1969) eye-opening account of Richard Nixon's media campaign in 1968, has become such a familiar part of the American political landscape that it now commands attention only when it threatens to get entirely out of hand—as it did in 1984 and 1986, when a spate of negative campaign ads began to appear. Slick advertising campaigns remain a favorite target for critics who despair that candidates are being packaged and sold to the American people like underarm deodorant, but no one can seriously doubt that in the coming years candidate advertising will continue to play a leading role in electoral politics in the United States and, increasingly, worldwide.

But political advertising encompasses far more than candidate-centered ads sponsored by political parties, political action committees, or the candidates themselves. Political advertising for ostensibly nonpolitical purposes by purportedly nonpartisan sponsors is also commonplace, even though it has attracted much less attention, and much less criticism, than candidate-centered advertising. In this chapter we analyze this less-understood form of political advertising as it has evolved in the United States. Our focus is on *business*-sponsored political advertising, for the simple reason that political advertising has long been an area of intense activity on the part of business in general and big business in particular. When, at key points in

American history, business aims and practices have come under fire, business people have naturally been eager to stave off such attacks (Key, 1964; Lasswell, 1939). In defending and promoting their interests, they have naturally adapted advertising, a tool originally developed to market their goods and services.

Although business's basic goals in engaging in political advertising have never changed, over the years several different approaches have evolved for attaining these goals. In what follows, we begin with an overview of these approaches. Our main interest, however, lies in the most notable (and, some would say, the most worrisome) recent approach, which cropped up during the 1980 presidential campaign and has been clearly in evidence ever since. The keystone of this approach is an advertising campaign designed to complement a candidate's nomination or election campaign and therefore to influence election outcomes, although the advertisements themselves contain no explicit candidate endorsements. We explore the uses of this approach to political advertising by focusing on the onslaught in 1979 and 1980 of business-sponsored ads for issues and symbols with which Ronald Reagan was already identified or was seeking to identify himself.

3 APPROACHES TO POLITICAL ADVERTISING

Business's earliest and most direct approach to political advertising involved simple *self-defense*. In what may have been the very first business-sponsored political advertisements in this country, the Bell System tried to overcome the widespread hostility that had been evoked by its surprise use of the patent laws to maintain its monopoly, hoping thereby to counter any public pressure for hostile legislation (Pimlott, 1951, p. 236). In 1908, Bell began running a series of ads that announced rather stiffly that "agitation against legitimate telephone business . . . must disappear with the realization of the necessity of universal service" (Griese, 1976). Once Bell had opened the door, other companies rushed in, and this new lobbying soon grew so widespread that members of Congress railed against it (Anonymous, 1913). Before long, even President Wilson himself would complain that "The newspapers are being filled with advertisements calculated to mislead the judgment not only of public men, but also the public opinion of the country itself" (Lane, 1950, p. 16).

During the 1930s, advertisements exemplifying a second approach, the *promotion of the free enterprise system*, began to appear. Sponsored mainly by business groups such as the National Association of Manufacturers and the Chamber of Commerce, these ads initially amounted to little more than self-defense on a grander scale; rather than the interests of a single company or industry, it was now the interests of business at large that were being defended. Soon, however, self-defense evolved into offense, in the form of invidious comparisons between business, which was invariably depicted as the sole engine of American prosperity, and government, which was typically lambasted as a threat to American freedom (Green, 1939; Tedlow, 1976). Labor unions, especially the leftist CIO unions, were likewise disparaged as subverters of the American free enterprise system (Seldes, 1947). These new antigovernment and antiunion thrusts marked a turning point for business, which had previously balked at using advertisements to attack government or labor outright (Pearlin & Rosenberg, 1952, p. 26).

A third approach to political advertising, which began to gather momentum just after World War II, involves the *advocacy of specific public policies*. From the outset, advocacy advertising was employed for both offensive and defensive purposes. For instance, the steamship interests advertised extensively to promote free trade, while the National Association of Real Estate Boards advertised just as vigorously to oppose government-subsidized housing (Schriftgiesser, 1951). Later, the concrete, steel, and earthmoving equipment industries advertised heavily for new road construction, as did aircraft manufacturers to promote American air power and then to celebrate the space program.

While showing no great reluctance to advertise for a variety of political purposes, business had almost always drawn the line at overtly partisan advertising. Although the very first Bell System ad was obviously written with the 1908 election in mind, advertisers still tried to avoid the appearance of partisanship. Only the maverick Henry Ford dared to break publicly with this tradition when he used commercial airtime during the Ford Sunday Evening Hour's 1936 radio season to criticize the Roosevelt administration for everything from demagoguery to effeminacy. Company spokesman W. J. Cameron, claiming to have toured the country and found people everywhere fed up with the New Deal, used Ford's commercial minutes to try to pave the way for a Republican restoration in the 1936 election. Even in the wake of the Republicans' humiliating defeat, Cameron kept up his partisan barrage, invoking the "corrective and sobering influence of an intelligent and active minority" as the rationale for his continued criticism of the Roosevelt administration (Cameron, 1937, p. 27).

However, the overt partisanship of Ford's radio commercials proved to be the exception, not the rule. Other businesses did not follow Ford's lead, and even during the Truman administration, a high-water mark of business political advertising, partisanship was generally downplayed during election periods. Only the American Medical Association's massive 1950 campaign against Truman's national health care plan was directly aimed at turning Democratic incumbents out of office, and even then care was taken to obscure the advertising campaign's true sponsorship (Kelley, 1956).

POLITICAL ADVERTISING SINCE 1970

And there matters stood—with business political advertising normally in evidence but not not sensationally so—until 1970. Then, suddenly, all this began to change. Political advertising by business quickly rebounded to the very high visibility it had commanded during the Truman years. Numerous magazine articles were written describing it, exposing it, decrying it, or defending it. *Fortune* magazine began sponsoring annual seminars to teach business people how to use it. And the U. S. Senate, always alert to new political trends, wanted to find out everything it could about whether the extravagant claims being made for and against it had any basis in fact (U. S. Senate, 1972, 1978).

Why this sudden upsurge of interest and activity? Largely because during the late 1960s and early 1970s, the American public's opinion of business and business leaders plummeted to a point that threatened the probusiness climate that had long prevailed. Congress was on the brink of passing new environmental, consumer protection, and health and safety legislation, all of which were bitterly opposed by business. Business was widely perceived to be in trouble, and business leaders shared in that assessment (McGrath, 1976; U. S. Senate, 1978, pp. 145–155).

Throughout the 1970s, business stuck with its time-tested approaches to political advertising. Starting with defensive advertisements, it later intermixed messages promoting the free enterprise system and advocating various public policies. Early in the decade, the oil, paper, chemical, and steel industries spent enormous sums of money on defensive ads whose message was that through the untiring efforts of industry, the pollution problem was being solved, eliminating the need for government regulation. These ads, many critics charged, served mainly as a smokescreen behind which the industries continued to pollute while fighting the new environmental regulations in court and elsewhere. Indeed, some of this advertising was so patently bogus—a prime example was a Chevron ad that misidentified the Palm Springs County Courthouse as the nonexistent Chevron "Pollution Research Center"—that it contributed to a widening skepticism about the entire practice of political advertising by business (U. S. Senate, 1972, p. 103; Weiss, 1970).

Recurring energy crises kept the level of defensive advertising unusually high throughout the 1970s. In 1979, all the major oil companies were still using their ads to deny charges that they were creating artificial shortages [Exxon, *Newsweek* 6/25/79], to defend their windfall profits [Mobil, *Newsweek* 4/23/79], to claim that they were preserving the environment [Gulf, *New Yorker* 4/2/79], or simply to reiterate how hard they were working to serve the public interest [Texaco, *Newsweek* 4/30/79]. But defensive advertising was by no means restricted to the oil companies. As health care costs soared, the insurance industry began to run advertisements about its tireless efforts to hold down costs (U. S. House, 1978, pp. 595–611). There was also constant advertising about the safety of chemicals [Monsanto, *Harper's*, 11/80]. Chrysler President Lee Iacocca personally signed advertisements defending the Chrysler loan guarantee in 1979 [*Time* 12/3/79], the same year the Tobacco Institute weighed in with a series of advertisements against "anti-smokers" [*Newsweek* 7/16/79].

As the pace of defensive advertising quickened, advertisements extolling the virtues of the free enterprise system also gained new momentum. The oil companies, which had suffered the greatest public obloquy, were the foremost celebrants of free enterprise. By 1975, Conoco was memorializing free enterprise as the "neglected freedom" in an ad that featured the likenesses of, and quotations from, Jefferson and Madison [*Newsweek* 8/25/75]. During the bicentennial anniversary of the American revolution, such advertising blossomed. Phillips Petroleum produced television ads (pretested to meet "performance norms in positively influencing viewer attitudues toward free enterprise") that it then sold at cost to smaller companies for their advertising campaigns (Sethi, 1977, p. 49). Such ads were neatly described by Representative Elliott Levitas during a House investigation of political advertising:

> There is an ad I see on television nowadays with an eagle flying around and picking up a fish, telling us how great the free enterprise system is and that we ought not to do anything to mess around with it. (U. S. House, 1978, p. 189)

On a more down-to-earth plane, Allied Chemical began a "Profits Are For People" campaign (Sethi, 1977, pp. 24–25), a sure sign that business interests believed that profitmaking had become associated in the public mind with profiteering. More imaginatively, Penn-

walt—which sponsored ads in business periodicals attacking government, labor, welfare recipients, and anyone who complained of discrimination (Sethi, 1977, p. 48)—pointed up small flaws in the free
enterprise system as a means of disarming readers and bolstering
the credibility of its primary message: Free enterprise is superior to
any other system.

As time passed and public antipathy toward business abated, the
free enterprise advertising became more assertive. Alcoa pointed out
that only a "free market system" could have sent a man to the moon
[*U. S. News & World Report* 7/23/79]. Insurance companies began to
tie the free enterprise theme into their defensive advertising [Crum &
Forster, *Time* 11/5/79]. The Statue of Liberty was featured so often in
ads that one might have thought it a monument to American business [Reliance Group, *Fortune* 12/1/80; Westinghouse, *Fortune* 12/
29/80]. By the time of the Reagan administration, Getty Oil was likening free enterprise to mountain climbing and other expressions of
rugged individualism, while vaguely warning of dire consequences
should "someone" decide that government ought to "protect us"
from anything [*U. S. News & World Report,* 10/19/81].

The energy crisis also stimulated a great deal of advocacy advertising. The American Electric Power System used the shock of the first
Arab oil embargo to press for the mining of coal on public lands and
the abandonment of many environmental regulations (Sethi, 1977,
pp. 138–179). As oil prices rose, many coal-related companies
formed a chorus of voices pleading that coal be liberated from the
clutches of "fanatical environmentalists" and of an Environmental
Protection Agency "blinded by a distorted vision of righteousness"
(Sethi, 1977, pp. 159, 172). Environmentalists in and out of government also bore the brunt of a bitter advertising attack by proponents
of nuclear power (U. S. House, 1978, p. 586).

Hints of the partisan advertising that would soon be forthcoming
cropped up in the course of this energy advertising campaign. During
the oil crisis of 1973–1974, the oil companies couched their disagreement with President Nixon in extremely tactful prose but labeled the
recommendations of the Democratic Congress a "disaster" (Sethi,
1977, pp. 119, 28). Once President Carter was in office, though, any
hesitancy about attacking the White House fell by the wayside. The Edison Electric Institute disparaged Carter's 1977 energy plan as "unfair"
and "needless" (U. S. House, 1978, p. 650), and Mobil castigated Carter's energy policy as an active threat "to you and your children"
against which members of the public should warn their elected representatives (Lewin, 1978, p. 29). Another hint of the partisanship to
come in 1980 was the emergence of advocacy advertising with a very

broad scope. Narrow-gauged policy advocacy ads continued to flourish, of course. Besides the energy ads, the steel industry, for example, advertised for "fair play" (i.e., protectionist legislation) for steel (Sethi, 1982, pp. 191–193). However, in 1975 Chase Manhattan launched a much broader campaign, promoting a six-point economic plan in a series of ads with such titles as "Uncle!," "Wolf!," "Ouch!," "Squawk!," and "Scream!". While Chase's advocacy of tax breaks for savers and investors and of lower taxes on capital gains constituted narrow advocacy for the bank's interests, its proposals to "stabilize" fiscal and monetary policies and to "do away with outmoded government regulations and agencies that restrict our free market economy" went far beyond narrow advocacy (U. S. House, 1978, pp. 675–678).

In many ways, and especially on the economic front, the Carter administration was relatively conservative. Paul Volcker, an advocate of tight monetary policy, was appointed to head the Federal Reserve Board, deregulation was emphasized, and the "antibureaucratic" Paperwork Reduction Act was signed into law. In this climate, political advertising began to wane after the intensive advocacy advertising in early 1977 over the energy crisis. During the last half of 1977 and all of 1978, most of the oil companies limited themselves to image advertising. As health care costs became an issue, the insurance industry did run some ads about its efforts to hold down costs. But even Carter's health care plan inspired little counteradvertising, with only American Medicorp venturing any policy advocacy in newspaper ads (U. S. House, 1978, pp. 588–593). The steel industry advertising mentioned above was fairly prominent around this time, too, as was free enterprise advertising of the "flying eagle" variety. And there was some antigovernment advertising by Mobil in a series of ads urging liberals and idealistic young people to side with business instead of striking a "trendy-left," "antibusiness posture" [Atlantic, 11/78]. All in all, however, readers of magazines and newspapers encountered less political advertising during this period, and what they did encounter tended to be less blatantly partisan. But even though relatively little political advertising was being run in 1977 and 1978, a great deal was being planned.

ADVERTISING FOR REAGAN: BUSINESS ADVERTISEMENTS AND THE 1980 ELECTION

The Early Campaign

As the race for the presidency began to heat up in 1979, various business interests initiated advertising campaigns that touched on, and in some cases directly confronted, the themes being articulated by the presidential contenders. Even more of these advertising campaigns got under way in 1980. In large measure, these campaigns amounted to unaffiliated arms of the Reagan for President effort. To avoid running afoul of campaign spending laws, businesses could not advertise for the explicit purpose of putting their stamp of approval on candidate Reagan or stamping their disapproval on his opponents in the primary or the general election. At most, they could use their advertisements to reiterate their favored candidate's positions or to take issue with the other candidates' ideas (as well as issuing pointed, and ostensibly nonpartisan, reminders about the importance of voting). Some business advertising campaigns in 1979 and 1980 reiterated and some took issue, but most did both. The themes reiterated were those of Ronald Reagan. The themes with which issue was taken were those of Jimmy Carter.

Early on, the Reagan program had three main thrusts. First, government was depicted as the major culprit behind inflation, the nation's foremost economic problem. Government programs—"miracle cures for which there are no known diseases"—were criticized for generating excessive spending (Clymer, 1979, p. 50), and the money supply was said to be out of control, thereby fueling further inflation. The second thrust was simplistic but very effective: the nation in general and business in particular, Reagan claimed, were being "regulated to death." More than anything else, the answer was to "get government off our backs." The third thrust derived from President Carter's lamentations about a national crisis over energy, inflation, and the budget. The only real crisis, Reagan charged, was in the White House. The nation was doing fine, or would be if only government would unleash the private sector, which would put people to work, solve the energy crisis, and generate enough wealth to balance the budget (Clymer, 1979). In November, 1979, when Reagan formally entered the race, he unveiled his economic program of reducing federal spending (largely by eliminating "unnecessary" regulations and the agencies that enforced them) and imposing supply-side tax cuts in order to spur enough investment and growth to balance the budget. He also proposed to pay greater attention to the nation's national defense needs, expanding the "crisis in the White House" theme to explain the nation's supposed military decline (Lindsey, 1979). These ideas would remain largely unchanged throughout Reagan's campaign for the nomination. The only modifications were of tone, not substance, as Reagan escalated his attack on Carter, whom he accused of having given up and written America off. Reagan rejected the hopelessness he attributed to Carter, and spoke glowingly of a "new beginning" in which the government would hardly be hardly noticeable at home but formidable abroad (Reagan, 1980; Smith, 1980).

In March of 1979 the Savings and Loan Foundation got the advertisers' campaign season into gear with a normal advocacy ad. Asking "Isn't it time to give a tax break to savers?," the foundation began its pitch for an supply-side tax cut [*Newsweek* 3/26/79]. By September an updated version of this ad blamed "INFLATION!" for low savings levels and repeated the pitch for a tax cut to keep inflation "from getting completely out of hand" [*Newsweek* 9/17/79]. These ads continued with increasing urgency over the next few months, and the last one in the series—widely published during the week before the election—added ominously, "Why can't you buy the home you want? Or sell the one you have?" The answers: "Short-sighted regulation, inflation, and an antiquated tax system." Hinting darkly that the government had willfully undermined the security of homeowners through "a concerted effort . . . to divert funds away from the main sources of mortgage lending," the ad pointed out in its tag line that "If we all speak up, Washington *has* to listen" [*Smithsonian* 10/80]. The National Association of Realtors agreed. In its "American Dream" ads, the realtors fixed the blame for soaring housing prices squarely on the government. Inflation, a "big factor" out of control, was pushing all prices up [*Newsweek* 6/11/79], and housing prices were rising even faster than most due to "excessive regulatory red tape" [*Newsweek* 5/7/79]. *Even worse, the regulations on builders were so cumbersome and unreasonable as to "reduce their incentive to build"* at all [*Newsweek* 6/11/79]. Government, then was the culprit in the housing shortage that "endangered [the] American bungalow" [*Newsweek* 6/18/79].

Citibank opened 1979 with an attack on the regulation of banks and, more broadly, on all attempts to regulate "land, labor, and money," which, however "well-intentioned," never work and are "potentially disastrous for all concerned" [*Saturday Review* 1/20/79]. Chase Manhattan was more Reaganesque in its rhetoric:

> America once had a vision of its future. And that vision led us to become the most productive nation on earth. . . . [But now] our vision of the future appears to have narrowed to include only that which is politically fashionable and expedient for the short-term.
>
> (*Atlantic* 9/79)

The "politically fashionable" vision to which the bank objected included attacks on corporate profits, demands for more "governmen-

tal 'safeguards' . . . [that] cost our society . . . about $100 billion"
each year, and spending "billions of taxpayer dollars on over-regula-
tion." This vision, if it became reality, would ultimately "lessen the
quality of life not only for us today, but for our children tomorrow."
Updating its seven-point plan of 1975, Chase advocated a balanced
federal budget, supply-side tax cuts, and an end to the overregulation
"that raises costs, lowers productivity, and provides no real benefit to
society" [*Harpers* 10/79].

Other companies moved in 1979 from narrow-based to broad-
based advocacy. The National Cotton Council, which since 1977 had
been advertising for fewer regulations on cotton, shifted into a
stronger, more generalized antiregulation mode. Overregulation
would, the cotton growers repeatedly claimed, "cost you the shirt off
your back" [*Saturday Review* 9/29/79] or "cost your family a home of
your own" (not that it mattered much, since people would be "eaten
out of house and home by federal regulations" even if they could buy
one) [*Atlantic* 7/80]. Likewise, Bethlehem Steel abandoned its earlier
narrow focus on steel policy to address the more encompassing issue
of inflation. From November through March, Bethlehem sponsored
its "Take It to the Top" series. On the surface, these ads promoted
Bethlehem's program of letting workers suggest ways to cut costs in
order to fight inflation. But despite any efforts at cost-cutting, each
ad reminded the reader that "When you get right down to it, deficit
spending by government is the chief engine of inflation. . . . Unfettered spending must be brought under control" [*Atlantic* 11/79]. The
last ad in this series invited readers to take their ideas to the top,
"to someone who can do something about it. That someone may be
President Carter. . . ." [*Atlantic* 3/80].

Around the same time, the American Council of Life Insurance also
abandoned narrow advocacy in favor of a broad-gauged campaign
against inflation. Drawing a fine distinction between "we, as a nation
of individuals" and the government, the ACLI declared that "we" are
not "helpless in the face of inflation" [*Newsweek* 7/30/79]. Self-control coupled with cuts in government spending would do the trick.
Despite this emphasis on self-control, inflation was billed as almost
totally a product of governmental profligacy. Headlines such as
"Warning: either we lower the pressures for government spending or
we blow the lid off the economy" made the point flatly [*Newsweek*
10/1/79], but even when the headlines featured the "consumers who
consumed themselves," the actual blame was affixed on a "national
spending spree" by government, which permitted the money supply
to expand too rapidly in order to cover its deficits [*Newsweek* 10/22/
79].

The most partisan advertising campaign initiated in 1979 was the SmithKline Corporation's "Forum for a Healthier American Society," whose four-page, red, white, and blue "Commentaries," written and signed by well-known Americans, graced the center of *Newsweek* eight times a year. Former Treasury Secretary William Simon set the tone for the series with "The Malignant Growth of Federal Spending," in which he examined "the true cause of the inflation that can put an end to our way of life." Simon focused his attack on "the small group of professional officeholders who continuously take wealth from everyone and redistribute it for purposes they alone deem important." How to "rid ourselves" of these people and avoid the impending "financial collapse" and "economic dictatorship"?

> We must save our votes for politicians committed to . . . a plan to reduce the growth of federal spending, match the growth of the money supply to the true growth of the economy, reduce taxes, and eliminate unnecessary regulation.
>
> [*Newsweek* 4/2/79]

Not to be outdone, commentator Ben Wattenberg linked "promiscuous" government spending not only with "the unraveling of the economic system," but with the decline of our "national potency" as well. "We're told," wrote Wattenberg, alluding to President Carter's speeches, "the American century is ending. Harrumph!" [*Newsweek* 4/30/79]. This was actually rather mild language for Wattenberg, who, in an earlier ad for Mobil, had decried America's' rancid feast of condemnation" and the "chorus of failure, guilt, and crisis" [*Atlantic* 5/78]. But Wattenberg closed the SmithKline ad with a flourish, likening Carter to the appeaser Neville Chamberlain, Reagan to Winston Churchill, and 1979 to 1939. America, the ad implied, was hovering on the brink of an abyss, with an obvious choice of leaders.

As the year went on, SmithKline touched all the bases of what would soon become the Reagan Revolution. In "Freedom. The Reliable Energy Source," economist Herbert Stein argued that the cure for the energy crisis was to unleash the free market, which has "as many brilliant successes to its credit as government has failures." Martin Feldstein, who would soon head Reagan's Council of Economic Advisers, made a pitch for enacting a supply-side tax cut, reducing government expenditures, and slowing the growth of Social Security benefits [*Newsweek* 6/25/79]. Walter Williams waged a serious attack on the minimum wage ("maximum folly") and on affirmative action and the Equal Employment Opportunity Commission [*Newsweek* 9/79]. Eric Schellin's attack on the regulation of business by "The Potomac Strangler" closed out the first year of SmithKline's campaign. Schellin, a delegate to the White House Conference on Small Business, conjured up images of Nero's "flames and fiddle music" in faulting President Carter for willful negligence in the face of disaster [*Newsweek* 12/79].

By the time Ronald Reagan officially entered the race for the presidency in November, these advertisers and several others were singing his tune. The themes that surfaced time and again in their ads were that inflation was caused by government's penchant for " 'creating money' out of thin air" [Amway, Inc. 1/80], that taxes were supporting "big government" at the expense of the productive private sector [Mobil, *Newsweek* 4/23/79], and, of course, that "overlapping, cumbersome, and often inane" regulations were tying business in knots [National Rural Electric Cooperative Association, *Atlantic* 5/79]. Every aspect of the Reagan solution was featured in these ads: balancing the budget, controlling the money supply, supply-side tax cuts, a stronger military, and above all, unleashing the private sector. No dissenting voice from the business community was to be heard in this chorus. The tone of the Reagan campaign was also faithfully reflected in these ads: confidence, not crisis; free enterprise, not regulatory red tape; toughness, not malaise. These contrasts became more and more vivid as the year went by. And 1980 would witness more of the same.

The Campaign Intensifies

All the major advertising campaigns of 1979 carried over into 1980 except those by Citibank and the American Council of Life Insurance. In March of 1980, however, the ACLI started a new, even more election-oriented campaign. Retaining its ungrammatical slogan, "Inflation. Let's Self-Control It," the ACLI undertook an "election" of its own, in the form of monthly magazine ads featuring "ballots" readers could mark and send to ACLI headquarters. These ballots offered voters only one alternative: to vote against inflation. Again, confidence was a primary theme—the idea being that only in Washington was there a crisis of confidence. Inflation "must be stopped. But is there anything we—each one of us—can do to stop it?" the premiere asked. "Absolutely!," it answered. "But only if we're ready to make the necessary sacrifices." One could mark on the "ballot" the "sacrifices" one was prepared to make:

> I will not ask government for any new programs that require deficit spending and will expect our elected representatives to do the same.

I will support a sound monetary policy by restricting my personal use of credit.

I will not expect or ask for government regulations unless the social benefit justifies the cost.

[*Newsweek* 3/30/80]

As this "citizens' crusade against inflation" gathered momentum, readers were instructed about the causes of inflation: environmental regulation, the minimum wage, wage increases, government spending, and declining productivity. Around election time, one such ad admonished "If you don't vote, don't put all the blame for Inflation on Washington" [*U. S. News & World Report* 11/3/80], while another announced the results of this anti-inflation referendum in an ad headlined "Hundreds of thousands vote: Inflation, no. self-control, yes." Over half a million people, the ad announced, had volunteered to make all the sacrifices required to stop inflation [*Harper's* 11/80.]

Union Carbide also invoked public opinion data. In an ad addressing the issue of economic growth versus a "no-growth future," the company cited findings from a 1979 survey that found that Americans, by a four-to-one margin, favored growth over no-growth [National Review 5/30/80]. This finding served as a springboard for propounding the company's specific policy preferences: that government spending be limited to "a certain percentage of GNP, thereby restraining inflation and restoring . . . economic stability"; that business taxes be lowered; and that "the cost and uncertainty of government regulation" be reduced [*Atlantic* 6/80].

The combination of Reaganomics and deregulation as the ads' main topic was not surprising, since the advertising was sponsored by the private sector, which, whether it believed in the abstract merit of the proposals or not, certainly had something to gain from their enactment. This unanimity of purpose is underlined by the degree to which advertisers took up one another's issues. For example, the National Cotton Council bemoaned the impact of overregulation on the housing and health care industries [*Atlantic* 7/80]. Even Union Carbide, a major energy consumer with a 1979 energy bill of more than $2 billion, joined the oil companies in their call for the elimination of price controls [*Harper's* 10/79].

In 1980, SmithKline's status as the most vociferous business supporter of Ronald Reagan came under serious challenge from United Technologies, which launched its campaign with an ad about the crisis of confidence entitled "Where's the gumption gone?" In a vigorous attack on the anti-growth forces that Union Carbide had exposed as such a small minority, United Technologies opined in its folksy way: "Sometimes it seems to us—maybe to you too—that there's an awful lot of negativism around. Wherever one turns, it's anti-this and down with that. Naysayers are loud in the land" [*Atlantic* 3/80]. The personification of these naysayers was consumer advocate Ralph Nader, who was promoting Big Business Day to draw attention to "Corporate Democracy" legislation. United Technologies hired Herbert Stein to evaluate "anti-business bigots" such as Nader. Stein's assessment: "If there is anything America's faltering economy doesn't need, it's a new set of business-stifling rules, controls, restrictions, and regulations. There's already enough strangulation by red tape" [*Atlantic* 4/80].

Nor did the United Technologies ignore national defense, where current policies had left the nation "second best." America was waking up after having been "beguiled" into letting down its guard, but "the awakening comes late. For years the Kremlin has been exploiting every opportunity for political and military advantage around the world" [*Atlantic* 5/80].

Some milder ads that ran during the summer led into more explicitly election-oriented ads in the fall. In September, readers were given United Technologies's view of what was on the minds of America's young people:

> The so-called me generation sees the American dream slipping away
> from its reach as inflation soars ever higher. The young wonder whether
> they will be able to afford a house and children. Many of them decry
> the rising welfare load, or rail against federal deficit spending. They're
> frustrated and afraid, and they're starting to blame the politicians.
>
> [*Atlantic* 9/80]

In October, in an appeal to apply cost–benefit analysis to federal regulation, United Technologies inveighed against the "regulatory jungle [that] stifles the economy, inhibits productivity, feeds inflation, closes plants, causes jobs to dry up" [*Atlantic* 10/80]. And in November, just in time for the election, readers were reminded of the "Goals for Americans" set forth by President Eisenhower's Commission on National Goals—goals that were strikingly similar to those being advocated by candidate Reagan [Atlantic 11/80].

Just as United Technologies used the lack of "gumption" to kick off its 1980 campaign, SmithKline turned to Michael Novak, who saw the greatness of democratic capitalism imperiled by leaders who "never perceived, never expressed, and too poorly defended its moral ideals." Novak reiterated Ben Wattenberg's idea from an earlier

SmithKline ad that 1979 was a replay of 1939, with the world poised at the edge of the abyss [*Newsweek* 3/80.]

This sense of emergency was by no means restricted to Wattenberg and Novak. In fact, everyone who wrote SmithKline's "commentaries" viewed the nation's situation as desperate. James Davidson of the National Taxpayers Union felt that "overtaxation" along with "other types of government mismanagement . . . have virtually halted the growth of America's economic output." Explicitly rejecting President Carter's idea "that we have reached environmental or other 'limits,' " Davidson laid out the standard business program for revitalizing the economy: lower business taxes, substantial deregulation, and cuts in federal spending. The policies of the current administration, Davidson claimed, had succeeded only in overturning the "traditional American values of hard work and thrift." Does this, Davidson wondered aloud, "disturb you? Does it disturb our elected representatives? If it did, they could easily do something about it" [*Newsweek* 3/31/80].

Throughout the campaign season, the failure of the Carter administration's policies was the recurrent theme of SmithKline's advertisements. America "wanders in a desert of failed education" because of a bloated education bureaucracy that can be eliminated only by a shift to tuition vouchers [*Newsweek* 4/80]. The nation's defense policy, according to John Lehman, soon to be named Reagan's secretary of the navy, "is failing to deter," as evidenced by "spreading Soviet adventurism . . . Cuban forces in Africa, the spectacle in Iran, the invasion of Afghanistan." Recovery from this dismal state of affairs "is possible only by drastic action now" [*Newsweek* 4/80]. Domestically, Amitai Etzioni mused, "we could probably get away, for a few more years, with pouring our money into a growing plethora of social programs. . . . We cannot, however, shore up our weakened economy at the same time" [*Newsweek* 9/80]. As the election neared, the messages became even more pointedly partisan. In October, Allan Meltzer introduced the threat of "Big Government. Democracy's Deadly Creation." "Will we," Meltzer asked, "continue on the path to bigger government, more redistribution, and slower economic growth? Only the voters can decide" [*Newsweek* 10/80].

Finally, in the week before the election, Walter Laqueur raised the big question of "The Crisis of Leadership." Leaders, Laqueur explained, "are those few who illuminate the society's urgent problems and successfully beckon its people toward solutions." Then, for the fourth time in 15 commentaries, the bulldog image of Winston Churchill was used as a surrogate for Ronald Reagan:

Did vision and courage die with Churchill and DeGaulle? Where, it is asked, have the great democratic leaders gone? . . .

Awareness spreads that our society . . . faces not just some passing difficulties but a struggle for survival. Hence the present resounding call for strong leadership.

At the moment all our options are open. Americans possess . . . public spirit and political will . . . enough to prevail over the moral and intellectual confusion spread by false prophets of decline.

[*Newsweek* 11/80]

Across the spectrum of business political advertising, the nation's condition was protrayed as critical. The American economy was crumbling, the energy future was bleak, inflation was out of control, and the only force for progress, American business, was struggling under the yoke of excessive taxation and regulation. President Carter was depicted as either standing helplessly by, chattering about "limits," or, worse, as indulging in "inflammatory rhetoric that buried any hope for rational legislative consideration" of the nation's problems [Mobil, *Saturday Review* 2/29/79]. The only hope, it was hinted again and again, was to turn Carter and the Democrats out of office and bring in the Reagan team. Robert Dee, chief executive officer of SmithKline, summed it all up in "An appeal" appended to the November 1980 commentary:

On Tuesday, November fourth, all able and eligible Americans will make momentous choices. . . . [N]o citizen should imagine that his or her votes cannot make important differences in election results and in government.

We hope the ideas presented—on inflation, taxes, energy, defense, education, regulation, and other subjects—will be useful as you join in deciding the character of American leadership in the Eighties.

The choices . . . are not between one party and another but between responsibility and negligence. . . .

[*Newsweek* 11/80]

After the Election

Ironically, the degree to which business advertisers had promoted the Reagan candidacy became even more apparent after the election, when campaign laws were no longer of concern. "With the induction of Ronald Reagan," rhapsodized United Technologies in its Inauguration Day ad:

Americans look for new directions and new visions. They long for an end to national drift and decline.

They yearn for a restoration of America's primacy.

They hunger for greater hope for the future of themselves, their families, and their country.

[*Atlantic* 2/81]

Suddenly, the sense of national desperation that had pervaded the pre-election ads vanished. In 1980, Michael Novak had feared that:

The course of democratic capitalism will be all too like that of a meteor flashing briefly across the centuries. . . . Perhaps the tyrannical central state will once again swallow the sectors of liberty, and history will relapse into its traditional torpor and backwardness.

[SmithKline, *Newsweek* 3/80]

But after only a few months of the Reagan administration, these dragons had seemingly all been slain. Far from being in desperate straits, democratic capitalism, buttressed by the "limited state," was now, in Novak's view:

A magnificent conception. It stands as a defense against all forms of collectivism. No matter how sweeping or how total the claims of these states may be, these claims crash into impenetrable walls at the boundary of individual conscience.

[*Newsweek* 9/81]

Things also looked much better to Ben Wattenberg, who joyfully beheld the "Gross National Spirit groping its way back" from the "decline" and "malaise" of the Carter years [United Technologies, *Atlantic* 11/81]. Not every postelection ad was so hyperbolic, but all did express a readiness for a "new era of American prosperity" [Smith Kline, *Newsweek* 10/21/81] now that America had become "a winner" again [Motorola, *Newsweek* 10/21/81].

To help ensure that the Reagan program would be a winner in Congress, business kept up its advertising efforts for some time. In these ads, President Reagan and his team were always pictured as being firmly in command of situations that, it was implied, had gone untended for some time. United States Steel, one of the many firms that had been pushing for a rollback of environmental regulations, was pleased to note that "President Reagan and EPA administrator Anne Gorsuch have proposed to update the Clean Air Act." This "updating" (a euphemism for relaxing clean air standards) was vital for the "economic recovery to which the President has committed his administration" [*Time* 10/26/81]. United Technologies credited Reagan and his secretary of health and human services, Richard Schweiker, for their timely attention to the Social Security problem [*Harpers* 5/81], and W. R. Grace praised Reagan for "offsetting Bracket Creep with a tax cut" [*New York Times* 7/14/81]. Union Carbide was so taken with the Reagan administration's new economic program, "an essential first step in making America more competitive," that it quoted the President's economic address to Congress in one of its ads [*Atlantic* 6/81].

But even more than they praised the new President, the postelection ads berated Congress. Many of them went so far as to single out the House of Representatives as the problem, now that the Republicans had gained control over the Senate. W. R. Grace, for example, did not specify just who were the "certain Congressmen, who place bigger government ahead of a productive private sector." It did, however, suggest that readers direct their complaints to Democratic Representative Dan Rostenkowski [*New York Times* 7/14/81]. Shortsighted [Dresser, Business Today Winter 1981], lacking the courage to stand up to special-interest groups [SmithKline, *Newsweek* 5//81], and still obsessed with taxing and spending [Mobil, *New York Times* 6/17/82, Time 8/30/82], Congress needed prodding. And readers were frequently encouraged to do just that [Grace, *New York Times* 7/14/81; American Council of Life Insurance, *Atlantic* 4/81, 5/81, 6/81; U. S. Steel, *Time* 10/26/81]. If prodding was not sufficient, Mobil reminded readers just before the 1982 congressional elections, "it only takes a few minutes to pick candidates who will bring government spending down" [*Parade* 10/31/82].

CONCLUSION

The presidential campaign of 1979 and 1980 triggered the loudest explosion of covertly partisan advertising in the history of the United States. Still, one can legitimately ask what difference it all made. After all, Ronald Reagan won a landslide victory over Jimmy Carter, and no one can seriously doubt that he would have done so had not even a single political advertisement by business appeared in the nation's newspapers and magazines. After the election, Jimmy Carter could trace his defeat to many different sources, but the concerted pro-

Reagan advertising campaign that business launched would not have been high on the list. The ads appeared, and Reagan won. But were the ads even noticed, let alone important?

We know of no reliable evidence one way or another that speaks to the effectiveness of the types of advertisements we have been describing. There is, however, abundant evidence that advertisers know how to reach their target audience—politically active, well-educated people—for their political ads (Anonymous, 1977; Garbett, 1982; Sethi, 1979). There is also evidence that advertising can change people's minds by presenting one-sided information on complex issues (U. S. Senate, 1978, pp. 32–36; Sethi, 1982, pp. 162–180; Stroetzel, 1982). More than a half million votes were cast in the American Life Insurance Council's mock plebiscite against inflation, according to the last ad in that campaign. Most of these people had doubtless already made up their minds, but some of them may have had their opinions influenced by the way the items were worded, especially since the credibility of the exercise had been enhanced by *Newsweek*'s official stamp of approval and encouragement for readers to participate. Still, the impact of the massive barrage of business political advertising, even if it could be measured, would not equal the margin of victory Reagan enjoyed in 1980.

One the other hand, it must be borne in mind that Ronald Reagan was not regarded as a certain winner until the late summer of 1980. In the early going, when George Bush was still assailing Reagan's "voodoo economics," the ads may have helped. And even had Reagan led from the beginning, the political advertising on his behalf still constituted a considerable expenditure of money by many corporations. SmithKline, probably the biggest spender, exceeded by many tens of thousands of dollars the amount it could have legally contributed to the Reagan campaign. Moreover, most of the corporations that advertised for Reagan—or at least against Carter—routinely categorize political advertising as "corporate" or "image" advertising. Thus classified, the costs of these ads could be deducted from the corporate income tax, and so, in effect, subsidized by other taxpayers (U. S. House, 1978). Thus, even though the impact of business advertising on the outcome of the election cannot be determined, such advertising raises a host of thorny political and legal issues.

All the other approaches that business had historically taken to political advertising (defensive advertising, promotion of free enterprise promotion with attacks on government and labor, and advocacy advertising) have undergone periods of surge and periods of decline—declining when there seemed little need for them, but surging anew whenever the need arose. It is reasonable to assume that the next time a President is roundly disliked in the business community and a challenger is well regarded, or vice versa, partisan political advertising will emerge again, as it did in 1980. Next time, it may be a close race.

REFERENCES

Anonymous. (1913, July 5). Hunting the insidious lobbyist. *Literary Digest,* 3–5.

Anonymous. (1979, November). Measuring corporate advertising effectiveness. *Public Relations Journal,* 19–22.

Cameron, W. J. (1937). *A series of talks given on the Ford Sunday Evening Hour.* Dearborn, MI.

Clymer, A. (1979, July 29). Reagan: The 1980 model. *New York Times Magazine,* 23–25, 47, 50.

Garbett, T. F. (1982, March-April). When to advertise your company. *Harvard Business Review,* 100–106.

Green, T. S. (1939). Mr. Cameron and the Ford Hour. *Public Opinion Quarterly, 3,* 669–675.

Griese, N. L. (1976, November). AT&T's quest for public understanding. *Public Relations Journal,* 34–36.

Kelley, S., Jr. (1956). *Professional public relations and political power.* Baltimore: Johns Hopkins University Press.

Key, V. O. (1964). *Politics, parties, and pressure groups* (5th ed.). New York: Thomas Y. Crowell.

Lane, E. (1950). Some lessons from past congressional investigations of lobbying. *Public Opinion Quarterly, 14,* 14–32.

Lasswell, H. (1939). The propagandist bids for power *American Scholar, 8,* 350–357.

Lewin, T. (1978). *The power persuaders.* Washington, DC: Common Cause.

Lindsey, R. (1979, November 14). Reagan, entering presidency race, calls for North American "accord." *New York Times* 1, 24.

McGinniss, J. (1969). *The selling of the president.* New York: Trident.

McGrath, P. (1976). *Managing Corporate external Relations.* New York: Conference Board.

Pearlin, L. I., & Rosenberg, M. (1952). Propaganda techniques in institutional advertising. *Public Opinion Quarterly, 16,* 5–26.

Pimlott, J. A. R. (1951). *Public relations and American democracy.* Princeton, NJ: Princeton University Press.

Reagan, R. (1980, July 18). Address accepting Republican nomination for presidency. *New York Times,* 8.

Schriftgiesser, K. (1951). *The lobbyists.* Boston: Little, Brown.

Seldes, G. (1947). *One thousand Americans.* New York: Boni & Gaer.

Sethi, S. P. (1977). *Advocacy advertising and large corporations.* Lexington, MA: D. C. Heath.

Sethi, S. P. (1982). *Up against the corporate wall* (4th ed.). Englewood Cliffs, NJ: Prentice–Hall.

Smith, H. (1980, July 15). Reagan is promising a crusade to make nation "great again." *New York Times*, 1, B7.

Stroetzel, D. S. (1982). Why Mobil does what it does . . . and how. *Public Affairs Review, 3,* 32–33.

Tedlow, R. S. (1976). The National Association of Manufacturers and public relations during the New Deal. *Business History Review, 50,* 25–45.

U. S. House of Representatives. (1978). *IRS administration of tax laws relating to lobbying.* Committee on Government Operations, 95th Congress, 2d session.

U. S. Senate. (1972). *Advertising 1972.* Committee on Commerce, 92d Congress, 2d session.

U. S. Senate. (1978). *Sourcebook on corporate image and corporate advocacy advertising.* Subcommittee on Administrative Practice and Procedure of the Committee on the Judiciary, 95th Congress, 2d session.

Weiss, E. B. (1970, August 3). Management: Don't kid the public with those noble ads. *Advertising Age,* 35–38.

6

The Stuff of Politics Through Cinematic Imagery: An Eiconic Perspective*

Robert L. Savage
Department of Political Science,
University of Arkansas

Political leaders look to the popular media for appropriate imagery with which to spread their messages and invariably find much in the way of pertinent material there. Motion pictures, for whatever reason, seem especially prized for such purposes. Indeed, Walter Lippmann (1922, p. 92) presciently pointed to the likelihood of such usage by political communicators as early as the era of silent films:

> The moving picture is steadily building up imagery which is then evoked by the words people read in their newspapers. In the whole experience of the race there has been no aid to visualization comparable to the cinema. They seem utterly real.

One category of political communicators, for example, the editorial cartoonists, have been found to reflect this attention to films as a source of inspiration for their commentaries on the foibles of contemporary political figures and institutions (Savage, 1987). *Star Wars, War Games, Jaws, Rambo, Ghostbusters*—these are just a few recent films providing notable iconic structures for the simple (but not necessarily simplistic) presentation of political ideas or events in a particularly graphic way.

Moreover, not only given motion pictures of recent vintage provide this iconographic shorthand for political communication. Major film stars of past and present (especially the great comic performers of

* I should like to thank Carlos Cortés, Lee Sigelman, and Jim Combs for cogent and encouragingly constructive readings of an earlier version of this essay. For the present version, nonetheless, I assume full responsibility.

the 1920s and 1930s) and sundry other film-related objects (the Oscars, the theater marquis, etc.) are also often utilized. In other words, whatever the actual level of the general public's awareness of cinematic phenomena, popular and political communicators are aware of them and assume a similar awareness on the part of their own audiences. Ronald Reagan, the former actor, may appreciate the dramatic intensity of Clint Eastwood's line, "Go ahead, make my day," but Ronald Reagan, the President, can also appreciate the graphic message of that same line in a given political context.

The more basic concern of this essay, however, is to look directly at commercial motion pictures as a reflection of societal values and, as in all human communication, transactionally a purveyor of those same values. More explicitly, the very stuff of politics, interest conflict and consensus, is exhibited in cinematic re-presentations over and over again at theaters, on television, and more recently through videocassettes (cf, Nimmo & Combs, 1983). That political communicators so often utilize cinematic sources should only serve to heighten interest in the messages and their presumable meanings conveyed through these filmic re-presentations to millions of people each day.

Assuredly, film critics and other literati may despair at what they perceive to be the meanings that underlie these flickering messages. Yet, even these cultural elites are not generally immune to all cinematic offerings, as the continuing successful career of Woody Allen without a major box-office hit, clearly attests. While some may be highly selective in their film choices, relatively few people in the developed nations can truthfully say that there are not at least a few movies that "really hit me where I live."

The first concern in the study of politics and film, then, is not a matter of measuring impact whether through analyzing the messages of political communicators in a search for cinematic references or through surveying the citizenry for movie-based information or beliefs. Rather, we need a stronger understanding of the potential messages to be found in popular cinema, that is, what do films tell us about societal values and institutions? After all, what we see in films are more or less compelling narratives of who we are, what we are and want to be, and sometimes even why we are. In other words, the movies are parasocial vehicles revealing the very parameters of human society.

IMAGERY, NARRATIVE, AND THE POLITICAL QUEST

There are no doubt many factors contributing to the disdain of social scientists generally, and political scientists more particularly, for the study of politics through the popular media.[1] The chief reason for this disdain, however, lies in some notion of distinguishing and preserving institutional boundaries. That is to say, experiences of individuals not defined to be specifically germane to the social institutions that are the focus of study tend to be ignored. This is the case even within that small subgenre of political communication research devoted to "politics and film."[2] Such films as *Mr. Smith Goes to Washington, Twelve Angry Men, The Candidate, The Last Hurrah,* and *Rambo,* pointed at specific political institutions or events, are included, but others that deal more generally with the definition of community such as *The Grapes of Wrath,* the interplay of social responsibility and personal risk as in *High Noon,* or the changing matrix of social values like *The Wild One,* are more often ignored in these studies.

Moreover, these studies are "hung up," shall we say, with the degree of verisimilitude these cinematic images have to "reality." But does it really matter whether Frank Capra's *Mr. Smith Goes to Washington* depicts the U. S. Congress and the legislative process any less realistically than Otto Preminger's *Advise and Consent?* The concerns of such studies all too often ignore the central role that the shaping of "perspectives," to use the general term proffered by Lasswell and Kaplan (1950), plays in the political process on the one hand, and on the other, that humans can only know their environment through imagination in any event (Boulding, 1956). A focus on some conception of how closely filmic narratives approach the scholar's notion of "real politics" leads to a pedantic educationalism that ignores the "real story," that is, what are the changes that may be provoked in the images held by audience members? In such changes lie the meanings of messages (Boulding, 1956, p. 7). None of this is to say that reality should be ignored, for, unless you know a trick or two, the hot coal *really* burns. Still, each person's reality is simply different, depending upon the store of images he or she has. Moreover, individual images are shaped by both the fundamental physical character of human existence and human cultural evolution. Both of these place limits upon what we can imagine in the presence of any given stimulus but neither necessarily gives any special warrant to rationalistic discourse over emotional discourse.

The recognition that human communication is at bottom a process

---

[1] Assuredly, there are many social science studies of popular communication as entertainment but relatively few go beyond this perspective, save for some highly circumscribed topics, such as the impact of violence in popular media.

[2] See, e.g., Thompson (1982); and Genovese (1984). The latter does include "problem" films as relevant for teaching politics but mentions them only in passing. There are contrary examples assuredly; see especially Combs (1984).

of imagination underlies Boulding's suggestion of *eiconics* as a valuable perspective in the study of human behavior generally and political behavior particularly, so essentially a human activity fraught with symbolic manipulation.[3] The problem with his construction of eiconics, in its original formulation as a metatheoretical proposition explaining human communication in terms of perceptual processes, is that he provided no dynamic to explain what hold's one's images together over time or, alternatively what provides a criterion for change in those images, beyond a functional typology of human activity, essentially an institutionalist perspective.

As it happens, however, there are other metatheoretical perspectives today that assist in providing such a dynamic. Perhaps the most widely recognized one is the dramatistic approach of Kenneth Burke.[4] A notion of *homo dramaticus* seems particularly compelling as the basis for investigating political eiconics where cinema is the empirical focus of that inquiry. A more recent view built upon the metaphorical conception of human beings as *homo narrans,* however, is also illuminating. Walter Fisher (1984, 1985, 1987) has cogently argued that human communication is best understood as a narrative enterprise, stories to be told.

> The central point here is that there is no genre . . . that is not an episode in the story of life (a part of the "conversation") and is not itself constituted by *logos* and *mythos.* Put another way: Technical discourse is imbued with myth and metaphor, and aesthetic discourse has cognitive capacity and import. The narrative paradigm is designed, in part, to draw attention to these facts and provide a way of thinking that fully takes them into account.
>
> (Fisher, 1985, p. 347)

Take, for example, a "how-to" film on the legislative process. While such a film will likely adopt some overtly narrative form of the "This is Representative John Doe and he wants to pass a law to reclaim land denuded by surface mining" variety, it may be shorn of all such aesthetic artifices and yet it will remain a narration with all its utilitarian, technical appearance. The film will be filled with the *mythos,* albeit implicitly, of representative democracy at the very least, whatever the emphasis upon *logos.*

---

[3] Eiconics, the study of imagery as process, is distinguished from iconography, the study of icons, or symbols, as particular stimulants of symbolic responses. Iconography would be at most, then, a subfield of eiconics.

[4] See, e.g., Burke (1955, 1966, 1969); Combs (1980); and Combs and Mansfield (1976).

That most people communicate about politics most of the time in largely mythic terms emphasizing *sentiments*, frequently underlain by primordial attitudes, is hardly a new idea.[5] Public opinion studies, however, typically treat their respondents as rationalistic communicators (and then often decry the seeming lack of "rationality").[6] These studies fail to take into account that respondents are simply telling *their own stories as citizens*, stories that reflect their self-images as citizens at the moment of conversation. The failures of opinion analysts lie in their insistence that there is only one mode of discourse proper to politics; indeed, they fail to understand that the generally superficial responses that they gouge from those who are surveyed reflect longer narratives that may or may not yearn to be told. Those underlying narratives have their sources in the general culture and the particularized experiences of the individuals who hold them. It is this meeting of culture and experience that suggests the important role that popular communication, including cinema, plays in shaping the politics of the people.

The movies as communication channels provide messages both explicitly and implicitly which help to define social identity, explore the parameters of social relationships, and evaluate social goals and events. Whatever meanings these messages may have depends upon the viewers ultimately. Despite such potential variability in meaning, however, students of politics need to explore the more salient images emanating from films so as to understand better the stories that arise in the body politic. This narrative perspective on political imagery is all the more compelling when we recognize that certain stories are told again and again in motion pictures, whatever the twists in plots and settings.

What, precisely, then are we to look for if we pursue the study of political eiconics through a narrative perspective focused on the cinema? Students of fictional literature might point to their "pentad" of setting, characters, plot, mood, and point of view. While this pentad may be of considerable utility for rigorous comparative analyses of films, it does not help in focusing upon politically relevant narratives. And we have already rejected the institutional emphasis common to the academics since it stresses *logos* when it is *mythos* that provides

---

[5] See, e.g., the all too long ignored study by Wiebe (1958) on opinion response to a televised Congressional hearing.

[6] See McGee (1985, pp. 168–174) who suggests that social scientists are embarked upon a mythical quest for "truth" and consequently make war upon whatever seems contrary to the "technical reasoning" that underlies their understanding of the social and political realm.

the emotional drive of narration. The proper focus, then, is the representation of political myths through motion pictures.

Michael Calvin McGee (1985), while addressing the political rhetoric of political leaders, journalists, and academics, nonetheless provides an important insight into the nature of political myth that is just as relevant for the understanding of popularly mediated politics. He stops just short of asserting that political myths universally center upon a quest. Whatever validity the more universal generalization may have, the present effort focuses only upon American film. The notion that American politics is fundamentally a romantic quest for a political paradise lost is sufficiently compelling that the more universal argument can be saved for a later day.

As McGee relates, the quest as political mythos provides the underlying context for ideological differences. Any given ideology points to an array of "ideographs," specific values that are more or less related. The liberal democratic ideology prevalent in the United States reflects values that largely began to be articulated in England's Elizabethan Age, and thus the nation's quest is essentially a conservationist one, a seeking to restore a golden age through heroic endeavors. The direction of that search, however, is defined in terms of ideographs such as "liberty," "individualism," "equal opportunity," the "rule of law," and "property." Thus, opinion leaders encourage the narrativization of values through *stories about ideographs.* The mythic quest ultimately is the search for "The American Dream."

Assuredly, not all American films reflect this particular mythic quest. Yet, it is highly unlikely that any film that rejects that quest will find any appreciable audience among Americans.[7] The setting, characters, plot, mood, and point of view may vary drastically but whatever ideographs that may be addressed in commercial films tend to be limited by the prevailing political culture. The problem for political eiconics, then, is the identification of dominant ideographs in whatever cinematic guises but with a sensitivity for the narrative pentad so as to be aware of relative valuations of these ideographs over time and among specific audiences.

Particularly central are the characters to the extent that they emerge as heroes, villains, and, yes, even fools. Especially notable in American films is the long line of comedic stars (foolish heroes, heroic fools?) who, through perseverance, audacity, or just sheer zaniness, overcome adversity, especially that placed in their way by the rich and/or powerful, and attain some proximate version of The American Dream, that is, life, liberty, and happiness. Charles Chaplin, the

---

[7] See McGee (1985, pp. 157–160) on the problematics of transporting ideographs.

Marx Brothers, and the Three Stooges best exemplify this celebration of Everyman, the humble hero resiliently defiant in the face of any authority save one's own sense of right and wrong. No authority is superior to the wisdom of the folk, ideographically speaking.

Such culturally pertinent cues notwithstanding, however, there is no proven technique or method for analysis of politically relevant imagery in film. Moreover, none of the available techniques feature the quantitative rigor so fashionable in the social sciences today. Still, there are several research approaches that can be utilized (Cortés, 1984, 1985; Savage, 1985). Two of these approaches, each of which richly assists in revealing political narratives in American cinema, are presented here.

GENRE STUDY: THE WESTERN AS AMERICAN POLITICAL FABLE

An approach long used by critics and scholars to assess certain bodies of film is the genre study. If, however, as some critics assert, a given genre must be more or less rigidly defined in terms of some fundamental "essence," the genre perspective has a much reduced utility for political eiconics.[8] Understood, instead, as a group of films having some common setting, the genre study can be extremely useful in exploring cultural movement over time, and all the more so when whatever themes emerging from that genre are placed in the changing context of the audiences' experiences.

This is especially apparent with that most American of genres, the Western. The history of the genre extends back more than 80 years and in some respects it seems that the genre has come full circle, perhaps explaining its often-proclaimed demise. In any event, much change occurred during that period, change that reflected and sometimes, perhaps, prefigured alterations in Americans' politically relevant perceptions.

The most important theme emerging from the Western revolves about the very basis of its setting, the *frontier*. That is to say, by the time cinema emerged, the land frontier had largely disappeared. The first Western movies came at a time when civilization had already come and largely conquered the frontier. Still, the confrontation was not clearly recognized as such until much later. Indeed, the only Western to win an Oscar as best picture, *Cimarron* (1931), depicted

---

[8] See Hardy (1984) who considers and rejects this "essentialist" view. Hardy's encyclopedia is, by the way, a veritable treasure chest of information on the Western.

the great Oklahoma land rush as a great entrepreneurial venture. Note, however, that the protagonist is reclaimed by wanderlust at the end, a suggestion that, carried to its logical conclusion, implied that the days of the frontier were drawing to a close. The peculiar irony of the introduction of postfrontier technology, such as the merging of science fiction and Western in Gene Autry's serial, *The Phantom Empire* (1935), and six-guns versus machine guns in an early movie starring William Boyd, *Gun Smoke* (1931), only confounded matters.

Nonetheless, civilization persistently bore upon the Western as it had the West earlier. Brashly and triumphantly it conquered *Dodge City* (1939) as Errol Flynn with all his swashbuckling verve fought to pave the way for *organized* society: the railroad, journalism, and gangsterism. This cinematic tale is loosely based upon the Wyatt Earp legend and thus provides an excellent counterpoint to the retelling by John Ford, the greatest director of the genre, in *My Darling Clementine* (1946). Ford resorts to stylization to make the same point about the inevitable coming of civilization by stringing together cultural rituals and artifacts as icons symbolizing civilized society, presenting them as seemingly incidental to the unfolding drama. As a consequence, his early depiction of the coming of civilization subtly stresses its inevitability and yet contains a certain wistfulness that presages more direct treatment of the confrontation in some of his later films.

The confrontation is presented somewhat more circumspectly in films that directly pit the the urban East against the pastoral West, usually with a comic touch. *The Cowboy and the Lady* (1938), with Gary Cooper as a less taciturn Westerner than he was to be in his more notable pictures later, preaches the pastoral morality. More conciliatory was *Ruggles of Red Gap* (1935) in which Charles Laughton as an English butler and the folks of one Western community come to some understandings of their common humanity.

By the 1950s this conflict between the raw frontier as wilderness, as nature, and its settlement as garden, as civilization, had become a decidedly self-conscious aspect of Western films. Ideographically speaking, the conflict pitted freedom against order, individualism against cooperation, ready justice against due process. Or, not altogether metaphorically, the cowboy versus the farmer, the horse verse the ox, the six-gun versus the plow. Perhaps the most famous of these films is the allegorical *Shane* (1953). More clearly and much more dramatically satisfying, John Ford's greatest masterpiece, *The Man Who Shot Liberty Valance* (1962), tells the story of how Tom Doniphon (played by John Wayne) unknown to anyone kills the outlaw Valance (Lee Marvin), allowing the lawyer (Jimmy Stewart) to be credited for the act. Law books and irrigation schemes subsequently lead the latter to a seat in the United States Senate while Doniphon slips into obscurity. History, and civilization, win over against the quintessential Western hero. Assuredly, there is strong irony here but, politically speaking, the film pits two versions of the American quest directly, and Ford's realism (at least in this film) compels him to allow the historically stronger vision to win.

A related version of this same theme focuses upon the "end of the Westerner," on the necessary demise of those who cannot or will not adapt or, like Tom Doniphon, at least accept the coming of civilization in whatever its guise. Indeed, this type of tale appears as early as 1919 in John Ford's *The Last Outlaw* starring Hoot Gibson. Harry Carey played the lead in a 1936 version of the same story. The classic telling, however, is *The Gunfighter* (1950). This seminal film presents Gregory Peck as an aging gunman who wants to put his pistol away but his very adeptness in its use has left him unprepared for any "civilized trade" and marked him as a hero for emulation or confrontation by any delinquent. As Hardy (1984, p. 194) points out, "the film forms a midpoint between *My Darling Clementine* which sees the transformation of Wyatt Earp into a solid citizen and Sam Peckinpah's more worried accounts of a 'civilized' West that has no place for old-fashioned heroes." Indeed, Peckinpah's only solution is violence on a heightened scale as in *The Wild Bunch* (1969) which set violence—and the end of the Westerner—as the basic theme for the next decade of Western films, and in, penultimately, *Pat Garrett and Billy the Kid* (1973), couched in utter cynicism as the law officer kills his friend Billy to preserve his own freedom behind the mask (badge) of law and order.[9]

If these related themes ultimately point to pessimistic conclusions for the Western as a source of inspiration for American political and social values, it is well to recognize that similar currents have flowed into most other genres that centrally feature the singular hero in pursuit of a mythic quest—the private eye, the spy thriller, the police

---

[9] In the 1970s the "end of the West" films are especially notable, including *The Ballad of Cable Hogue* (1970), *Monte Walsh* (1970), *McCabe and Mrs. Miller* (1971), *Wild Rovers* (1971), *The Life and Times of Judge Roy Bean* (1972), *The Shootist* (1976), and *Mr. Horn* (1979, a two-part telefilm originally). This theme would also include films set in the "modern" West such as *The Lusty Men* (1952), *Hud* (1963), and *Junior Bonner* (1972), among others. Certainly, these Westerners unable to adapt could, as in *Shane*, simply be allowed to drift away, to remain outside, but after John Ford's *The Searchers* (1956) where John Wayne stops and folds his arms after the fashion of his late friend Harry Carey, watching the others—who will adapt—walk inside the house and close the door, that seems a much less tenable conclusion.

story, the pirate film, and so forth. Even science fiction in recent films such as *Alien* (1979), *Outland* (1981), and *Blade Runner* (1982) reflects this pessimistic turn.[10]

This line of development, however, pointing to the denouement of the Western genre, is not the whole story of its political relevance in American life. The Western has been an outlet for commentary on contemporary political events, a reflection of general social and political values in American society, and a potential agency of liberal democratic socialization.

In the first case, one need only look to the many B Westerns of the 1930s featuring bankers as villains as in the classic *Stagecoach* (1939); the anti-Nazi Westerns of the early 1940s; for example, *Riders of the Northland* (1942); the antitotalitarian film of the early Cold War period, *The Fabulous Texan* (1947); the thinly veiled plea for a stand against McCarthyism in *High Noon* (1952); and the latently anti-Vietnam war films such as *Journey to Shiloh* (1968), *Little Big Man* (1970), and *Soldier Blue* (1970). On the other hand, the one clear instance where a distinctively radical political view has been espoused in a Western, the class struggle underpinning Michael Cimino's *Heaven's Gate* (1980), suggests that there are definite limits upon social and political commentary that American audiences will respond positively to in the Western.

In terms of evolving social values, allow me to point to one example for which Americans may be less sanguine in the Reagan era. In the 1930s the villain's evil was largely unmitigated, truly black against the stark white of the hero. In the 1940s legendary American outlaws became popular subjects for biographical treatments, often pointing to sociological forces as a factor contributing to their outlawry. In the 1950s the outlaw often was a juvenile delinquent. In the 1960s the outlaw, in that era of countercultures, became less and less distinguishable from the hero.[11] The Western has yet to resolve this problem and may remain an endangered species until it affords a way of presenting villains with distinctively black hats in a society that desires such stark contrasts but is too sophisticated to accept them.[12]

---

[10] Perhaps the Asiatic martial arts genre, so well received in American ghettos, has not yet been afflicted but this author must plead ignorance.

[11] Actually, the roots of this blurring of hero and outlaw lie in the "psychologizing" of the 1950s. Jimmy Stewart is manic as the hero of the *The Naked Spur* (1953), and Sterling Hayden is obsessive-compulsive as *Johnny Guitar* (1954). Indeed, the latter film is a brilliant exposition in character studies for a wide array of neurotic and/or sociopathic conditions, suggesting that civilization may be only a thin veneer covering natural human savagery. Only Clint Eastwood's *High Plains Drifter* (1972) has subsequently approached this view of civilized society in the Western genre.

Finally, the Western has had considerable potential as an agency of political socialization. A number of films could be pointed to here, but two Western parables are of particular note: *High Noon* (1952) and *Once upon a Time in the West* (1968). Gary Cooper as Will Kane, the town marshal in *High Noon,* may well be the ultimate Western hero. He is torn by his personal desire to satisfy his Quaker bride's pacifism, not to mention the fear of death, on the one hand, and his sense of civic responsibility on the other, even when all the other citizens "forsake" him. Nevertheless, he walks tall down Main Street as the fateful hour approaches. Though the drama as a whole may be stilted, in large part due to the caricature characterizations (save for the great Katy Jurado appearing as the marshal's former mistress), Will Kane's walk down that street epitomizes the ideal image of American political stewardship and social conscience, a lesson sorely needed by the nation at the high point of McCarthyism.[13]

More equivocal on the surface, perhaps, is Sergio Leone's masterpiece in the Western genre, *Once upon a Time in the West.*[14] Certainly, the characters are caricatures, even archetypes, but in no other Western is there such a rich array of archetypes. The film, related in an almost fairy-tale fashion, combines the time honored Western motif of revenge with what we have already seen as just as time-honored as a theme, the coming of civilization. There are five major protagonists-antagonists in the film but only one of these emerges as truly heroic. The characters are a railroad tycoon, presented as a 19th-century robber baron of the first order (played by Gabriele Ferzetti); the hired gunman who does the tycoon's dirty work (Henry Fonda); the mysterious solo gunman seeking revenge (Charles Bronson); the romantic, almost fool-like bandit (Jason Robards); and the prostitute

---

[12] The relative success of *Silverado* recently, especially in contrast to Eastwood's *Pale Rider,* may belie that "sophistication," however. Rushing's (1983) examination of two recent "modern" Westerns, *The Electric Cowboy* (1980) and *Urban Cowboy* (1980) points to related conclusions.

[13] Although reflecting different political origins and certainly more exotically, Emiliano Zapata as portrayed by Marlon Brando in *Viva Zapata!* (1952) provides a similar lesson in reluctant stewardship. On the "Americanization" of this Mexican revolutionary hero, see Vanderwood (1979).

[14] Some may object to the inclusion of "spaghetti Westerns" here. However, while American audiences have not been overly responsive to foreign films, Western films from Italy, especially by the master craftsman Leone, have had wide popular appeal in this country as well as having had a major impact on the further development of Westerns produced by the American film industry. A more serious complaint would be that Americans have only recently been able to view this particular film uncut, as Leone intended it. Still, the concern here is with the ideographically based socialization potential of the film.

who turns to marriage only to become widowed before she arrives at the homestead (Claudia Cardinale). Without dawdling over the intricate plot, it is the woman who emerges as heroic, for each of the four men is flawed in a way that dooms him once the seeds of community life are planted. The woman, however, ripens, recognizing her role as the "mother" of the town that is sprouting on either side of the railroad bed. Leone and his cowriter, Sergio Donati, are in full command of American ideographs as we see the community taking root through the industriousness of the common worker as well as that of the woman whose entrepreneurship will, little wonder, leave her not only the premier matron of the community but rich as well. The lesson, then, is that the fruits of the earth belong to the ordinary law-abiding folks—if they are industrious and conscientious.

The Western, while often relating much else of relevance to American politics, has most of all pursued this romance of community building and its fragility in a raw environment where individualism, rugged or not, is a central ideograph. That the Western is recognized here as the premier American genre should surprise no one, since this has been asserted frequently, most often on the basis of the nation's historical tradition as a frontier society.[15] A corollary explanation, however, is the essentially martial character of the genre. As McGee (1985) has argued, public address has typically been presented in terms of war, of crusade. Likewise, the Western is a struggle to "tame" the frontier, an extension of American hegemony whether against nature, the Indians, or anyone else not persuaded by the American civil religion. The denouement of the Western may lie not only in the ultimate triumph of civilization but in our own growing doubts about our nation's "manifest destiny" as well.[16]

SOCIAL PORTRAYAL: STEREOTYPY AND SOCIAL STIRRINGS

At various points in the discussion of the Western above, allusions have been made to typical depictions of some social groups or cate-

---

[15] See, e.g., Combs (1984, pp. 40–55); and Rushing (1983). For the strongest explication of the frontier thesis as applied to American politics, see Elazar (1984, pp. 123–131).

[16] *Broken Arrow* (1950) is the seminal film here. Its sympathetic treatment of American Indians was a notable departure, although not altogether without precedent and not without ambiguities. With regard to the latter, after all, Debra Paget as the Indian bride of Jimmy Stewart was fated to die before the end of the film.

gories of individuals, for example, the American Indian and the banker. This suggests a very different approach to the eiconic analysis of politics in cinema: social portrayal. Such inquiry focuses upon the images projected of specific categories of people which is a vital concern if we are to learn about, in Lester Milbrath's (1964) terms, who is *central* and who is *peripheral* to the life of the community, at least as depicted by Hollywood and other film capitals.

The social portrayal approach has most often been used in the study of stereotypes, especially as related to ethnic and racial groups and more recently to women. While stereotypy is of interests to students of politics as a matter of both empirical and prescriptive concern, a more general orientation toward *social typology* is of greater utility. If we become too concerned with the limitations and the negative connotations of stereotypes, we may overlook the forest in searching for the trees. There are larger concerns, such as whether a given group of people are portrayed much at all, let alone positively (Erens, 1984; Cortés, 1985). It is no doubt small consolation for members of a group to see themselves portrayed in unfair and distorted ways, but if they are never seen they are not, for all practical purposes, recognized as members of society; they are beyond even the periphery of community. Moreover, a focus on stereotypy may blind one to subtle, even salutary, changes in social portrayal of the group over time.

Still, stereotypy is of considerable importance in such analyses, most especially because of its tendency toward unidimensionality in depicting given groups. This aspect of stereotypy belies much of our experience but assuredly not all of it. That is to say, many of us have little or no contact with members of such groups in our daily lives. This is no justification for stereotypical distortion but in a very real sense, filmic stories are not unlike our own stories in that the first issue must be *narrative truth*. What do other people contribute to our stories, or to the stories enacted on the silver screen?

These concerns, then, point toward the figure–ground distinction in social perception. To the extent that members of given social groups do not emerge from ground very strongly, they are likely to be portrayed at best as a flashing icon and in a unidimensional fashion often emphasizing some negative quality common to the folklore of other groups. In "spooky" films of the past, for example, if a Black person is shown only a few seconds at some scary turn of events, the cinematic convention was for him or her to become white-faced. Presumably this conventional treatment refers to a person's becoming "ashen" in the face of stress but the audience could also recognize the stereotypical trait of inordinate cowardliness attributed to

Blacks.[17] While the same stereotypical convention may subsequently be used for characters emerging to become more important figures in unfolding dramas for some time afterward, there is likely to be a movement away from the extreme unidimensional aspect of the representation that may be evident when members of the group are little more than the ground of perception.

We can and should denounce inane stereotypy such as the "cowardly Black" image, but the more interesting inquiries in social portrayal occur when groups move forward as major figures in films. At this point they can be categorized broadly as heroes, villains, and fools/foils. Ethnic minorities are most often depicted as fools or foils but in particular genres and/or at particular times they may be regularly presented as villains. With few exceptions prior to 1950, the American Indian was most often portrayed as a villain. His—for Indian women and children were rarely more than background figures—only consolation as a rule was that he usually did not literally wear a black hat. Occasionally he might play the fool, especially if he came into contact with the white man's "firewater." Only rarely was he heroic, as in *The Last of the Mohicans* (1936), and then he was likely juxtaposed with an exceptionally villainous Indian antagonist.[18] Generally, a charting of the ratios of hero/villain/fool for social groups as depicted in American films would throw much light on the treatment of various social groups, and, in combination with histories of contemporary social movements, would exhibit the extent to which cinema reflects the larger society. But the charting needs to be done for more than just ethnic/racial groups. Occupational groups, for example, would be just as important in a society that generally attempts to paper over class differences. Moreover, some important generational differences could be documented. In speaking of generational differences, what about age groups as portrayed in films? If Hollywood has become so youth-oriented as often proclaimed, have the elderly actually been presented in different ways in the past?

American films, however, are more sophisticated today even if that mostly reflects only the fact that with far fewer movies being produced annually, more care can be taken in their production. Just how much sophistication is suggested by Sylvester Stallone's superschlock *Rocky* series (1976, 1979, 1982, 1985). As Daniel Leab (1979) asserts, the first *Rocky* was conceived by Stallone to be a testament to and an affirmation of blue-collar ethnics in America. Leab

---

[17] Black stereotypy in films has received notable attention from scholars; see, e.g., Bogle (1973); Leab (1975); and Cripps (1977).

[18] On cinematic images of American Indians generally, see Bataille and Silet (1980).

also directs our attention to the not-very-latent racism of these eth-nics for Rocky is the Great White Hope, a mythic hero whose quest is much more than a boxing crown. The irony and, yes, the sophistica-tion become all the more apparent in *Rocky III* when Apollo Creed, the former champion, also acquired heroic status as he helps Rocky to defend his crown against a truly villainous Black antagonist. The *Rocky I* and *II* Blacks are more or less villainous, but in *Rocky III* Black Americans have truly arrived for while some are villains, others are heroes, just like white people. The culmination of the series is obvious; in *Rocky IV* the Great White Hero becomes the Great Ameri-can Hope who does battle with the seemingly inhuman Russian, more stereotypically portrayed than Apollo Creed and other Black charac-ters in the first *Rocky*.[19] (If there is a *Rocky V*, what can he be but Earth's Great Hope battling the greatest space monster of them all?) In any event, *Rocky IV* takes a much more comfortable position for Hollywood in presenting America as the great melting pot, however much the cinematic tendency for social stereotypy over the decades belies that stance.

Pluralism, albeit distorted, rather than a melting-pot image, has been the actual standard as far as ethnic and racial portrayals are concerned in American films. American cinema has also occasionally provided clear statements supporting a pluralist position and thereby moving determinedly away from stereotypes (Erens, 1984). One such exceptional example is *Norma Rae* (1979) where the heroine interacts with the Jewish labor organizer, Reuben Warchovsky. When she dis-covers that Jews do not have horns as she has been told, Norma Rae professes that she cannot see any differences between Jews and other people. Reuben, however, contradicts her simply by saying "History." *Norma Rae* is also an exceptional film in its depiction of class struggle, and Reuben Warchovsky is all the more exceptional as a character because he is both Jewish *and* a union organizer, neither social category having been treated so sympathetically in American films as a rule.

If American films have come a long way from the shallow stereo-

---

[19] And thereby hangs another tale. Russians, particularly when identified as "Bol-sheviks" or "Reds," have not usually been cast in a very favorable light. Yet, when the American government saw a need to present our temporary allies to the American public in a more positive light during World II, Hollywood was up to the challenge; see Culbert (1979). Nor is this the only foreign policy consideration to have had an impact upon the portrayal of other nationalities as witnessed by the making of the film biogra-phy of Zapata (Vanderwood, 1979). Paradoxically, however, the U. S. government has not been so interested in interceding in film projects when these same nationality groups are American ethnics.

typy of racial and ethnic images of the past, there are other types and categories of social groupings where such changes are not so evident and in some instances not so well studied. Class, gender, and age, among others, represent lines of social cleavage that are still suspect in terms of their portrayal in American cinema. Of the three mentioned here, only the gender distinction has received much scholarly attention (see, e.g., Mellen, 1973; Haskell, 1974; Sochen, 1979; Kaplan, 1983). Social portrayals in film do reflect the stirrings of social conscience but American film makers seem to require continuous agitation to sustain whatever advances they make in re-presenting the plural character of American society.[20]

A CONCLUSION: POLITICS THROUGH THE MIND'S EYE, OR ART AND ARTIFICE AS POLITICS

In the end we do want to learn what audiences take from films, how the flickering images of the cinema may shape people's imaginations as they look beyond to reality. This is the other side of the coin in the study of political eiconics. This science of eiconics, however, must remain sensitive to emotion as well as cognition, to *mythos* as well as *logos*. Studying politics through film may especially be advantageous in this regard since

> Cinematographic drama is, so to speak, finer-grained than real-life dramas: it takes place in a world that is more exact than the real world. But in the last analysis perception permits us to understand the meaning of the cinema. A movie is not thought; it is perceived.
>
> (Merleau–Ponty, 1964, p. 58)

The art of the cinema is a reflection of life, our stories, and yet it is larger than life. Movies most of all reflect possibilities, not as well-laid plans or schematics for action, but as suggestive perceptual parameters for future stories to be told.

If *The Candidate* (1972) reveals important political truths to its viewers such as that campaigning is not governing or that political power can be an aphrodisiac, its real importance for understanding

---

[20] A more audience-centered perspective on social portrayal, as suggested by Nimmo's essay on magazines earlier in this volume, would also be highly welcome in the study of politics and film. One small example comes from the 1950s. How many teen-agers, delinquent or otherwise, of that reputedly nonpolitical generation knew that they were rebels without causes until James Dean so vividly provided the archetype for them (and for a great many motion pictures afterward) in *Rebel without a Cause* (1955)?

American politics finally lies in its revelations about the paradox of the political hero in a democratic society. That is to say, the hero's quest is always subject to seduction. Young Senator-elect Bill McKay has momentarily succumbed to the deadening impact of his winning campaign at the film's conclusion, and we are left to imagine if and how he will continue. Yet, we are also left with a firmer understanding of the seductiveness of life's complexities for all of us, including politicians. At the same time, we should not overlook Merleau–Ponty's observation, for the candidate in reality is a human being telling his or her story for a lifetime and living the stories of others as well. The candidate has acquired a set of images and values in that process that will carry through. Whether the rest of us will appreciate that understanding is another set of stories. Still, *The Candidate* opens our eyes to the art, and the artifice, of political heroism.

In any event, if we are to understand the impact of cinema upon political behavior, we must first comprehend what cinema projects. While millions of words have flowed about what we know of film content, still our words most often seem inadequate. "Perhaps it is just this—that visual media are addressed to the *eye*—that ironically keeps us from 'seeing.' As rhetoricians, we are more familiar with the word than the image, the enthymeme than the myth" (Rushing, 1985, p. 199). Our understanding must be related in rational discourse but, at minimum, we can insist that our rationalizations not be superimposed so as to altogether obscure the objects of our discourse, the stories of the people whatever their channels of communication.

REFERENCES

Bataille, G. M., & Silet, C. L. P. (Eds.). (1980). *The pretend Indians: Images of Native Americans in the movies.* Ames: Iowa State University Press.

Bogle, D. (1973). *Toms, coons, mulattoes, mammies and bucks: An interpretive history of Blacks in American films.* New York: Viking.

Boulding, K. E. (1956). *The image: Knowledge in life and society.* Ann Arbor: University of Michigan Press.

Burke, K. (1955). *A rhetoric of motives.* New York: Braziller.

Burke, K. (1966). *Language as symbolic action: Essays on life, literature, and method.* Berkeley: University of California Press.

Burke, K. (1969). *A grammar of motives.* Berkeley: University of California Press

Combs, J. E. (1980). *Dimensions of political drama.* Santa Monica, CA: Goodyear.

Combs, J. E. (1984). *Polpop: Politics and popular culture in America.* Bowling Green, OH: Bowling Green University Popular Press.

Combs, J. E., & Mansfield, M. W. (Eds.). (1976). *Drama in life: The uses of communication in society.* New York: Hastings House

Cortés, C. E. (1984, Fall). The history of ethnic images in film: The search for a methodology. *MELUS, 11,* 63–77.

Cortés, C. E. (1985). Chicanas in film: History of an image. In G. D. Keller (Ed.), *Chicano cinema: Research, reviews, and resources* (pp. 94–108). New York: Bilingual Review/Press.

Cripps, T. (1977). *Slow fade to black: The Negro in American film.* New York: Oxford University Press.

Culbert, D. (1979). Our awkward ally: *Mission to Moscow* (1943). In J. E. O'Connor & M. A. Jackson (Eds.), *American history/American film: Interpreting the Hollywood image* (pp. 121–145). New York: Frederick Ungar.

Elazar, D. J. (1984). *American federalism: A view from the states* (3d ed.). New York: Harper & Row.

Erens, P. (1984). *The Jew in American cinema.* Bloomington: Indiana University Press.

Fisher, W. R. (1984). Narration as a human communication paradigm: The case of public moral argument. *Communication Monographs, 51,* 1–22.

Fisher, W. R. (1985). The narrative paradigm: An elaboration. *Communication Monographs, 52,* 347–367.

Fisher, W. R. (1987). *Human communication as narration: Toward a philosophy of reason, value, and action.* Columbia: University of South Carolina Press.

Genovese, M. A. (1984, Winter). Teaching politics with films. *News for Teachers of Political Science, 1* (40), 4–5.

Hardy, P. (1984). *The encyclopedia of Western movies.* Minneapolis: Woodbury Press.

Haskell, M. (1974). *From reverence to rape: The treatment of women in the movies.* New York: Holt, Rinehart, & Winston.

Kaplan, E. A. (1983). *Women and film: Both sides of the camera.* New York: Methuen.

Lasswell, H. D., & Kaplan, A. (1950). *Power and society: A framework for political inquiry.* New Haven, CT: Yale University Press.

Leab, D. J. (1975). *From Sambo to superspade: The Black experience in motion pictures.* Boston: Houghton Mifflin.

Leab, D. J. (1979). The blue collar ethnic in Bicentennial America: *Rocky* (1976). In J. E. O'Connor & M. A. Jackson (Eds.), *American history/American film: Interpreting the Hollywood Image* (pp. 257–272). New York: Frederick Ungar.

Lippmann, W. (1922). *Public opinion.* New York: Harcourt, Brace.

McGee, M. C. (1985). 1984: Some issues in the rhetorical study of political communication. In K. R. Sanders, L. L. Kaid, & D. Nimmo (Eds.), *Political communication yearbook 1984* (pp. 155–182). Carbondale: Southern Illinois University Press.

Mellen, J. (1973). *Women and their sexuality in the new film.* New York: Horizon Press.

Merleau–Ponty, M. (1964). *Sense and non-sense* (H. L. Dreyfus, Trans.). Chicago: Northwestern University Press.

Milbrath, L. (1964). *Political participation.* Chicago: Rand McNally.

Nimmo, D., & Combs, J. E. (1983). *Mediated political realities.* New York: Longman.

Rushing, J. H. (1983). The rhetoric of the American Western myth. *Communication Monographs, 50,* 14–32.

Rushing, J. H. (1985). *E. T.* as rhetorical transcendence. *Quarterly Journal of Speech, 71,* 188–203.

Savage, R. L. (1985). *Popular film and popular communication.* Paper presented at the annual Convention of the International Communication Association, Honolulu.

Savage, R. L. (1987). *Heroes, villains, and fools, fools, fools: The popular media as referential sources in editorial cartoons.* Paper presented at the joint meeting of the Central States Speech Association and the Southern Speech Communication Association, St. Louis.

Sochen, J. (1979). The new woman and twenties America: *Way Down East* (1920). In J. E. O'Connor & M. A. Jackson (Eds.), *American history/American film: Interpreting the Hollywood image* (pp. 1–15). New York: Frederick Ungar.

Thompson, R. (1982). *American politics on film.* Paper presented at the annual convention of the Popular Culture Association, Louisville.

Vanderwood, P. J. (1979). An American cold warrior: *Viva Zapata!* (1952). In J. E. O'Connor & M. A. Jackson (Eds.), *American history/American film: Interpreting the Hollywood image* (pp. 183–201). New York: Frederick Ungar.

Wiebe, G. D. (1958). The Army–McCarthy hearings and the public conscience. *Public Opinion Quarterly, 22,* 490–502.

7

The Politics of Monogamy and Romance: Ideology and the Soap Opera

Jeremy G. Butler
Broadcast and Film Communication Department,
University of Alabama

One ideologically overheated scene in the 1955 film *All That Heaven Allows* neatly conflates the patriarchal repression of a woman's sexuality/identity with the introduction into the domestic arena of a television set.[1] A smarmy TV salesman carries the immense "table model" toward Cary Scott, a widow who has just sacrificed her one chance for romance in order to placate her monstrously middle-class teenage children. At Christmas the two teen-agers announce their imminent departure from the home of their deceased father (whose sports trophy still stands on the mantel). Insensitive to Cary's suffering, they present her with the television set, the final nail in her well-appointed bourgeois coffin of a house. As Cary's reflection is captured within the picture tube, the salesman guarantees, "All you have to do is turn that dial and you have all the company you want, right there on the screen. Drama, comedy, life's parade at your fingertips." Cary, and the viewer, recognize that her existence has become an imitation of life.[2] Her sacrifice of romance has been rewarded with a superficial simulacrum of "life's parade."[3] And what, if we may extend this film's

---

[1] Douglas Sirk (director). (1955). *All That Heaven Allows.* Cast: Jane Wyman (Cary Scott), Rock Hudson (Ron Kirby), Gloria Talbott (Kay Scott), William Reynolds (Ned Scott).

[2] To invoke another Douglas Sirk-directed film: *Imitation of Life* (1959). Copyright by Universal Pictures, a Division of Universal City Studios, Inc. Courtesy of MCA Publishing Rights, a Division of MCA Inc.

[3] Or, as Laura Mulvey (1986) argues, "The television set becomes charged with metaphor and connotation linking middle class interior, motherhood, prosperity and repression" (pp. 81–82).

fictional world, do we suspect the lonely widow will use to fill her unhappy afternoons? The soap opera.

It seems appropriate to begin this consideration of the ideological structure of soap opera with a short detour into the Sirkian world of film melodrama because Douglas Sirk's films form the foundation upon which a reorientation of the analysis of melodrama and soap opera has been built. Thomas Elsaesser (1972/1985), Laura Mulvey (1977/1978), Paul Willemen (1971, 1972/1973) and others initiated a rediscovery of Sirk and the 1950s melodrama that has eventually led to a restructuring of the terms of analysis applied to melodrama and its close relation, television soap opera.[4] Tania Modleski (1979/ 1982), Ellen Seiter (1981, 1983), Jane Feuer (1984), Ien Ang (1985), Robert C. Allen (1985) and Annette Kuhn (1982, 1984), among others, have detached this work on Sirk from its auteurist biases and mixed in elements drawn from contemporary feminism, textual analysis, "ethnographic" studies (see David Morley, 1980), Marxism, semiotics and poststructuralism. These writers have provided a fresh perspective on the lowly soap opera, which used to be solely the province of social scientists searching out the (presumably negative) "effects" of TV or attempting to reduce television's complex discourse to so many numbers in a content analysis computer print-out. Instead, this recent work on soap opera has emphasized other aspects of the genre: its ideological and narrative structures, its televisual style, and the possibly gendered positioning of its spectator/subject. In short, the soap opera is no longer viewed as a mere sociological artifact, but rather is now recognized as a television *text:* a signifying system constructed of sound and image, encoded with ideology, and addressing a particular spectator position.

DISCOURSES IN CONFLICT: IDEOLOGY MEETS THE TEXT

The main project of this chapter is to articulate the functioning of ideology in the soap opera apparatus. In other words, I will show how contemporary U. S. society—presumably middle-class, presumably patriarchal—signifies its basic assumptions about the family, woman's sexuality, and labor in the soap opera text. In so doing I will be following the lead of recent ideological criticism which, as Mimi White (1987) succinctly summarizes,

---

[4] For an analysis of the development of recent British media studies, see John Fiske (1987). For an overview of writings on melodrama, see Christine Gledhill (1985).

Is concerned with the ways in which a particular text or group of texts functions as a part of ideological practice and offers a system of knowledge or a way of experiencing the world for a viewer. Ultimately its goal is to understand how textual systems, with their relative autonomy and unity, also function within the dynamics of a given social formation. (p. 142)

To approach ideology in this fashion avoids the inadequacies of the traditional Marxist notion of ideology as "false consciousness" or the standard humanist view of ideology as a system of ideas which may be divorced from social structures. Rather, it recognizes that all popular culture products are part of a somewhat autonomous semiotic system, linked in complex ways with socioeconomic structures. Ideology is but the pattern of *seemingly* natural customs, beliefs, taboos, and so forth, that bind a culture together; "a society's representations of itself within and for itself and the ways in which people both live out and produce those representations" (Kuhn, 1982, p. 4). These signifiers/representations, however, are not *politically* neutral—understanding the term "politics" to refer broadly, as Millett (1970) does, "to power-structured relationships, arrangements whereby one group of persons is controlled by another" (p. 43). Ideology signifies a society's power structure. Ideological signifiers inevitably underscore the hegemonic interests of the class holding economic and/or police/military power.

Hegemony, however, is not as monolithically oppressive as, say, T. W. Adorno or Max Horkheimer (the Frankfurt School) would have us believe. It would be inaccurate to assume the "facts" that because (a) television is produced by money-seeking capitalists that (b) television programs must homogeneously "reflect" capitalist beliefs, and that (c) viewers will accept these beliefs unquestioningly. This statement may be contested on a least two levels. First, television's "flow" (Williams, 1974) betrays a remarkable degree of heterogeneity. Television does not transmit one ideological discourse but *many*, fissured discourses, some of which obviously contradict one another. Examples of these internal contradictions are many. A *Bunny's Tale* (1985), a "feminist" TV movie, was intercut with commercials for antifeminist cosmetics products. An AIDS public service announcement urging more care in sexual activity segued into Mike Hammer seducing a young woman.[5] One must not, however, mistake television's seeming cacophony for total pluralism. Television does not transmit *all* possible discourses. Much is left unsaid, repressed, in television's ceaseless flow. Additionally, that which *is* represented must be trans-

---

[5] In a scene broadcast in the 1986–1987 season of *The New Mike Hammer*.

lated into the televisual idiom, must be made to fit TV's fragmented signifying system. An ideological analysis of the television text, therefore, needs to account for the *limited* pluralism of the television product, for the impact of television style, and for the text's significant absences.[6]

The second problem with Adorno's and the traditional leftist condemnation of popular media is its construction of the spectator as the unthinking receptacle into which is poured the dominant class ideology—a position also shared by both right wing Moral Majority members who fear that "satanic" rock songs will pervert the young, and social scientists operating under the largely discredited *hypodermic needle* theory of media effects. Despite the seeming passivity of the television viewer (he or she *receives* the active transmission of the TV program, which one cannot control or even directly respond to) the viewing situation is actually the site of ideological *decoding*, where the meaning of the program is *actively* constructed. Morley (1980) contends, "The message [or text] in social communication is always complex in structure and form. It always contains more than one potential 'reading.' Messages propose and prefer certain readings over others, but they can never become wholly closed around one reading. They remain polysemic" (p. 10). His ethnographic approach examines the production of meaning by "readers" whose belief systems may or may not duplicate the prevalent ideology. The reading of a television text, therefore, becomes "that moment when the discourses of the reader meet the discourses of the text" (Fiske, 1987, p. 268). The result of this encounter varies according to the reader's socioeconomic status, psychological makeup and televisual literacy. Stuart Hall (1973/1980) has grouped these variations in terms of their relationship to dominant ideology. In his terms, the reading may be *dominant, negotiated,* or *oppositional* (1980, pp. 136–138). The dominant reading shares completely the beliefs of dominant ideology—to the point where the ideology itself submerges into the "natural" or commonsensical. It becomes invisible to the reader because of its status as the "obvious." The oppositional reading, in contrast, occurs when the reader shares none of the ruling class precepts. Typically, this reader is alienated from society and belongs to a subcultural group, for example, Jamaicans in London, punks in New York City, Amish in Pennsylvania. In practice, few readings are wholly dominant or wholly oppositional. More commonly, a reader negotiates his or her interpretation of a television program.

---

[6] The style of soap opera sound and image will not be discussed here as I have attempted its articulation elsewhere. See Butler (1986).

He or she inhabits the dominant ideology, but also recognizes some of its elements as constructed, "unnatural," "false" representations. Or, in Hall's words:

> Decoding within the *negotiated version* contains a mixture of adaptive and oppositional elements: it acknowledges the legitimacy of the hegemonic [dominant ideological] definitions to make the grand significations (abstract), while, at a more restricted, situational (situated) level, it makes its own ground rules—it operates with exceptions to the rule. (1980, p. 137)

In this fashion, a feminist could derive pleasure from the Miss America Pageant if she selectively focused on the portions where the women are strong and independent, and downplayed the sexism of the swimsuit competition.

Although remaining distant from conventional empirical research methods, Hall, Morley and others associated with the Centre for Contemporary Cultural studies at the University of Birmingham, are not alone in their efforts to recenter media criticism on the spectator's role in the process of signification. Indeed, 1980s writing on the soap opera has been led toward a consideration of the viewer–text relationship by Modleski's (1979/1982) influential, feminist rethinking of the genre. Her approach stresses the feminine spectator's position *vis-à-vis* the text. A number of writers have elaborated this aspect of her argument—either directly or indirectly. Robert C. Allen (1985) has constructed an entire "reader-oriented poetics of the soap opera" (chap. 4). Ellen Seiter (1981) applies semiotician Umberto Eco to soap opera in order to hypothesize the genre's "openness" to feminist counterreadings. Dana Polan (1986), incorporating concepts of Fredric Jameson, suggests that mass culture objects, such as "Blondie" cartoons and "Dallas," may be mined for "allegorical" levels of interpretation by the creative reader. Ien Ang's (1985) study of the "melodramatic imagination" and "Dallas" is centered on 42 viewers' written responses to the program. Rounding out this eclectic group of reader-centered methods, is Annette Kuhn's (1984) psychoanalytically inflected exploration of "women's genres" (melodrama and soap opera), which poses the questions: "Do these 'gynocentric' forms address, or construct, a female or a feminine spectator? If so, how?" (p. 19).

The present study is more circumscribed in its aspirations. Lack of resources and, more crucially, the absence of a fully developed method for empirical discourse analysis restricts this writer's ability to research actual viewers' responses to soap operas. What I propose instead is to detail the ideological problematic of the soap opera, to articulate what I perceive to be the ideological encoding of the genre's preferred, dominant reading and then to suggest alternative (negotiated, oppositional) readings. In this effort I will appropriate a portion of Morley's (1980) method: "Analysis of messages [texts] attempting to elucidate the basic codes of meaning to which they refer, the recurrent patterns and structures in the messages, the ideology implicit in the concepts and categories via which the messages are transmitted" (p. 23). In soap operas these patterns are constellated mostly around issues of *personal* politics—the family, male–female relationships—which contain denotative and connotative discourses of race, class, religion, consumer capitalism, and so forth. The notes that follow propose, initially, a preferred reading suggested by the soap opera text—a reading that inhabits dominant ideology and promotes its "natural" representation of societal and personal politics.[7] This preferred reading, however, must take account of the contradictions within ideology that facilitate negotiated and even oppositional pleasure in the soap opera.

THE IDEOLOGICAL PROBLEMATIC

In her analysis of the British soap opera, "Crossroads," Charlotte Brunsdon (1981) writes, "The ideological problematic of soap-opera—the frame or field in which meanings are made, in which significance is constructed narratively—is that of 'personal life'" (p. 34). The television soap opera has been historically the only TV genre to deal—some would say obsessively—with narratives of personal relationships: friends and lovers, husbands and wives, parents and children, and so on. Where other TV genres detail the *actions* of (usually) men in the world of work and adventure, soap operas contend with the *passions* of women (as often as men) in the world of emotion. One may rehearse the by now familiar scenario of the socioeconomic forces nurturing the genre's emphasis on the emotional/personal, on family and romance. The U. S. soap opera was developed originally on radio in the late 1920s and 1930s by sponsors looking for a market to sell cleaning products. They didn't need sophisticated demographic analyses to tell them that that market was to be found in daytime radio, reaching the detergent-purchasing, presumably female

---

[7] Hence, my sense of the political is quite broad, but I agree with Roland Barthes's (1957/1972) contention that "One must naturally understand *political* in its deeper meaning, as describing the whole of human relations in their real, social structure, in their power of making the world. . . ." (p. 143).

consumer in the home, where and when she worked. What was needed, therefore, was a narrative form that dealt with so-called women's concerns that might lure the "housewife" to the radio. Soap opera evolved, then, as one of the few TV genres specifically designed for the female listener. This female listenership—which has dominated to the present day—has attracted the interest of feminists currently writing on mass media. Drawing on their recent work, one can better understand ideological structures within soap opera.

Personal Politics: Sacrifice and Suffering in the Domestic Zone

In ideological terms, one of the most interesting antecedents of the soap opera was Irna Phillip's "Thought for a Day," a series of short, regionally broadcast (WGN, Chicago), nonnarrative treatises on the value of home and motherhood. Phillips soon moved into narrative form with the soap opera "Painted Dreams."[8] So began her long and significant influence on soap opera, both during radio's "Golden Era" and continuing into the age of television. Her early soap operas continued the bald-faced ideological task of "Thought for a Day": proselytizing that the woman's place is solely in the home. Consider the advice of Mother Moran, from "Today's Children," when one of her daughters strayed from motherhood toward a career as an artist:

> Frances, you are paintin' your dreams, yes. And you hold the brush and must be choosin' the colors to use. . . . There are three colors that have stood the test of all time. They are the colors that are the foundation of all dreams of all men and women in the world—the colors of love . . . family . . . home.

>   (Edmondson & Rounds, 1976, p. 39)

"Today's Children" provided a sympathetic, identification figure (Mother Moran) and placed in her mouth the ideology of the dominant class. Women were not permitted a personal identity, but rather defined themselves through the nurturing of their family. Radio soap opera stories detail over and over again the virtues of maternal suffering and sacrifice.[9] The family is at the center of the radio soap opera and its televisual successor.

---

[8] "Painted Dreams" premiered on WGN in 1932 and was reworked as "Today's Children" when broadcast nationally on NBC.

[9] This conclusion, as others, about radio soap operas must be understood as tentative. In truth, we know precious little about radio soap opera. In lieu of a comprehensive ideological or aesthetic analysis of the genre we are forced to rely on received wisdom that cannot be proven or disproven. The situation is not likely to improve, either, since the texts themselves have dissipated into the ozone; radio soap opera was not deemed worthy of preservation.

In conventional middle-class society, the wedding serves several functions: It marks the integration of the couple into the social order; it legitimates sex as a function of reproduction rather than recreation; and it inaugurates one cornerstone of consumer capitalism, the nuclear family, with its many material needs. Indeed, Marxists since Engels (1884/1972) have seen the bourgeois family as a historically specific social structure, a microcosm and essential component of capitalism. Marriage and the family form the bedrock upon which TV soap opera is constructed. Unlike the film romance, which leads us up to the altar and then rolls the end credits, the soap opera articulates the eternally *ongoing* struggles of wife, husband, and children. The Hughes family of "As the World Turns" and the Bauers of "Guiding Light" have had their stories related over decades of narrative. Superficially, soap opera presents marriage as the ideal state for woman and man. Characters obsessively pursue matrimony; occasionally returning from the grave to consummate the marriage. And after the frequently delayed weddings, some must go to extreme lengths just to maintain their marriages. For example, in "As the World Turns," Craig faked paralysis and his wife Betsy was constrained by guilt from leaving him. Pregnancy and parenthood are treasured above all else, with normally villainous characters scrapping tooth and nail for custody of babies with little thought for the inconveniences of caring for a small, needy infant. Time and again characters speak of the importance of "love . . . family . . . home," in Mother Moran's words. But the representation of family in soap opera is not without its contradictions.

Marriage is extremely hazardous in soap opera. The core families are constantly threatened from within and without. These threats range from the pedestrian (lack of "communication" between husband and wife) to the ludicrous: The head of an international drug ring almost killed Brooke ("All My Children"), even though, as it turned out, she was Brooke's mother. As Jane Feuer (1984) points out,

> Marriage—with its consequent integration into the social order—is never viewed as a symbol of narrative closure as it is in so many comic forms. Indeed to be happily married on a serial is to be on the periphery of the narrative. (pp. 12–13)

The genre thrives on the disruption of the family, not its representation as the ideal, *stable* condition. As Mulvey (1986) has argued, "At one and the same time, the family is the socially accepted road to respectable normality, an icon of conformity, and the source of deviance, psychosis and despair" (p. 95). Not surprisingly, the mother is most often at the center of all this despair and narrative aperture. Modleski (1979/1982) notes that the good mother (e.g., Maeve Ryan, "Ryan's Hope"), as opposed to the scheming one who manipulates her children (e.g., Phoebe on "All My Children"), sacrifices for her children and suffers the indignities of her weak husband's indiscretions. Modleski continues, "the function of the mother is unchanged: she is there to console her children and try to understand them as they have illegitimate babies, separate from their spouses (miraculously obtaining annulments instead of divorces), and dispense birth control information in the poor neighborhoods" (p. 92). Thus, at the same time the dialogue extols the glories of family and motherhood, the narrative presents a catalog of the horrors that may befall a family. In the cinema, the family is the safety zone, the enclave, to which the protagonist retreats from the cruel vagaries of the outside world. In soap opera, the family is the site of emotional upheaval.

At the heart of the representation of soap opera motherhood are two intimately intertwined components: paternity/maternity and pregnancy. As Derry (1983) has illustrated, one of the central issues within the family structure is the search for paternity. Few soap opera characters know who their biological father is, and many do not even know who their true mother is. During 1986–1987, "As the World Turns" has chronicled an astonishingly convoluted story line involving multiple instances of mistaken paternity and maternity. The controversy swirls around teen-aged Lily Walsh. Lily has just learned that she is adopted and thus that the woman who raised her, Lucinda Walsh, is not her biological mother. (This information surfaces soon after Lucinda learns that she has a daughter she never knew about, who was raised in the fictional Central American country of Montega.) The biological mother is Lily's best friend, Iva, who herself learned only recently that not only was she (Iva) adopted, but the cousin who raped her 18 years ago was *also* adopted. Consequently, the rape was not additionally incestuous.[10] Lily's situation is an extreme example but far from unique. Approximately a dozen of the 25 or 30 current "As the World Turns" characters do not, or did not, know who

---

[10] "As the World Turns" producer Michael Laibson explained that the writers invented the multiple adoptions so that Iva's adoptive brother could date her biological daughter without it being incestuous. Author's interview with Michael Laibson, August 6, 1986, Athens, Ohio.

their true parents are or were. Each of these revelations of true paternity/maternity disrupts and realigns the soap opera's dense, intricate familial structure. Best friends become mothers; acquaintances become brothers; and, not infrequently, spouses-to-be become brother and sister. (E.g., Erica almost married her half-brother Mark on "All My Children.")

Many paternity conflicts begin at the pregnancy itself, for pregnancy is no simple matter in soap opera. Every pregnancy almost miscarries at least once and, indeed, miscarriages themselves are quite common. As Derry (1983) notes, soap opera pregnancies are dangerous, mysterious events, both feared and obsessively pursued. One other facet of pregnancy has been discussed by Modleski (1979/ 1982). She observes that the soap opera villainess reverses traditional male–female roles by skillfully manipulating pregnancy:

> If she decides she wants to marry a man, she will take advantage of him one night when he is feeling especially vulnerable and seduce him. And if she doesn't achieve the hoped-for pregnancy, undaunted, she simply lies to her lover about being pregnant. The villainess thus reverses male/female roles: anxiety about conception is transferred to the male. (p. 95)

In terms of sexual politics, then, pregnancy becomes a source of woman's power rather than a weakness that prevents her from acting "like a man." The fact that it is often an evil character that uses pregnancy in this fashion does not vitiate this point, according to Modleski. She contends, "The extreme delight viewers apparently take in despising the villainess testifies to the enormous amount of energy involved in the spectator's repression and to her (albeit unconscious) resentment at being constituted as an egoless receptacle for the suffering of others" (p. 94). The villainess thus *contradicts* the middle-class ideological premise of woman as long-suffering martyr.

One final aspect of soap opera's representation of pregnancy deserves consideration. During the 1970s abortion was gingerly dealt with as a special "issue" in liberal soaps such as "All My Children," which has similarly presented stories about rape, cocaine addiction, lesbianism, diabetes, and so on. Since that time, however, abortion has gradually evolved into a soap opera taboo. No positive character will have an abortion in current soaps—no matter what the source of the pregnancy: rape (e.g., Estelle, raped by Billy Clyde, married to Benny—"All My Children"), one night's indiscretion that will now ruin the person's life (e.g., Cliff's liaison with Sybil that produced a child that kept him and true-love Nina separated—"All My Children), and so on. Instead of abortions, characters suffer through long, at-risk pregnancies resulting in children that burden them and/or their lovers. Only weak or evil characters abort a fetus. Once again, patriarchal ideology sends mixed signals: On the one hand, characters are told that pregnancy is joyful and that, even in cases of rape, abortion is to be abhorred. On the other, they are shown pregnancies that are horrific and emotionally destructive, doing no one any good. From these pregnancies result offspring whose existence generates additional pain and suffering.

Marriages often do not survive all these manipulated pregnancies and endless searches for paternity—not to mention drug ring mothers and other dangers. Divorce, consequently, is surprisingly common on television soap opera.[11] Moreover, soap opera's abundance of divorces distinguishes it from most other genres in television and film. The cinema has timidly offered a few films on divorce such as *Kramer vs. Kramer* (1979) and *Shoot the Moon* (1982), but cinematic narrative codes are designed to bring (disparate) couples together, not split them apart.[12] U.S. prime-time TV has avoided the topic of divorce until recently. It has occasionally included divorced characters since 1961 and the divorcee Vivian Bagley of "The Lucy Show," but it wasn't until 14 years later that a successful prime time program would be centered on a divorced character ("One Day at a Time"). It seems curious, therefore, that soap opera, a genre that devotes so much energy verbally promoting marriage, would be the film and TV genre that spends the most time chronicling divorces. A character such as Erica ("All My Children") has been divorced so many times that by now even the most devoted fan must have lost count. In some respects, soap opera divorce is represented as a punishment for evil characters. Erica, during the 1970s, was a conniving, manipulative, selfish woman. Divorce suited her. It served as her frequent punishment, causing her loneliness and isolation. However, soap opera divorce frequently does not discriminate between good and evil. It punishes positive characters who are truly in love, but against whom circumstances have conspired. In this regard, divorce is no different from most other negative aspects of life in soap opera, it affects the good as much as the evil. As Derry (1983) observes "Indeed, perhaps the most important aspect of soap opera is the way the genre reflects some of our most profound fears: that is, that the universe is hostile, that fate conspires against us, that every life leads inevitably to

---

[11] Apparently, divorce was almost unheard of in radio soap opera.

[12] See Seiter's (1983) consideration of these films as a retrogressive step for modern melodrama.

death. . . . No one stays happy" (p. 11). Or, as we might amend Derry's observation with slight exaggeration, no one stays married.

In terms of sexual politics, middle-class divorce is a double-edged sword. It frees the woman from dependence on a specific man and liberates her from a social structure, marriage, that supports her sexual and economic subjugation. But, most divorces result in the woman's assuming primary care for the children, with the man's participation in the work of child rearing largely reduced to financial support. After a divorce the man becomes a de facto bachelor once again while the woman becomes a *single parent.* As a single parent, often working at a full- or part-time job, she may find her options more limited than when she was married. This result of divorce is seldom observed in contemporary soap opera. Instead, a rather utopian view of divorce is represented. Untraditional groupings of children from various marriages live together under one roof with minimal discord. Women with young children seldom have trouble attracting new lovers or obtaining child care when they start jobs as TV talk show hosts, computer firm executives, or investigative reporters. New jobs and new romances are begun and the main imperative of soap opera—that the story continues—is sustained. The soap opera form does not lend itself to stories about the negative, statistically common product of divorce: a woman who divides all her time between menial work and child care, and cannot afford the effort, time, or money required for new romance. Such a woman is too isolated from the social mainstream to permit the constant interpersonal activity necessary for soap opera romance. She is one of the significant absences of the soap opera text. Due to this narrative gap, soap opera divorce is somewhat anomalous. It destroys the glorified unity of the middle-class family, but divorced women and men do not seem to suffer or be stigmatized for that destruction.

Personal Politics II: Sex and Love Outside of Marriage

It would appear that domestic relations dominate 1980s television soap opera as they did 1930s radio soap opera. Since the 1970s, however, there has been a conscious trend to incorporate more of what Derry (1983) calls *romantic and sexual adventures*—adventures that do not necessarily result in matrimony. Premiering March 26, 1973, "The Young and the Restless" is generally considered the progenitor of this new emphasis on younger characters in "restless" sexual escapades. "General Hospital" has rivaled and perhaps even surpassed its success with this technique, a sample of which is described by Derry: "Diana loved Phil, who loved Jessie, who was married to Peter, who offered to marry Diana, who was much later jealous of Leslie, who loved Rick, who loved Monica, who was married to Jeff, who became enamored of Diana . . . and so forth" (p. 13). Although it would be misleading to assume that 1980s soap opera has eclipsed domestic narratives with tales of wild youth in Dionysian revels, it would be equally misleading to ignore those elements of sexual politics residing outside the perimeter of the family.[13]

As might be expected, the most common sex and love outside of marriage is that which is leading up to it. The road to matrimony is a rocky one, however, for the soap opera couple that is pure of heart. Indeed, at any particular time, most soap operas are developing at least one story of a hapless pair of lovers struggling to reach the altar: Luke and Laura ("General Hospital"), Greg and Jenny ("All My Children"), Steve and Betsy ("As the World Turns"), Bo and Hope ("Days of Our Lives"), and so on. At this point, premarital sex between mature adults is widely practiced, acknowledged, and accepted in the world of the soap opera. The fact that the man and woman plan to marry provides a certain validity to their sexual activity.

The values of the genre are congruent with those of contemporary U. S. society in this respect, but a shift seems to be occurring. It may be too early to generalize, but a few soap opera women and men have consciously decided to refrain from sex until they are officially wed. In the instances observed so far (Betsy and Steve, Frannie and Seth, "As the World Turns"), the woman instigates their abstinence, even though both parties are already sexually experienced. It may well be that in these days of AIDS hysteria and "safe sex" we are witnessing a new discourse regarding sexuality. In particular, Betsy and Frannie seem to be signaling a regression to the patriarchal belief that the woman is responsible for limiting sex to that which is performed within monogamy, solely for the purpose of reproduction. Any other female sexuality is considered dangerous and branded taboo. As custodians of the domestic, these women repress sexual desire outside of the familial structure. This attitude toward women's sexuality in soap opera is just now emerging and is not without its counterexamples. In the very same program, "As the World Turns," one may witness couples (e.g., Casey and Lila) engaged in premarital sex and appearing perfectly satisfied—or rather, as satisfied as one may be in soap opera.

---

[13] Indeed, there has been a distinct backlash to "The Young and the Restless"-style adventures. From the start those story lines met resistance from older viewers and currently, in an aesthetic regression, many shows are re-emphasizing family story lines.

Extramarital sex—whether adulterous or wholly detached from the context of marriage—has increased in visibility over the past 15 or 20 years, but its ideological function has changed very little. Sexually active men (*womanizers*—e.g., Jack, "The Young and the Restless") and sexually active women (known euphemistically as *witches* on soaps—e.g., Tina, "One Life to Live") are presented in a very negative light. Seldom are sexually active women or men positive characters. They're at best weak and selfish, and, at worst, destructive, untrustworthy, and villainous. By ignoring or even mocking matrimony they sin against that patriarchal institution and become what Derry (1983) terms *taboo breakers*. Our relationship to these characters, he maintains, is conflicted and dialectical.

> Although we may wish that the taboo-breaker be punished, our response is complex, because we spend so much time in secret empathy that our hope is eventually replaced by a dread of the inevitable outcome. . . . The genre rejects any simple concepts of justice and rarely punishes the taboo-breaker at the moment of his or her most arrogant act. What happens more frequently is that circumstances begin to change the behavior of the taboo-breaker—who is not punished until her or his life has already begun to become more conventional. (p. 10)

(Derry uses Karen, "One Life to Live," as his principal example.) The longevity of soap opera serves to complicate our reading of it. "All My Children's" Phoebe and Erica were two of the program's toughest, most manipulative taboo breakers of the 1970s, but in the 1980s their characters have become more vulnerable and hence more empathetic—in preparation for their punishments with bad marriages and men more manipulative than they.

The Economics of Soap Opera Life

The soap opera adopts certain strategies in its representation of class and work. Rather than address directly these topics, they are either displaced into terms of personal politics that the genre may absorb, or else they are totally repressed and left unsaid. Unlike some British soap operas which are centered in a working-class milieu, U. S. soap opera characters are predominantly middle-class and often work as professionals, especially doctors, lawyers, journalists and vaguely defined "business" people. Soap opera tends toward this social class because its politics are invisible; as middle-class characters they bear the society's (dominant) ideology through commonsensical and thus unquestioned values.

Unions and labor disputes are absent from a world of doctors, lawyers, et al. Though their work may occasionally be dangerous, no one dislikes or is alienated from his or her job; work is challenging, rewarding, invigorating. Indeed, work as actual labor is rarely presented. Moreover, as Charlotte Brunsdon (1981) has noted, "the action of the soap-opera is not restricted to familial or quasi-familial institutions but, as it were, *colonizes* the public masculine sphere, representing it from the point of view of the personal" (p. 24). The doctors and nurses of General Hospital spend more time talking about personal relationships than patient care. And personal emotions often intrude directly into the public space—as when Dr. Cliff Warner of "All My Children" was forced to operate on Palmer, a man he detested. Pine Valley, Oakdale, Port Charles, and other soap opera communities are very small worlds in which the personal and the public are inevitably compounded, with the former crowding out the latter. The repression of job alienation, unions and other aspects of working life fits easily into the middle-class discourse on (ennobling) work that underpins much of bourgeois ideology.

Into this overriding middle-class homogeneity, however, are mixed working-class and *lumpenproletarian* figures. Class conflict—deflected into *romantic* conflict—has been a favored story device since the genre's radio days when "Our Gal Sunday" opened with the familiar refrain:

> The story of an orphan girl named Sunday, from the little mining town of Silver Creek, Colorado, who in young womanhood married England's richest, most handsome lord, Lord Henry Brinthrope. The story asks the question, Can this girl from a mining town in the West find happiness as the wife of a wealthy and titled Englishman?
>
> (Edmondson & Rounds, 1976, pp. 44–45)

Sunday's marriage to Lord Brinthrope is but one, early example of romance bridging a social gap. Indeed, in 1985, "As the World Turns" incorporated its own "wealthy and titled Englishman" and matched him with a woman of humble origins (Marcy). More typically, however, today's soap opera doesn't resort to European royalty to show class differences. The wealthy heiress falls in love with the stableboy (Lily and Holden, "As the World Turns"), or the juvenile delinquent from the streets becomes involved with the bourgeois young woman studying to be a doctor (Jessie and Angie, "All My Children").

In each of these instances, socioeconomic differences are used to drive the narrative forward, providing a major source of conflict. In the cinema, the resolution of these class differences in the couple's eventual union serves a major ideological effect. It unites two classes and suggests that, in the U. S., class differences are merely superficial and may be overcome by love, that all citizens are basically equal. The cinema's "happily-ever-after" marriage of two people from different classes thus signifies the bourgeois fiction of a classless American society, or at least one in which classes may melt into one another. In television soap opera the union of men and women from different class positions can have one of three results. First, the couple may leave the narrative entirely, providing film-like closure of their story line—as was the case with Marcy and her English lord. Second, the formation of a couple may mark the blending together of their class differences. In the case of Jessie and Angie, Jessie became more "civilized" and middle-class while Angie acquired some of Jessie's street-smart toughness. Third, the couple's differences may continue to erupt in the narrative—causing ongoing conflict even after the couple is ostensibly united. In "As the World Turns," working-class Steve, for example, continued to feel socially inferior to his wife, Betsy and her affluent American family (doctors, lawyers, etc.) even after they were wed. This inferiority complex eventually led to his flight from Oakdale and the breakdown of their marriage. In this third instance one may observe once again how, in contrast to the cinema, the soap opera's lack of narrative closure unsettles middle-class ideology. Rather than blending class differences into a smooth marital homogeneity, the soap opera marriage may contain a heterogeneous class mix that continues to generate narrative enigmas: "Will Steve and Betsy resolve their class differences and reunite?" The bourgeois premise that love destroys socioeconomic barriers is contradicted. Lack of narrative closure permits self-perpetuating ideological fissures.

The Unseen, the Unheard: Signifying Absences

Some significant elements of late-twentieth-century U. S. life are slighted or fully repressed in the soap opera. Their invisibility is a function of the inability of middle-class ideology to cope with them. A brief consideration of these repressions suggests themes that society would rather leave unsaid. Chief among these signifying absences are racial minorities and homosexuality.

Blacks and another minorities began appearing regularly in soap operas in the 1960s, but a fear of miscegenation has kept them from being fully incorporated into the genre's narrative discourse. Romance between minorities and whites remains a soap opera taboo, which has caused some remarkably twisted story lines. In 1967, Irna Phillips created one of the first international romances in soap opera: a Eurasian woman (Mia) dating Anglo men (Paul, Jim) in "Love is a Many Splendored Thing." The resulting controversy caused the quick termination of the Eurasian character and her replacement by troubled, young, white women.[14] Similarly, and more recently, "All My Children" began cultivating a romance between a young white woman (Jenny) and a young Black man (Jessie), but then Jenny's interest suddenly and without motivation shifted to a white man (Greg).[15] The most convoluted narrative complication involving an interracial couple would have to be a story line developed on "The Young and the Restless" in 1985. Tyrone, a light-skinned Black cop with a Black lover, went undercover as a *white* gangster, and became engaged to a white woman, Alana, the daughter of the syndicate boss, Mr. Anthony. The story teased the viewer with the possibility of the taboo marriage of Tyrone with Alana, a possibility that was maintained right up to their wedding. Though they were wed, the marriage was never consummated. Tyrone's true identity was revealed on the day of the wedding when Mr. Anthony was killed and his syndicate disbanded. Alana then left Tyrone because he had deceived her. In so doing, "The Young and the Restless" avoids the issue of interracial marriage by developing a reason for the couple's breakup that has nothing to do with race—that is, Tyrone's betrayal of Alana's trust. In a sense, the issue of miscegenation has been displaced onto one of personal honor. The result, however, is de facto racism: The Black man and the white woman are not permitted to consummate the marriage.

Because minorities are excluded from marriage to white characters and thus from white familial structures, they inhabit a parallel romantic/familial universe. Black families exist on most soaps, but their story lines of, say, romance or paternity involve only other Black characters. They intersect with white characters solely at work, and work

---

[14] The program was based on the film of the same name and the novel, *A Many Splendored Thing.* For more details, see Schemering (1985, pp. 140–141).

[15] Subsequently, "All My Children" has developed two interracial sexual narratives that were surprisingly blind to the characters' races. (1) A young white woman, Dottie, developed an infatuation with the aforementioned Jessie. He did not return her affections, however, and eventually married a Black woman, Angie. (2) Angie was the victim of attempted sexual abuse by her white doctor/professor while she was in medical school. Neither of these story lines was that of a positive or consummated romance, but they do signal that Black and white characters *could* be successfully mixed in interpersonal narratives.

as discussed above, is removed from the central concerns of soap opera. Consequently, Black characters are subordinate in terms of screen time spent chronicling their stories. They are inferior narrative elements because they are forbidden entry into a soap opera's core familial structures. A simple example of commutation illustrates my point. When unknown white newcomer Josh entered the Oakdale of "As the World Turns" he disrupted several white familial structures by turning out to be Lily's true father and Iva's rapist cousin; and by developing a romantic attraction to the married Betsy, which may or may not be mutual. If, hypothetically, we substitute a Black actor for Josh then none of these disruptions would have been possible. Josh would have been permitted only to interact with the (two or three) Black characters currently on the program. Soap opera's solution to the "problem" of incorporating minorities has been to adopt a "separate-but-equal" approach that delegates minority performers to the status of minor characters. The near-invisibility of minority characters signifies middle-class ideology's inability to represent alien cultures, the other, the outside.

Like minorities, homosexuals are excluded from the center of soap opera discourse because of the primacy of the bourgeois family and romance, but, unlike with minorities, the soap opera does not construct a parallel universe for gay romance or gay families. The reason for this is obvious, gay men and lesbians represent the ultimate threat to the middle-class family. They are, in a sense, *afamilial;* they exist outside of the parameters of heterosexual courtship and its culmination in monogamy and family. Consequently, there is no point of entry for them into the middle-class family and no framework upon which to build a parallel familial structure. Their rare appearances in daytime soap opera have been bracketed off as story lines dealing with a social "issue," as when "All My Children" (1983) featured a lesbian psychologist (Lynn) in a short-lived story involving the confused and abused-by-men Devon. Devon became sexually interested in Lynn, but Lynn gently rejected Devon's interest as a mere rebound from bad experiences with men. "All My Children" used the story didactically; Lynn would explain to Devon (and the viewer) that lesbians are not evil or perverse, and that they share many of the desires of heterosexuals. Lynn was not a long-term character, however. Once this "liberal" argument about lesbianism was made, her character left town. As Seiter (1983, p. 22) contends, regarding homosexuality on "Dynasty," "Since good sexuality must always be directed towards marriage and children in the family melodrama, homosexuality must either be associated with villainy and neuroses, or banished altogether." Daytime soap opera has chosen near-total banishment.

PROVISIONAL CONCLUSIONS: A STRUCTURED POLYSEMY

Can one draw a single specific political message from the soap opera's representation of family and romance? I would suggest not. Soap opera is clearly, in Morley's (1980) term, a *structured polysemy*. There is not one meaning, but many available to the soap opera reader—although these multiple meanings are not limitless. Broadcast television's internal contradictions facilitate pleasurable viewing by spectators belonging to oppositional, subcultural groups as well as those inhabiting dominant ideology. The vast majority of soap opera viewers—as well as critics and scholars of the genre—*negotiates* an understanding of the genre that is neither wholly within dominant ideology nor wholly oppositional to it. This negotiated reading brings the viewer's symbolic system to bear upon the discourses of the soap opera text. As I have argued, these textual discourses are marbled with contradictions, facilitating a wealth of negotiated readings and thwarting the analyst's desire for simple homogeneity.

REFERENCES

Allen, R. C. (1985). *Speaking of soap operas.* Chapel Hill: University of North Carolina Press.

Ang, I. (1985). *Watching "Dallas": Soap opera and the melodramatic imagination.* New York: Methuen.

Barthes, R. (1972). *Mythologies* (A. Lavers, Trans.). New York: Hill & Wang. (Original work published 1957)

Brunsdon, C. (1981). "Crossroads": Notes on soap opera. *Screen, 22*(4), 32–37.

Butler, J. G. (1986). Notes on the soap opera apparatus: Televisual style and "As the World Turns." *Cinema Journal, 25*(3), 53–70.

Derry, C. (1983). Television soap opera: "Incest, bigamy, and fatal disease." *Journal of the University Film and Video Association, 35*(1), 4–16.

Edmondson, M., & Rounds, D. (1976). *From Mary Noble to Mary Hartman.* New York: Stein & Day.

Elsaesser, T. (1985). Tales of sound and fury: Observations on the family melodrama. In B. Nichols (Ed.), *Movies and methods: An anthology* (Vol. 2, pp. 165–189). Berkeley: University of California Press. (Original work published 1972)

Engels, F. (1972). *The origin of the family, private property, and the state.* New York: Pathfinder Press. (Original work published 1884)

Feuer, J. (1984). Melodrama, serial form and television today. *Screen, 25*(1), 4–16.

Fiske, J. (1987). British cultural studies and television. In R. C. Allen (Ed.), *Channels of discourse: Television and contemporary criticism* (pp. 254–289). Chapel Hill: University of North Carolina Press.

Gledhill, C. (1985). Melodrama. In P. Cook (Ed.), *The cinema book* (pp. 73–84). New York: Pantheon.

Hall, S. (1980). Encoding/decoding. In S. Hall, D. Hobson, A. Lowe, & P. Willis (Eds.), *Culture, media, language* (pp. 128–138). London: Hutchinson. (Original work published 1973)

Kuhn, A. (1982). *Women's pictures: Feminism and cinema.* Boston: Routledge & Kegan Paul.

Kuhn, A. (1984). Women's genres. *Screen, 25*(1), 18–28.

Millett, K. (1970). *Sexual politics.* New York: Avon.

Modleski, T. (1982). *Loving with a vengeance: Mass-produced fantasies for women.* New York: Methuen. (Original chapter on soap opera published 1979)

Morley, D. (1980). *The "Nationwide" audience: Structure and decoding.* (BFI Television Monograph No. 11). London: British Film Institute.

Mulvey, L. (1977/1978). Notes on Sirk and melodrama. *Movie, 25,* 53–57.

Mulvey, L. (1986). Melodrama in and out of the home. In C. MacCabe (Ed.), *High theory/low culture: Analysing popular television and film* (pp. 80–100). New York: St. Martin's.

Polan, D. (1986). Brief encounters: Mass culture and evacuation of sense. In T. Modleski (Ed.), *Studies in entertainment: Critical approaches to mass culture.* Bloomington: Indiana University Press.

Schemering, C. (1985). *The soap opera encyclopedia.* New York: Ballantine.

Seiter, E. (1981). Eco's TV guide—The soaps. *Tabloid, 6,* 35–43.

Seiter, E. (1983). Men, sex and money in recent family melodramas. *Journal of the University Film and Video Association, 35*(1), 17–27.

White, M. (1987). Ideological analysis and television. In R. C. Allen (Ed.), *Channels of discourse: Television and contemporary criticism* (pp. 134–171). Chapel Hill: University of North Carolina Press.

Willemen, P. (1971). Distanciation and Douglas Sirk. *Screen, 12*(2), 63–67.

Willemen, P. (1972/1973). Towards an analysis of the Sirkian system. *Screen, 13*(4), 128–134.

Williams, R. (1974). *Television: Technology and cultural form.* New York: Schocken.

8

Political Themes and Images in Music Videos

Anne Johnston Wadsworth
Department of Radio, Television, and Motion Pictures, University of North Carolina at Chapel Hill

Lynda Lee Kaid
Department of Communication, University of Oklahoma

In the music video, "Land of Confusion" by Genesis, a (Spitting Image) puppet character resembling Ronald Reagan dreams of being Superman and of living in the age of dinosaurs. Interspersed with these dream sequences are scenes of puppets which resemble other world political figures. As the visuals of these political figures and the Reagan dream sequence continue, the song's chorus tells viewers/listeners that people need to make the world a better place in which to live. At the end of this music video, the Reagan puppet wakes up next to a Nancy Reagan puppet and comments on the strange dream that he had. As he reaches to push a button to call for a nurse, he accidentally pushes a red button above the nurse button, marked NUKE. When he pushes the button, the video shows a large mushroom cloud growing on the screen as the Reagan puppet remarks, "That's some nurse!"

Not all music videos that contain political themes are this blatant in their satire and criticism of government and power plays between nations. However, this particular video is similar to numerous others that have an antinuclear theme and a focus on the "power figures" which, according to the artists, manipulate the average citizen into making war. Nuclear war is only one of the several political themes that has been found in the audio and/or video message of music videos.

159

MUSIC VIDEOS AND POLITICS

Since their origin, music videos have provided a mass-based forum for artists to comment on the political environment. While the method of expression may be new, videos are certainly not the first music forms to address political issues; music has always been an important means for artists to express dissatisfaction with some political stances by government.

The importance of music in the political system was evident in the writings of Plato, and songs and jingles have long played a specific role in political campaigning (Jamieson, 1984). Music's most direct role in modern politics can be traced to the political rock or "protest rock" popularized in the 1960s by artists such as Bob Dylan (Orman, 1984). The early protest music of the 1960s had a strong peace, freedom, antiwar, and/or antiestablishment tone (Robinson, 1976).

During this same period, "soul" music highlighted the political and social struggles of the Black community and has been credited with bringing group cohesion, political activism and self-help to that portion of American society (Maultsby, 1983). Even modern country music sometimes contains sociopolitical messages specifically related to distinct conditions (Smith, 1980).

Outside of the United States, music also has been used as a vehicle for messages of protest. One of the best examples is Jamaican rock music, also known as Reggae. Reggae is the music of a subculture in Jamaican society which abhors the government and the established way of life in Jamaica. The lyrics of Reggae have traditionally served as sermons protesting this established way of life and advocating the subculture's beliefs (Winders, 1983).

Characteristics of Music Videos

Music, then, has been and continues to be an important form for expressing political views. Videos provide music with a new dimension for expressing these political themes and images. Songs with political messages can now be dramatized for viewers, and political messages which may have been "lost" on listeners in the past can be visually demonstrated or enhanced for viewers. Before videos, an artist or group might compose a song to express a political viewpoint, but the basic interpretation was largely left to the listener. Now, through the video elements of a song's presentation, the artist has a number of ways to structure the interpretation. In addition, scholars have suggested that the influence of music as a vehicle of political expression is difficult to assess because the lyrics may not be understood by the listeners (Meadow, 1980). But with videos, lyrics are interpreted for audiences through the visuals, providing, in some instances, a new message to the song.

Although not much is known about the influence of music videos, several scholars have attempted to describe the inherent characteristics in all videos and the implications these characteristics have for interpreting the messages. Videos most closely resemble commercials, because, at the most basic level their purpose is to sell the artist(s) and the music in the video. Some videos also promote a movie. Lynch (1984) argues that in addition to their function as a selling tool, music videos resemble commercials in that they are short and their aim is to engage the viewer in a direct and immediate experience. Others argue that, unlike commercials, which only "promise" an experience after one has used the product, music videos are "themselves primary experiences" (Aufderheide, 1986, p. 63). Music videos trigger emotions similar to traditional commercials, according to Aufderheide, and focus on moods which center around a lack, an incompletion, an instability, and a searching for location, for a sense to belong.

Categories of Music Videos

In addition to these general characteristics, several categories or formats for music videos have been identified. One category is the performance category, in which the majority of the visuals feature the artist or group performing the song, usually, though not always, in concert (Brown & Campbell, 1986; Kinder, 1984; Lynch, 1984). A second format is the concept video. Brown and Campbell identified the concept video as one that tells a story in which the song's artist is the main actor. The concept video has also been described as a video which features the performer or group singing a song, interspersed with a narrative version of the song (Gehr, 1983). Because of this emphasis on a narrative in addition to the performance of the artists, "concept" music videos are sometimes called narrative music videos (Kinder, 1984; Lynch, 1984). Lynch categorized a third type of videos, into those that are strongly influenced by experimental film and use abstract and modern film techniques.

A final format for music videos are "dream" videos which feature "incongruous visual images" (Kinder, 1984, p. 5). These videos, according to Kinder, resemble dreams in that they weave "loose narratives out of chains of incoherent images" (p. 5). Like dreams, these videos offer their own version of reality, providing viewers with a "a ready-made alternative to social life" (Aufderheide, 1986, p. 66).

Political Messages in Music Videos

Few scholars have attempted to assess systematically the themes and images of political messages in videos. One of the problems with identifying a "political" theme in a music video may result from difficulty in defining "political music." Orman (1984) suggested that several characteristics are common in all political rock music. According to him, political rock music contains messages which attempt to recruit people for specific social movements and messages which support a readily identifiable world-view. Although not much work has been done on the scope of political themes and images in videos, several scholars have identified recurring political messages.

In terms of the proportion of political messages in videos, a recent content analysis found that 14.5% contained references to political issues (Baxter, DeRiemer, Landini, Leslie, & Singletary, 1985). However the researchers coded only video elements in their sample, and no attention was given to the nature of the specific political issues mentioned or how they were visually portrayed in the video. Brown and Campbell (1986) found that 20% of their sample of music videos communicated some kind of social protest, ranging from protest of nuclear war, oppression of workers, and prejudice, to protest of the business establishment and of the decline of radio. Other political themes which scholars have informally identified in music videos include: apocalypse, nuclear fallout, and postholocaust themes and images (Aufderheide, 1986), oppression by authority figures (Aufderheide, 1986), liberation from oppression, and nature versus technology themes (Lynch, 1984).

Influence of Music Videos

Probably the area of least research on videos is that of their influence on the audience. In the past, scholars argued that music should be considered as an important vehicle for political socialization. As mentioned, the difficulty in understanding the influence of music is usually due to the numerous interpretations listeners can give to lyrics which may or may not be clearly heard or understood. Music's potential for shaping political feelings and images, according to Meadow (1980), result from its being mass-based, widespread and is focused on teen-agers who, according to political socialization experts, are reaching a critical period in their understanding and development of political feelings. In addition, music is repetitious; songs are frequently heard over and over in different contexts (Meadow, 1980).

Videos, like music, are also widespread, geared toward an adolescent audience, and found in different contexts. The audience for the cable channel Music Television (MTV), is mainly between the ages of 12 and 34 (Livingston, 1984). Of this group, teen-agers are the most targeted audience, with figures suggesting that MTV has a weekly penetration of 43% of the U. S. teen-age market (Sun & Lull, 1986). Like popular music, videos are pervasive, playing on several channels other than MTV, in addition to being featured in stores, in shopping malls, in the previews of films, and during rock concerts. A selection of an artist's or a group's videos can also be purchased now, much like a cassette or album.

While videos share a common ground with music, they offer a new dimension to "listening" to music by providing a visual intrepretation of lyrics. While audience members are certainly free to provide their own, alternative interpretation to the lyrics, videos conveniently package one for them. Because of the provision of a structured meaning to lyrics, "seen and heard" music, as a form of popular culture, may be better than "heard-only" music in helping viewers interpret and redefine the lyrics and better in creating, along with other forms of popular culture, "a world of meanings that communicate aspects of social and political myth" (Nimmo & Combs, 1980, p. 132).

This ability of the visual portion of videos to influence the interpretation of the lyrics and, consequently, the message of the song is an important influence about which several scholars have speculated. Kinder (1984) argued that the visual aspect of videos overrides the audio portion and allows the video to be interpreted for the audience. According to Kinder, the video provides images which the viewer then internalizes into his or her own fantasy life, "incorporating them into a private reservoir of dream images" (p. 11). She argues that "one of the most powerful aspects of music videos is its programming of viewers to retrieve specific visual images from memory every time they hear a particular song" (p. 14). Kinder, thus, attributes to videos an ability to structure an interpretation of the song and a potential to provide audiences with a collective dream about political and social myths.

In a study of adolescents' viewing of videos by Sun and Lull (1986), one category for viewing was related to the visual component of MTV, suggesting that adolescents liked the way the visuals interpreted the songs for them and the way the music was acted out. Sun and Lull found that young viewers used the visuals to help them interpret the song and enjoyed the way the "visual interpretations presented in videos helped them get 'the understanding' of songs" (p. 121), indicating that these viewers thought there was only one interpretation of the song and that the visuals assisted them in getting that interpretation.

Although the interpretation of the lyrics may be the single most unique contribution of videos, the overall package of videos contributes to audiences' involvement with the music and the visuals. Music videos are forms of popular culture, and, according to Nimmo and Combs (1980), popular culture dramatizes political myths and can "reaffirm or disturb our collective political identity" (p. 133). In order to explore the ways in which videos "dramatize" political myths, this study attempts to identify the dominant themes and images and the overriding messages in political videos.

METHODOLOGY

To investigate the political themes and images, samples of videos were taped from MTV during two separate time periods. One sampling was done during the week of November, 1984, when 2-hour segments between the hours of 8 A.M. to midnight were taped everyday during that week. This resulted in a sample of 109 different videos. The second sampling was done during a 6-week period October–November, 1985. Again, the hours were randomly selected, and the program was taped during 2-hour segments. This resulted in a sample of 155 different videos.

Initially, all of the videos were viewed and marked by several persons as to whether there were any political themes and images. The researchers then viewed the videos that had been marked and made the final decision about whether or not the video contained any political images and themes either in the video or in the audio of the music video. From the total sample, 36 videos were selected as having political themes and images. In addition, the researchers viewed other videos not included in the samples but which were seen as having definite political messages in order to see what themes and images were present.

A coding sheet was constructed to tap the various political messages and symbols present in the videos. The most important question asked of the coders was an open-ended question where coders were asked to write a phrase or phrases on what the political theme was. They were instructed to be as specific as possible in their discussion of the political theme. Coders were also asked to identify any political symbols or emblems presented in the videos. Other questions included: If the theme was portrayed mainly in the audio, the video, or equally in both; if the video was from a movie or TV show; if a particular country or region of the world was highlighted in the video; and the technique used to present the message.

Two coders were trained in the use of the instrument and each viewed all 36 videos. On most of the items coded, agreement was virtually unanimous since many of the items called for straightforward observation. However, some discrepancies arose when judging the dominant theme of a video, and these differences were arbitrated by the researchers. After the themes were identified by coders, the researchers viewed all of the samples in addition to the more recent videos.

FINDINGS AND DISCUSSION

Of the types or categories of music videos identified by scholars, videos from this study which contained political themes were typically of the narrative or concept type, depicting their political messages through some loosely linked story line. They most frequently involved either some form of conflict between nations, power structures, ideologies, cultures, or status levels or some type of manipulation of the "average citizen" by those in authority or power. Also, several specific political themes emerged from the analysis.

"Oppression" Videos

One of the most frequently found themes is probably best described as an Oppression theme, although this incorporated numerous subcategories or images, including anti-big business and corruption themes as well as messages making fun of the American work ethic. Several of these videos portrayed the average workers as slaves in some type of factory, working to the point of exhaustion while being supervised by some powerful authority. Examples of this type of theme included Rick Springfield's "Bop Till You Drop" and The Hooters' "All You Zombies." Another message was the corruption that money and the quest for money brings. These videos satirized the work ethic, showing people piled under paperwork, working to exhaustion, and striving to consume and take all that they could from life.

In some of these Oppression videos, the artist or group was the "hero," trying to break from the routine, break the bondage of this work ethic, or fight the corrupt, powerful authorities. John Cougar Melloncamp's "Authority Song" used the symbolism of a boxing match to depict his fight against authority and corruption as he took on military, corporate, and political leaders. In the video, the working-class people (represented by Melloncamp) sat on one side of the boxing ring while the powerful leaders and figures sat on the opposite side of the boxing ring. In this particular video, Melloncamp (and the working class) lost the fight against authority.

Oppression videos also addressed the problems of tensions and oppression between races, classes, and factions within a nation which sometimes result in violence. A particularly powerful presentation of this type of oppression theme from this sample of videos was the "Sun City" video by Artists United Against Apartheid. This video presented a strong anti-apartheid message particularly in the use of actual news footage showing some of the violence, oppression, and distinctions in South African society and politics. Another particularly strong video in this category was Mick Jagger's "Under Cover of the Night." This video presented a drama about the violence and terrorism in El Salvador. It is a brutal video in which several members of the group are not the heros but rather are terrorists who kidnap a man, eventually killing their hostage.

"War" Videos

A second popular political theme in the videos analyzed here was a War theme (or in most instances, an antiwar message). In some cases, war was simply used as a backdrop for a personal story or relationship between two people. For example, Elton John's "That's Why They Call It The Blues" video tells the story of young lovers in the 1950s who are separated when the man enlists in the military and goes off to war. The couple become estranged and begin to lead separate lives until they are reunited at the end of the video when he returns home. War is also used as a backdrop in Chicago's video, "Along Comes a Woman," which borrows story lines and sequences from the movies *Casablanca* and *Raiders of the Lost Ark*.

The majority of War videos presented a less romanticized version of war, depicting its horrors and destruction. Most contained strong antiwar messages, such as the music video, "War Song" by Culture Club which contained lyrics such as "war is stupid" and scenes featuring children dressed in skeleton costumes. Nuclear war was also a popular topic of War videos. Some of these contained a disturbing message that a nuclear war would be started through some accidental pushing of a button or firing of missiles (such as the video, "Land of Confusion" by Genesis). Videos such as Roger Hodgson's video "Had a Dream (Sleeping with the Enemy)" criticized political figures in power who manipulate nations into war. This video features the artist running aimlessly through clouds and haze, suggesting the hopelessness that would exist after nuclear war.

Some War videos focus not so much on worldwide problems but rather on the personal devastation and problems caused by war. Billy Joel's "Goodnight Saigon," which pays tribute to American soldiers in Vietnam, features visuals of these soldiers. "Born in the USA," by Bruce Springsteen, also comments, mainly through the lyrics, about the personal experiences of an American asked to fight in Vietnam and his experiences upon returning home. Another Springsteen video, "War," shows a father and son watching their television screen filled with news scenes of combat and war. Springsteen is shown in concert performing the song until the end of the video, when the audience is returned to the scene of the father watching the television news accounts of the war, but, this time, the son is missing from the scene (suggesting he is fighting in the war or dead).

A final subcategory of War videos dealt with tension between the East and West or between the United States and the Soviet Union. In "Burning Heart" (the theme song of *Rocky IV*) by Survivor, scenes from the boxing match between the *Rocky* and the Soviet boxer dominate the video. The visuals of Rocky's triumph suggest an overall American triumph over the Soviets in an international war or contest. Frankie Goes to Hollywood's "Two Tribes" also uses a boxing ring to simulate a fight between the Americans and Soviets but with a less optimistic outcome. In this video, a boxer resembling Reagan and one resembling Brezhnev begin boxing in a ring with an international audience looking on. As the fight continues, both boxers become bloodied and weak, and the international "community" of onlookers is drawn into the fight as well, suggesting a "no win" outcome to any fight between the two superpowers or tribes.

Peace Videos

Similar in some ways to the War theme, the third theme featured prominently in the videos in this sample was a World Peace theme

The message of these videos used antiwar sentiments, but focused mainly on world peace and acceptance of different nations and different views. U2's "Pride (In the Name of Love)" paid tribute to the individuals who fought and died for the cause of peace, while Jon Anderson's "Easier Said Than Done" carried the message of world harmony and cooperation. "Love is the Seventh Wave" by Sting presented a message of a "rising tide" of love and peace against war and destruction. As animated tanks, soldiers, and helicoptors moved across the screen, they were replaced with flowers, doves, and symbols of peace to signify the replacing of world hostility with world harmony.

American Values Videos

The final category into which several videos in this sample fell is best described as an American or Western Values theme. In some of these videos, the message was a patriotic one, and the videos themselves were typically very upbeat and included scenes from American life, such as those in Bobby and the Midnights' "I Want to Live in America."

Other videos with this theme were critical of the encroachment of American or Western values on other cultures or the interference of the West in other nations' affairs. In "Rock the Casbah" by Clash, the visuals show an invasion of Western products and influences into the Middle East and the tensions there. The group is singing in a desert as warplanes fly over and visuals of an American presence are shown. David Bowie's "China Girl" presents the promises of Westernization of Chinese culture and specifically of a Chinese woman.

Political Symbols used in Videos

Although the political themes in these videos were sometimes clearer in the audio than in the video or vice versa, for the majority, the political theme was evident in both. In some instances, the lyrics were not clearly political to the coders or researchers, and only upon seeing the video, did the video take on a political meaning. In these instances, the visuals seemed to offer a way for the artist to structure the viewers' interpretation of the song or to more clearly offer an interpretation for them. The artist or group, in a sense, created a political message that was not apparent from the words of the song. In most cases, symbols were used to enhance the message, but sometimes the symbols featured gave the lyrics "new" meaning.

In the War and World Peace videos, symbols such as tanks, military aircraft, soldiers, uniforms, and artillery were used extensively to represent aggression and hostility. As mentioned, a boxing ring was used in some videos with different themes to represent a fight against authority or a contest between two nations. For those War Videos which focused on nuclear war, mushroom clouds were used in the gloomy end of the narrative. World Peace videos used the peace symbol and doves.

Children were used in both World Peace and War videos to symbolize those things at stake in a world at war or at peace. Several U. S. symbols were used, such as the flag, the Capitol, Liberty Bell, and the Lincoln Monument. In one video, where the problems and tensions in American society are being addressed, the characters in the video struggle under the weight of the Liberty Bell in order to move it ("Hell in Paradise" by Yoko Ono).

CONCLUSION

It is difficult to know what the influence of these political messages is on their young audience. Music videos are only one form of popular culture through which political myths are, as Nimmo and Combs (1980) suggest, presented, interpreted, and validated. This study provides only information on the presentation of political myths through music videos.

The political messages of the music videos analyzed here suggest that there are popular themes which are being addressed by artists. Many of the videos, particularly in the War and Oppression categories, made strong, disturbing statements about the conditions in which humans live and the likelihood of an unpleasant (if any) future if those conditions persist. There are few happy endings in the story lines of the narrative videos, with the exception of some of the World Peace or patriotic videos.

If Kinder (1984) is correct about the ability of videos to provide audiences with a "collective dream," the dream is not a pleasant one in political music videos. It is filled with threats of oppression and the inevitability of nuclear disaster. Although the dream offers some hope that world peace might be achieved through a grassroots effort, its strongest and basic contention is that the average person's future is manipulated and controlled by powerful (and sometimes inept or comical) political or authority figures.

REFERENCES

Aufderheide, P. (1986). Music videos: The look of the sound. *Journal of Communication, 36*, 57–78.

Baxter, R. L., DeRiemer, C., Landini, A., Leslie, L., & Singletary, M. W. (1985). A content analysis of music videos. *Journal of Broadcasting & Electronic Media, 29*, 333–340.

Brown, J. D., & Campbell, K. (1986). Race and gender in music videos: The same beat but a different drummer. *Journal of Communication, 36*, 57–78.

Gehr, R. (1983, August). The MTV aesthetic. *Film Comment, 19*, 37–40.

Jamieson, K. H. (1984). *Packaging the presidency*. New York: Oxford University Press.

Kinder, M. (1984). Music video and the spectator: Television, ideology and dream. *Film Quarterly*, 2–15.

Livingston, V. (1984, August 20). Battle of the broadbands: Turner takes on MTV. *Cablevision, 9*, 11–12.

Lynch, J. D. (1984). Music videos: From performances to Dada-Surrealism. *Journal of Popular Culture, 18*, 53–57.

Maultsby, P. K. (1983). Soul music: Its sociological and political significance in American popular culture. *Journal of Popular Culture, 17*, 51–60.

Meadow, R. G. (1980). *Politics as communication*. Norwood, NJ: Ablex Publishing Corporation.

Nimmo, D., & Combs, J. E. (1980). *Subliminal politics: Myths & mythmakers in America*. Englewood Cliffs, NJ: Prentice–Hall.

Orman, J. (1984). *The politics of rock music*. Chicago: Nelson–Hall.

Robinson, J. P. (1976). The rhetoric of revolt: Protest rock and drugs. *Journal of Communication, 26*, 125–136.

Smith, S. (1980). Sounds of the South: The rhetorical saga of country music lyrics. *Southern Speech Communication Journal, 45*, 164–172.

Sun, S., & Lull, J. (1986). The adolescent audience for music videos and why they watch. *Journal of Communication, 36*, 115–125.

Winders, J. A. (1983). Reggae, Rastafarians and revolution: Rock music in the Third World. *Journal of Popular Culture, 17*, 61–73.

9

Diary of a Generation: The Rhetoric of 1960s Protest Music

Raymond Sprague
Department of Music,
University of New Orleans

Kathleen J. Turner
Department of Communication,
Tulane University

> They must throughout be watchful against innovations in music . . .
> counter to the established order, and to the best of their power guard
> against them. . . . For the modes of music are never disturbed without
> unsettling of the most fundamental political and social conventions.
>
> Plato, *Republic:* IV, 424b, c

Throughout the course of history, people have attributed much to the power of music. The Greeks declared it indispensable in the training of youth; Renaissance theorists noted its potential to sway emotions; and 19th-century philosophers and musicians believed that music was the most perfect art form because of its ability to communicate ideas and emotions. This essay examines the ways in which the 1960s urban folksingers attempted to harness the persuasive powers of music. The traditions of the 1930s, the changing styles of the 1960s, and the issues of Vietnam protest provide an understanding of the ways in which these urban folksingers used music to educate, motivate, and activate their audiences.

THE ROOTS

The urban folk movement of the late 1950s and 1960s, including the music of protest against the Vietnam war, had its political and artistic roots in the urban folk movement of the 1930s and 1940s. Ethnic music fitted with new texts had long been used by workers as a means of mobilizing support for a cause. It was not until the Depression and

Dustbowl days of the 1930s, however, that singers advocated the conscious use of *American* folk tunes for political purposes. By the end of the 1930s, such musicians as Pete Seeger, Woody Guthrie, and Huddie Ledbetter, as well as the collection of groups calling themselves the Almanac Singers, were crisscrossing the country singing folksongs for any union rally or political cause that would address the plight of farmers and industrial workers.

The 1930s urban folksinger saw American folksong to be useful in several ways. The most obvious was its entertainment value at rallies, for the music kept large crowds occupied and interested between speakers. More significantly, folk music also reinforced the speakers' points while actively involving the crowd. By outfitting a well-known American folk tune with new words that described a problem and offered a political solution, the singer could deliver a message while having the crowd sing along on a regularly recurring refrain. The use of folksongs thus created a sense of community among the participants, brought the rallies' purposes to light in another manner, and enabled the audience to take home the political charge as the refrains echoed in their heads.

One example of a good song for these rallies (or "hootenannies," as they were sometimes called) paired the folktune "East Virginia" with lyrics that asked for a simple job with dignity. The well-known melody lay in a limited and therefore easily singable range. In addition, the repetitiveness of the verse-refrain structure allowed for the performers' perspective to be articulated in the verses while inviting audience participation in the refrain. In this version, the verses blamed the unnamed "mister" for taking away jobs and indulging in yachts and Rolls-Royces while the workers' children suffered; between each verse, the refrain echoed disdain for the mister's millions while simply asking for a job. The words were easily understood and singable; while most of the verses provided numerous examples of the problem, the last verse offered the political solution of the Farm–Labor party.

This transformation of "East Virginia" into "I don't want your millions, mister" illustrates the conscious efforts of the 1930s folksingers to keep the musical performance of these songs simple. The reason for this decision was twofold. First, a simple song with very little musical ornamentation was not as likely to be approached as an aesthetic experience. While a *volkslied* or folksong by Schubert elicits an audience response of rapt and quiet attention to the encounter with fine art, an encounter with a simple union song implies little of that fine art detachment and far more of the folk art response of audience involvement. Secondly, and as important, the air of simplicity engendered by the performance lent credence to the implication that the performer was "jes' folks" like the audience—even if the performer actually happened to be from an urban area, with a college education, and without a union laborer's job.

The 1930s urban folk movement, then, relied heavily on folk tradition for its appeal. The style of performance and the simple, direct way in which the lyrics stated the problem entailed a notable lack of art consciousness, for messages of change needed to be stated bluntly and succinctly. This bluntness, and the confrontational style of these songs, relegated the majority of them to an underground existence. In a popular music industry designed to help people escape their problems, not confront them, the 1930s urban folk musician's encounter with reality was not considered commercially viable.

In retrospect, it becomes apparent that the 1930s movement redefined folk music. Traditionally, folk music had been any song preserved via the oral tradition by a group of people. Yet the urban folksinger viewed any song that was designed to unite people, raise their collective consciousness, and ultimately improve their lot in life as being music *for* the masses and, by implication, a folksong. Folk music, then, was not only music of the folk but also music on behalf of the folk.

With the onset of World War II and the concomitant economic growth, songs protesting the workers' plight lost their impact and their audience. Many of the urban folksingers, already left-leaning in their political views, turned to songs in support of the war against the Axis powers and in support of America's ally, Russia. Even after the war, when the Soviet Union changed from ally to adversary, the socialist and communist ideologues of the movement continued to champion the use of folk music for sociopolitical change. In 1946, for example, Irwin Silber founded *The Peoples' Song Bulletin* (later published as *Sing Out*), a monthly magazine dedicated to social change through folk music. As a consequence, the postwar urban folk movement returned to its underground existence.

The appearance of the Weavers in 1948 heralded the first commercial successes of the urban folk movement. In 1951 the Weavers's version of "Good Night, Irene" became the first recorded folksong to sell a million copies, and the group enjoyed a relatively large success by singing both traditional folksongs and union songs from the 1930s and 1940s. However, the burgeoning popularity of urban folk music was nipped in the bud during the McCarthy era by its association with socialist elements. A number of folksingers were called before the McCarthy hearings to testify about their beliefs and actions. As a result, many—including Pete Seeger of the Weavers—were blacklisted by the recording, radio, and emerging television industries. Others had difficulty finding an audience given the "pinko" stigma attached to folk music by this anti-communist hysteria.

THE URBAN FOLK MOVEMENT OF THE 1960S

In 1958 the Kingston Trio helped to rejuvenate folk music by proving its commercial viability with their hit single "Tom Dooley," which sold a million copies. The trio served as the perfect ambassadors for the urban folk music revival, for they were apolitical, clean-cut, and collegiate (in the best sense of the word). Moreover, they presented folk music in a style that drew heavily from contemporary pop vocal styles. The musical polish and appeal of their work is obvious in "MTA," one of their pop chart successes. The song traced the harrowing experience of a man named Charlie, who hopped aboard Boston's mass transit system and was relegated to an underground existence because he lacked an extra five cents for the recently increased subway fare. While listeners probably didn't notice, "MTA" offered a spoof of the 1930s protest song. The song used folk instruments for its accompaniment (specifically unamplified guitars, banjo, and string bass) and a verse-refrain structure to encourage participation. In addition, the lyrics dealt with a topical social issue, mass transportation, and provided a mock political solution at the end. All of these traits are characteristic of 1930s urban folk music. However, the absurdity of the situation and the verbal asides (such as murmurs about scandal and analogies to Paul Revere) reassured the audience that this song was not to be taken seriously.

Such treatments of the folk idiom soon led folk music critics to scoff that the Kingston Trio's music was not real folk music. True, the group was apolitical, uninvolved, and in the end, not singing on behalf of the folk. Yet its musical polish was in fact no greater than that of performers perceived as more "folklike," and their material often came from traditional folk sources. Moreover, their instrumentation and accompaniments drew heavily from the bluegrass tradition.

Whatever the perception of the Kingston Trio, it cannot be denied that their successes created recording opportunities for other folksingers. Taking their cue from their 1930s predecessors and President John F. Kennedy's exhortation to "Ask not what your country can do for you, ask what you can do for your country," some of these singers saw themselves as messengers of change and spokespersons for the new order. They identified folk music as a way to raise consciousness and to effect change. These musical messengers differed from their predecessors, however, in that their songs were aimed not at the working class, but rather at a generation of college students, tomorrow's leaders, who were disengaging themselves from the perceived frivolities of high school experiences and rock and roll. Consequently, the form and content of the 1960s songs were different. Both music and lyrics became more complex as the performers and songwriters affected an art consciousness heretofore not found in folk music.

Consider, for example, the Peter, Paul, and Mary rendition of the Bob Dylan classic, "Blowin' in the Wind." Their spoken introduction frames the way in which the song is to be received; it calls not for an active or visceral reaction, but a cerebral response. For such a response to occur, the receiver needs to ponder not only the words and their artfulness, but also the artistic presentation that envelopes the delivery of the text. A comparison with Bob Dylan's version underscores this intent. While both use the same text and melodic/harmonic contours, Peter, Paul, and Mary provide an accompaniment that hearkens back to classical guitar stylings, and their vocal delivery exhibits a refinement and polish that contradict the appellation of "folk." Bob Dylan, on the other hand, uses a straightforward, simple guitar strum, and his gravelly vocal quality draws heavily on the stylings of Woody Guthrie. While Dylan's lyrics work from an art consciousness, his performance encapsulates the immediacy of the folk tradition.

Similarly, Peter, Paul, and Mary's "A-Soalin" transforms folk music with a high art performance. The tune and lyrics are drawn from such well-known children's rhymes as "it's raining, it's pouring, the old man is snoring." Yet the delicate contrapuntal lines of the accompaniment compete for the listener's attention with a vocal texture that increases in complexity with the use of canonic devices and free counterpoint. As a result, the rendition demands a response that is neither vocal nor participatory, but rather one of aesthetic valuation, thus underscoring the conception of folk music as art.

Folk musicians of the early 1960s adopted this intellectualized, art-conscious approach in order to appeal to the perceived audience for these songs. In addition, the folk music from this era, even protest songs, exuded an understated optimism that was based on the belief that folksingers could improve the plight of the world by singing their songs. The "folkies" saw themselves, then, as superior to other singers of pop music because of their perceived mission; and they particularly disdained rock and roll, which at this time was in the throes of its "Teen Angel--Purple People Eater--3 Chipmunks" stage. With their meaningful and poetic lyrics, unamplified instruments, ethnomusicological scholarship, and art consciousness, they saw themselves as the moral keepers of musical America.

As early as 1962, certain folk musicians, dissatisfied with the snail's pace of civil rights progress and with public indifference to the American involvement in Southeast Asia, became disillusioned. Such singers as Pete Seeger, Joan Baez, Judy Collins, Phil Ochs, and Tom Paxton eschewed art consciousness and began to deliver more direct and pointed messages. With the assassination of President Kennedy in November of 1963, the movement shattered, for the utter sense-lessness of the act rammed home the point that certain events could not be changed by rational discourse. Indeed, irrational acts often had greater impact.

Bob Dylan led the way to yet a new conception of folksong in 1964 and 1965. Such earlier Dylan songs as "The Times They Are a-Chang-ing" and "Blowin' in the Wind" were anthems of the 1960s, and his "Masters of War" became the quintessential antiwar song. Yet his im-pact as a singer-songwriter reached full force with his album *Highway 61 Revisited*. On this record Dylan merged his folksong style with a rock medium, a combination that dismayed many folk traditionalists. Moreover, the songs on this album exhibited both a pessimism and a fascination with an existentialist outlook not apparent in the earlier music of the movement. With this album and with such songs as "Positively 4th Street" and "Like a Rolling Stone," Dylan had defined the direction that the urban folk movement would take.

"Sounds of Silence" provides an excellent example of Dylan's per-vasive influence. Originally released in 1964 as one of the songs on the album *Wednesday Morning 3 A.M.*, the original version by Simon and Garfunkle, with its acoustic guitar accompaniment, was never popular. Immediately following the successes of Dylan's new style, Columbia released another version of the same song as a single, this time with an accompaniment that added drums, electric guitar, and electric bass to the original track. Both the single and the album of the same name sold more than a million copies. Moreover, "Sounds of Silence" and "Like a Rolling Stone" shared more than folk-rock mu-sical stylings. The lyrics of both songs dealt with alienation, isolation, and the feeling of helplessness in an uncaring and unfeeling world. Thus both songs carried not only a musical, but also a rhetorical mes-sage that struck responsive nerves in the assembled consciousness of young America. The idealism of a few years earlier had gone, and was replaced by bewilderment, frustration about an inability to change the system, and a sense that the older generation was unre-sponsive. That the protests should now be couched in rock music also made sense: Rock was the music of a younger generation, and in itself implied a discarding of an older generation's values.

While Bob Dylan showed the way, Simon and Garfunkle were two of the more prominent artists to explore actively the musical implications of his shift. From 1965 to 1968, their albums helped define the musical and poetic parameters of the folk-rock style. Furthermore, such albums as *Sounds of Silence* and *Parsley, Sage, Rosemary, and Thyme* exhibit an eclecticism that finds parallels in the albums of the Beatles from this time. The music from this period ranges from the simple acoustic stylings of songs such as "Cloudy," "Kathy's Song," and "April, Come She Will" to the rock stylings of songs such as "Blessed," "I am a Rock," and "A Simple Desultory Philippic." The common denominators for all of these songs are lyrics that exhibit poetic aspirations, the extensive use of metaphor, and art consciousness in the crafting of musical accompaniments and forms. Their approach to protest runs the gamut, too. At one end of the spectrum are generalized statements that stress an existentialist point of view; at the other are blunt, often acerbic commentaries on the ills of society.

The music of Simon and Garfunkle is thus typical of the approach that applies an art consciousness to lyric and music. A personal statement by the artist is the end result, and this statement is to be prized as much for its artfulness in its manipulation of materials as it is for its message. Several albums that are representative of this approach are *Bookends* by Simon and Garfunkle, *Album* and *Album 1700* by Peter, Paul, and Mary, and Judy Collins's *Wildflowers.* Included in this musical landscape of the updated urban folk movement were folksingers who addressed the question of American involvement in Southeast Asia.

VIETNAM PROTEST MUSIC

The evolving urban folk tradition found a particularly salient issue in the Vietnam conflict. Give the nature of popular music during the 1960s as well as the nature of the Vietnam protest, however, anti-Vietnam songs can either be found almost everywhere or hardly anywhere—depending on how they are defined and where they are sought. Songs that were clearly anti-Vietnam rarely made the radio play lists or the pop industry's charts. As Peter, Paul, and Mary suggested in "I Dig Rock and Roll Music," to say something directly meant that the radio wouldn't broadcast the record, so strong messages of protest appeared between the lines at best. Folksingers who wanted to reach large audiences with their messages, then, could write ambiguous lyrics that masked the song's social significance, or use increasingly complex musical accompaniments that also served a masking function. The alternative was to reach far smaller audiences through the kind of blunt, confrontational, noncommercial music of the 1930s urban folksinger.

Not only did the channels of popular communication place constraints on the messages of protest music, but so too did the complex nature of the Vietnam protest itself. A peace movement with its roots in the 1950s joined with feminism, civil rights, the New Left, and students' rights, and the ideas, claims, and accomplishments of one group sparked the activities of others. Protesters thus viewed Vietnam as symptomatic of broader social evils with a host of interrelated concerns. This complexity can be seen in the music. A number of songs explicitly link Vietnam with hatred, discrimination, capitalism, and a range of social ills. Others address the concatenation of social problems in such ambiguous terms that listeners can supply any number of interpretations. In "Sounds of Silence," for example, what is the neon god that "they" made and to which "they" prayed? And who are "they"?

Thus few antiwar songs dealt overtly and exclusively with Vietnam, and they rarely made it onto the pop charts. However, songs considering Vietnam as part of a complex of social evils and personal disillusionments, with indirect allusions, are everywhere during the 1960s. The selection of the channel and the delineation of the issue were thus critical variables for the writers and performers of 1960s Vietnam protest music.

Phil Ochs's "I Ain't a-Marchin' Anymore" appeared on an album by the same name in 1965—the same year as the first teach-in against the war, and the same year as the revitalized "Sounds of Silence." A direct descendant of the 1930s urban folk style, it incorporated a simple, acoustic guitar accompaniment with clearly enunciated lyrics: The audience was supposed to hear and understand the song's delineation of the problem. It was a direct, straightforward statement about reality as Ochs saw it, presenting a revisionist's view of history. The young always died in wars because they followed the older generation's orders. When Ochs exhorted in the refrain, then, "I ain't a-marchin' anymore," the young heard that to stop being killed they had to stop going off to war. *They* were the political solution to the problem. The rhythm of the frenetic guitar accompaniment exhorted the audience to march—but to a different drummer. Listeners were to understand the lyrics, but the slight variations in the length of the stanzas and in the final lines of each discouraged audience participation. Like Peter, Paul, and Mary, Ochs asked for a thoughtful rather than a vocal response. The audience was thereby circumscribed from joining in on such specifically antiwar songs as "I Ain't a-Marchin' Anymore." In contrast, the repetitive structure of the civil rights anthem "We Shall Overcome" encouraged audience participation. With verses adapted to the issue of Vietnam, this song was one of the most commonly used litanies at antiwar rallies.

The claim of the foolishness of going off to war is shared by "Alice's Restaurant." First performed by Arlo Guthrie at the Newport Folk Festival in July of 1967, two years after Ochs's album appeared, this song elongated the proposition into a convoluted light satire. The 17-minute rendition started with the establishment of Alice's Restaurant by a commune, whose members then took the trash from this little enterprise to the dump, where they got arrested for dumping without a permit. After recounting various escapades, the lyrics brought the characters around to draft registration at the Selective Service office, complete with paperwork, uptight officers, and the astonishing discovery that the arrests for littering barred them from being drafted.

For the majority of the 17-minute performance, the music was the constant repetition of a stylized guitar accompaniment, punctuated by the intermittent return of a sung refrain. The lyrics of the verses were spoken in a style reminiscent of Woody Guthrie's talking blues. The accompaniment set a calm, gentle background for the light satire of the lyrics, which mocked not only the establishment but also the protest movement. The irony of a litterbug who was not considered moral enough to commit murder was paired with the additional (albeit gentler) irony of an Alice's Restaurant movement peopled by folks like Arlo's father, Woody, who believed that singing about a problem could resolve it. Yet the satire was neither stinging nor caustic, for the message was nestled amidst lots of humorous cushioning in this lengthy narrative. The sharpest articulation of the litterbug-versus-murder morality received a rapid-fire delivery that evoked the audience's laughter. After racing through the point, Guthrie returned to the mild, folklike melody and the apparently unrelated refrain on which the audience could, 1930s-style, join in. This rhetorical and musical masking helps explain why, unlike "I Ain't a-Marchin' Anymore," "Alice's Restaurant" received some air time as a novelty song, even though it never made it to the charts.

In contrast to the lightly satirical narrative of "Alice's Restaurant," 1967 also saw the bitter allegory of "Waist Deep in the Big Muddy," based on an actual training camp incident in which Marine trainees drowned. After 17 years of being blacklisted by national networks,

Pete Seeger turned this song into a *cause célèbre* when he attempted to perform it on the Smothers Brothers prime-time television show. When the powers that be at CBS learned of Seeger's intention to perform "Waist Deep," they strongly suggested in rehearsals that he cut the last verse. Seeger refused to expunge it, with its Nixonian technique of declaring that it wouldn't point to a moral and then pointing to one. CBS retaliated by cutting the entire song from the videotape of the show before it aired. In the resulting brouhaha, the network backed down, and Seeger was invited back to the show to sing the song *in toto.*

The song's lyrics used an allegorical approach that encouraged audience involvement in an enthymematic decoding of the metaphors. The Big Muddy of the lyrics was the Mekong River, a synecdoche for Vietnam; the Big Fool, both by his height and by the magnitude of his folly, was Lyndon Johnson; the trainees in danger symbolized not only the armed forces in Southeast Asia but the American public as well. The first line said it was 1942, but the audience translated from this ostensible time to the applicable time, as it later would with *M*A*S*H,* underscoring our failure to learn from the past without blindly repeating it. There was a little burst of pleasure as each part of the puzzle was translated, and that very process of translation pulled the listener into the logic of the lyrics.

This logic, or world-view, was reinforced by the music. The calm rhythms, low tessitura, and repetitious, predictable melodic structures tied in with the narrator's commonsense approach, which contrasted all the more strongly to the insane, macho bravado of the Big Fool. Only at the end, when the allegory turned to a warning of imminent threat, did Seeger change the pervasive mood with the introduction of a rhythmically more active accompaniment that underscored the urgency of the message. As with "I Ain't a-Marchin' Anymore," the limited means of accompaniment and clear enunciation bespoke of rhetorical intent; the predictable musical and lyrical structure established audience expectations and psychological involvement; yet the changes in the lyrics and the variation of the refrain precluded musical participation by the audience. Those who would like to stay healthy, as the ending suggested, were to listen and learn from the song.

The mildly satirical narrative of "Alice's Restaurant" and the more bitter allegory of "Waist Deep in the Big Muddy" were joined in 1967 by two Simon and Garfunkle songs that are telling in their contrasts. One is "Silent Night/Seven O'Clock News." This song pits the duo's sweet, simple rendition of the Christmas classic against an announcer's reading of the evening news: drug overdoses, white backlash against Martin Luther King, Richard Speck's gruesome murder of seven student nurses, the antiwar protest hearings of the House Un-American Activities Committee, and finally former Vice-President Richard Nixon's prediction that the Vietnam war would continue for another 5 years, especially if protesters kept opposing the American mission there. The newscast was sledgehammer-blunt, yet sharpened by its juxtaposition with the carol's evocation of quiet, peace, and love. The directness of "Silent Night/Seven O'Clock News" relegated it to relative obscurity: It received little airtime, and popular mythology holds that it was banned from the airwaves in several cities.

Contrast this confrontational approach to that of Simon and Garfunkle's "Scarborough Fair/Canticle." The basis of this piece is a nonpolitical 16th-century English folksong about unrequited love. Initially presented by unison voices accompanied by a solo acoustic guitar, the melody was then repeated several times in an everchanging musical tapestry. The accompaniment became increasingly contrapuntal, and the textural complexity increased as harpsichord, electric bass, and chimes were added. Contributing to this complexity was the addition of a descant to the original melody, which created a thicker harmonic fabric and provided a contrapuntal foil. The lyrics of this descant, sung above the melody, began with pastoral references, and concluded with generals who had forgotten why their soldiers kill. Yet the musical complexity made it increasingly difficult for the listener to understand the words of the descant, despite the fact that those words grew increasingly specific with each verse. Thus, the primary message of the song was hidden in the descant of verse 4, by which time listeners were as taken with the artfulness of the complex musical filigree as they were with the lyrics. Musical accompaniment and texture were manipulated to mask the message, as Simon and Garfunkle explicitly used a technique that was often implied in other urban folksongs of the mid-1960s.

The song's juxtaposition of a 16th-century folksong with an antiwar message implied that the issue had been going on for much longer than we would have liked to admit. This suggestion of historical guilt was not new; Ochs recast the American Revolution in "I Ain't a-Marchin'," for example, and Pete Seeger had also implied a perpetual cycle in "Where Have All the Flowers Gone." Yet Simon and Garfunkle took this one step further, using musical devices not only to create an artistic statement, but also to provide a powerful contrast to the message. Other songs would emulate this approach, but "Scarborough Fair/Canticle" stands as one of the most powerful and moving antiwar statements ever made. With its musically and lyrically masked message, however, it spent 5 weeks in the Top Twenty.

By 1969, the mixture of musical approaches had spawned yet another type with the "I-Feel-Like-I'm-Fixin'-to-Die Rag." As the title indicates, this song by Country Joe and the Fish provided a musical theater of the absurd. From the common vaudeville-like fanfare, to the
Fourth of July burst of fireworks that dissolved into machine-gun fire,
the audience was thrust onto the midway of a bizarre carnival, complete with calliope, kazoo, and vendors hawking their games of
death. The confidence of "I Ain't a-Marchin'," the bemusement of "Alice," and the artfulness of "Scarborough Fair" disintegrated here in a
bitter burlesque of American consumer values. Listeners were exhorted to be the first to receive their son in a coffin. The insanity of
"Waist Deep" and the cruelty of "Silent Night" exploded here into
black comedy. Instead of the simple guitar accompaniment, "Fixin'-
to-Die Rag" rocked with a convoluted, almost chaotic panoply of carnival instruments. The result was a nihilistic vision: Because of the
total absurdity of the situation, we might as well whoop it up, because
we'll all get killed anyway.

The music of the Vietnam protest examined here is indicative of
the changes in the tenor of the antiwar movement itself. In 1965,
before the extensive escalation was publicized, the urban folk movement's lingering faith in the power of song is evident. By 1969, their
bitterness over their inability to influence the course of the war led to
a music of futility and rejection. The antiwar movement, always an
amorphous collection, would have to wait for Johnson's war to become Nixon's war in order to marshal the venom necessary to revital-
ize the assault.

Perhaps from this vantage point it is not surprising that certain folksingers found another mode of protest. Members of such groups as
Jefferson Airplane and the Grateful Dead, who had paid their musical
dues earlier in the folk movement, enacted their dissatisfaction by
adopting a counterculture, drug-related life-style. Songs that extolled
this life-style, then, such as "White Rabbit," also functioned as protest
against the status quo.

SUMMARY

Drawing from its roots in the 1930s, the urban folk movement of the
late 1950s and 1960s moved through three overlapping stages. The
first saw traditional folk music being used for both entertainment and
social action. While the second stage of the movement retained this
idealism, some disillusionment clouded the earlier optimism. Moreover, music from this second period often exhibited an art conscious-

ness and existential outlook not found in earlier folk music. Finally, disillusionment set in following Kennedy's assassination. American society looked darker and solutions less probable as the urban folk-singer retreated into an existential state in which artistic statement was as important as social message.

By the late 1960s the movement had shattered on the rock of artistic pretension. While some found solace in the drug counterculture, others remained preoccupied with their existentialist, artistic musings. Still others escaped to the imagined blandishments of rural America. Yet even as John Denver traveled his "country roads," he too was offering not solutions, but retreat from a complex world.

That the movement should end like this was inevitable. The smug self-assurance of the early urban folk crusader was shattered by the cataclysmic events of the 1960s. The longer and the more deeply the folksinger pondered these events, the clearer it became that no one song or one person could effect change. In the end, the most fitting eulogy for this movement that questioned even itself was delivered by Judy Collins in 1968. In the song "Both Sides Now," she emphasized the fact that things she once thought seemed obvious were no longer comprehensible. In the final analysis, then, the urban folk-singer really did not know life at all.

DISCOGRAPHY

Judy Collins, "Both Sides Now," *Wildflowers*, Elektra EKS–74012.

Country Joe and the Fish, "I-Feel-Like-I'm-Fixin'-to-Die Rag," *I-Feel-Like-I'm-Fixin'-to-Die Rag*, Vanguard 79266.

Bob Dylan, "Blowin' in the Wind," *Bob Dylan's Greatest Hits*, Columbia ST 9463.

Arlo Guthrie, "Alice's Restaurant," Reprise 0877.

Jefferson Airplane, "White Rabbit," *Surrealistic Pillow*, RCA LSP–3766.

Kingston Trio, "MTA," *Kingston Trio at Large*, Capitol T1199.

Phil Ochs, "I Ain't a-Marchin' Anymore," *I Ain't a-Marchin' Anymore*, Electra 7287.

Peter, Paul, and Mary, "A-Soalin'," *Peter, Paul, and Mary in Concert*, Warner Brothers 1555.

Peter, Paul, and Mary, "Blowin' in the Wind," *Peter, Paul, and Mary in Concert*, Warner Brothers 1555.

Peter, Paul, and Mary, "Where Have All the Flowers Gone?," *Peter, Paul, and Mary*, Warner Brothers W1449.

Simon and Garfunkle, "Scarborough Fair/Canticle," *Parsley, Sage, Rosemary, and Thyme*, Columbia CS9363.

Simon and Garfunkle, "Seven O'Clock News/Silent Night," *Parsley, Sage, Rosemary, and Thyme,* Columbia CS9363.

Simon and Garfunkle, "Sounds of Silence," *Wednesday Morning 3 A.M.,* Columbia CS9039.

Simon and Garfunkle, "Sounds of Silence," *Sounds of Silence,* Columbia CS 9269.

10

Political Culture and the Rhetoric of Country Music: A Revisionist Interpretation

Stephen A. Smith
Jimmie N. Rogers
Department of Communication,
University of Arkansas

It has been said that any country might be governed at the will of one who had the exclusive privilege of furnishing its popular songs.

James Madison

The rhetorical power of popular music has been recognized by theorists (Booth, 1974; Burke, 1969;) and political practitioners have recognized, feared, and attempted to suppress that power (Danto, 1986). Southern politicians, at least since Madison's remark in 1828, have recognized the political implications of the relationship between lyrical narrative and the resulting construction of social reality. Senators Albert Gore, Jr., of Tennessee and Ernest Hollings of South Carolina were outspoken leaders in recent Congressional attempts to restrict exposure to certain rock music lyrics—basing their attacks on the nature of the values condoned by the lyrics—and may well have expected some personal political advantage from opposition to the messages of various rock stars. On the other hand, Roy Acuff, Jimmy Swann, and Jimmie Davis each attempted to parlay their country music stardom into political power by running for governor of Tennessee, Mississippi, and Louisiana, respectively. Country music has long been a traditional feature of political barbeques, fish fries, and campaign rallies in the South (Smith, 1985), and Senator Howard Baker's sending a telegram to be read at the funeral of Tootsie Bess in Nash-ville was indicative of contemporary political homage paid to country music.

As president, Jimmy Carter viewed country music as a product of the rural South, expressing the values of that region in the lyrics in much the same manner as he did at the lectern. He called country music "part of the soul and conscience of our democracy," and said it reflected "the greatness, goodness and diligence of hard working men and women" (1978). Consequently, Carter often invited country singers such as Charlie Daniels and Willie Nelson to perform at White House gatherings. Once he was scheduled to play host to a White House dinner for stockcar racers but missed the event in order to meet with Begin and Sadat at Camp David, and at least one journalist thought that was a mistake. Lewis Grizzard said Carter should have been in Washington with the drivers and the pickers and should have included Begin and Sadat in the activities. "Give them a cold beer, and let them listen to Willie Nelson," he said. "After 'Blue Eyes Crying in the Rain' who would still want to fight?" (1984, p. 77).

Richard Nixon and his political compatriots appeared to have be-lieved that all country music fans were "patriotic, red-blooded, all-American vote fodder for conservative Republicans, and any affirma-tion of redneckism [was] therefore assumed to be a plus for the Presi-dent" (Gaillard, 1974, pp. 49–50). Nixon, who was titillated by and frequently requested such songs as "Welfare Cadillac," appeared on stage at the grand opening of the new Grand Ole Opry House and said that country music "comes from the heart of America. It talks about family. It talks about religion. And as we all know, country mu-sic radiates a love of this nation, a patriotism. . . . Country music . . . make [s] America a better country" (1975). A critic called the trend to country music "the trend that gave Nixon his mandate" for it was indicative of "the nation clarifying basic premises—home, job, faith—after a dangerous and anarchic decade when music was pre-eminently the tool of the radicals" (Mano, 1974, p. 90).

Country music lyrics often express certain political sentiments. However, like beauty, truth, and pornography, the country music message means different things to different people, and its interpre-tation has often escaped precise measurement, even by scholars and critics who have applied the tools of their various disciplines. Casual observers often assume that Merle Haggard's "Okie From Muskogee" (1969b) is the quintessential political statement of country music. Even some journals and books have advanced articles with such sug-gestive titles as "The 100% American Songbag: Conservative Folk-songs in America" (Truzzi, 1969), "Country Music: The Ballad of the

Silent Majority" (DiMaggio, Peterson, & Esco, 1972), and "Fundamentalism, Racism, and Political Reaction in Country Music" (Lund, 1972).

The diversity of themes in recorded country lyrics is so broad that one can find examples to support almost any hypothesis by selectively searching and choosing certain titles. Rather than conducting a search of obscure album cuts, unsuccessful singles, "B" sides of successful singles, under-the-counter recordings, or even limiting the sample to lyrics reprinted in *Country Song Roundup*, this study presents an analysis of the 50 most popular and commercially successful songs for the years 1960 through 1986 as determined by *Billboard* magazine. Primary attention was given to those songs popular enough to appear on the top fifty charts for any year from 1960 through 1986; however, those songs successful enough to make the weekly "Hot Country Singles" charts were also used as examples and to provide additional data. Since country music is still primarily a musical message delivered on singles, we contend that these communication artifacts contain the messages which have the greatest impact. These lyrics narratively display and rhetorically amplify the attitudes, beliefs, and behaviors that are within a psychological latitude of acceptance (or at least are so inoffensive they will not be instantly rejected) of the greatest number in the commercial country music audience (e.g., Booth, 1974, pp. 166–182; Burke, 1969, p. 69; Holsti, 1969, p. 82; Horstman, 1986, p. 231; Rogers, 1983). Such a sample, even unadjusted for the quirks in compiling the most popular lists, will more likely reflect those messages to which the audience repeatedly exposed itself, based on record sales, radio play, and jukebox activity, from 1960 to 1986.

The range of themes found in the most popular country songs is not as wide as that found in all recorded country music. More than 60% of the successful songs are about love relationships (Rogers, Rodgers, & Beasley–Rodgers, 1981). Most of the other songs are concerned with living as it is, should be, or could be. It is from this second group of songs that we can discover the most widely accepted attitudes about social, economic, and political events in this country; through these narrative "fantasy themes" about life, we can also understand one perspective on political ideology. In the song lyrics used in this study, the political philosophy presented in country music was found to be much more libertarian than suggested by either previous studies or former Presidents.

DiMaggio, Peterson, and Esco identified and acknowledged certain populist themes in the 200 songs selected in their study of country lyrics for 1950 to 1970, but they concluded that populism was on the wane and that the lyrics contained "several means of rationalizing failure short of questioning the American dream itself" (p. 51). Jens Lund suggested that the country music message was essentially one of fundamentalism, racism, and political reaction (pp. 90–91). The results of this study, however, demonstrate that libertarian politics and populist economics are the values most frequently articulated in the rhetoric of popular commercial country music lyrics and that the rejection of authoritarianism, institutional structures, and even, at times, the "American Dream" is so pervasive as to border on anarchism. Such a philosophical stance, as demonstrated below, can be found and illuminated with regard to aspects of race relations, politics, and economics.

RACE RELATIONS: "WHITE MAN SINGIN' THE BLUES"

Several studies (Jellicorse, 1974; King, 1974; Rodgers 1981) have suggested that country music, as a convenient rhetorical vehicle which reflected Southern social norms, was a popular outlet for the expression of white racism. While one can cite under-the-counter records with limited sales or a few "put-on" albums, such as those by Kinky Friedman, to support that view, this analysis of the lyrics of the most popular country music revealed something quite different. Indeed, while not one song reflecting racist attitudes appeared on the annual charts of the top fifty singles, there were numerous songs with varying commercial success which reflected an interracial understanding that has developed from shared personal experiences and obvious class affinity. Bobby Goldsboro and Tanya Tucker each recorded in 1974 Bobby Braddock's "I Believe The South Is Gonna Rise Again," which posits a vision of interracial harmony much like that found in Martin Luther King, Jr.'s "I Have A Dream" oration. Other examples of this emerging genre are Tony Joe White's "Willie And Laura Mae Jones" (1969), Johnny Russell's "Catfish John" (1972), Kenny Rogers's version of "Reuben James" (1969), and Tony Booth's version of "Irma Jackson" (1970).

The most significant finding of the present study in the area of race relations is the discovery of only four songs on the annual top fifty charts which make specific references to racial minorities. Johnny Cash's "The Ballad of Ira Hayes" (1964) expresses sympathy for the plight of an Indian who was among the heroes of Iwo Jima, but who died a broken, forgotten man. Henson Cargill's "Skip a Rope" which was No. 1 on the charts for 5 weeks in 1968, suggested that there was nothing humorous about a children's game which parroted parents' philosophies concerning always playing to win despite any rules and also hating a "neighbor for the shade of his skin" (1967). Tom T. Hall's "(Old Dogs—Children And) Watermelon Wine," which achieved No. 1 status in 1973, tells a bit of advice which the songwriter received from an "old gray black gentleman" who says, "God bless the children while they're still too young to hate" (1972). In the most recent song in this category, the upbeat hit "America," Waylon Jennings declares that all his brothers are black and white and yellow. He also insists that red man has a right to expect "a little from you" and then admonishes America to "promise and then follow through" (1984).

It may be, as suggested by Tony Joe White in "Willie and Laura Mae Jones," that the people depicted in most country songs are so busy trying to survive they have little time to worry about the color of other people's skin (1969); it might be that they perceive themselves as a minority group in contemporary America and recognize shared discrimination with other minorities; or it may be that radio station managers have been concerned about minority challenges to their FCC licenses. Whatever the cause, racism cannot be said to be a major theme among the songs which achieved commercial success, and country music cannot be said to create or reinforce racism among its audience—just ask Charley Pride's accountant.

LAW AND POLITICS: "AMERICA COMMUNICATE WITH ME"

After hearing Merle Haggard's "Okie From Muskogee" (1969b) and "The Fightin' Side of Me" (1969c) some critics have suggested that the country music message is a lyric version of "My country, right or wrong" and have stereotyped the music and the audience as the epitome of the reactionary forces of "law and order." Numerous songs about prison life indicate that violation of the law is a rather common practice in the mythic reality of the world of country music. Respect for or obedience to the law is not one of the major themes, and the opposition ranges from a song which expresses a benign disrespect for a city ordinance (Billy Edd Wheeler's "Ode to the Little Brown Shack Out Back," 1964) to one which advocates the active violation of laws such as speed limits, toll charges, weight limits, and ICC logs in C. W. McCalls's No. 1 hit, "Convoy" (1975).

Predominant among recent songs which refer to the government and its actions is the theme that those who propose and enact the laws, even the "conservative" administration of Ronald Reagan, are viewed with skepticism and cynicism set to music. Hank Williams, Jr., in his song "I'm For Love," surveys the infighting among various levels of government, then observes that the people are "against the politicians, and the highway still ain't paved" (1985). In his satirical view of "The American Dream," Williams (1982) again focuses on the hypocrisy of politicians by describing Reagan's stated intention to control inflation and stop spending and then observes that the new tax increase is the biggest in history. The singer feels that the circular reasoning and behaviors of the politicians just leave the citizen in a hole.

Mac Davis, in "The Beer Drinking Song," also despairs over political solutions to the problems of the average citizen. He wants to know why the Social Security system is failing and asks "Where the hell's all the money we paid?" After the specific concern for a national problem, he gets more universal in scope and reinforces Williams's "hole theory" by lamenting that "if the commies don't take us, Reganomics 'll break us" (1982).

One reason that the *dramatis populi* in country music lyrics despair of political efficacy is that they see the federal government as being insensitive to their needs. Another explanation for the apparent disregard for government authority is the perception that the statutes and the system unfairly discriminate against the average country music citizen—a theme not uncommon in the populist rhetoric of the 19th century. Jerry Reed's "She Got The Goldmine (And I Got The Shaft)" (1982) is an obvious indictment of the "justice" dispensed by the legal system. Reed explains that he intended to be reasonable following the breakup of a marriage and to divide the joint property equally, but the court entered an order that the felt was unfair. The singer found that after the court ruled that his former wife was to receive the house, the children, and both the cars, the judge then began to discuss child support. He was sure it was some kind of mistake because, if his addition was correct, the court ruled that he was to give much more than he had. Similar sentiments about a stacked deck are also expressed by John Conlee in "Working Man," when he complains about a policeman's vigilance with a radar gun and a notice from the IRS telling him that his taxes are "a big mess." He wonders, "is this the way the good life's supposed to be" (1985).

Executive agencies are also seen as operatives for the wealthy and as opponents of the average citizen. Johnny Paycheck's 1978 hit, "Me And The I.R.S.," is an example of this theme. He begins his narative by insisting that he is to going to tell the IRS that he has had enough of them, for the "big man rakes it in" while the "little man coughs it up." He repeats this primary objection to the different treatment of the "big man" and "little man" and his inability to survive with "Uncle Sam's hands" in his "pants." After deciding not to pay any more he insists that the IRS does not intimidate him. He then suggests he will reconsider his decision not to participate in the process if the government will require everyone to pay his or her fair share, but since this is not the case he tells the IRS to "put your 1040 form where the sun don't shine." In an afterword to the song, Paycheck calls the IRS agents "bloodsuckers," and asks "Did you ever see Dracula in a gray flannel suit?" Not only is he angered at the policies on collecting taxes, he is outraged at the way revenues are spent. "Hell, you could take what they spent to study the sex habits of the South American swamp rat and keep us in beer for the next hundred years!"

Guy Drake (1969) also expresses his opposition to government spending in "Welfare Cadillac," but not all country songs reject the social and economic programs of the New Deal era. In his 1961 hit "Po' Folks," Bill Anderson laments that his granddaddy's pension of $1.33 "was ten dollars less than the landlord wanted for rent" without any suggestion that $1.33 was too much money or a wasteful government expenditure. He further admits that the Salvation Army provided clothing for the family and "a man from the county came to cut our hair." Bob McDill's populistic "Song of the South" not only discussed participation in New Deal programs but also venerated them as a salvation from an unrewarding economic system. The songwriter described a situation that was rather typical for the times when he relates how a family was told that Wall Street fell. The family was "so damn poor we couldn't even tell" (Russell, 1980). After they suffer sickness and the loss of the farm, the family moved to town. The father gets a job with the Tennessee Valley Authority after the move, and they are then able to survive.

ECONOMICS: "NOTHING BEHIND YOU, NOTHING IN SIGHT"

Without having to consult census data to confirm the demographics of the population in the rhetorical vision of the country music world, one can understand that the working poor are predominant. In "Forty Hour Week," after eulogizing an itemized who's who of the proletariat, Alabama sings they "work hard every day" and proclaims that the "fruits of their labor are worth more than their pay" (1980).

DiMaggio, Peterson, and Esco also suggested that the lyrics of country music bemoan the economic structure but fall short of rejecting the system and the American Dream of success through hard work. Two songs in this study seem to lend support to their thesis. Bill Anderson's "Laid Off" portrays the plight of a man and his wife who both lose their jobs on the same day, but says they will make it even though they will be on their knees asking the Lord to help while they are out of work (1982). Merle Haggard's "If We Make It Through December" tells of a man who "can't afford no Christmas" because, despite his diligent efforts and hard work, "got laid off down at the factory" (1973). Although he feels that "their timing's not the greatest in the world," he expresses hope for the future if his family can just make it through the winter. Haggard is less optimistic, however, in this 1969 hit, "Hungry Eyes," in which he concludes that "another class of people put us somewhere just below," and he laments that their prayers and hard work only brought a loss of courage (1968).

Hopelessness is more clearly expressed in Charley Pride's "Down on the Farm." He bemoans the plight of farmers who "never thought of giving it up," but who are now "staring out a factory window, trying to understand it all." Despite their hard work, they discover that "a way of life can be auctioned off," and despaired, "It was only the family farm, who really cares if it's gone." Poignantly, Pride acknowledges that, "somebody's dreams are gone" (1985). As Hank Williams, Jr., sang of the situation, the "banker's against the farmers; the farmer's against the wall" (1985). John Conlee brought Harlan Howard's classic "Busted" back on the charts in 1981; it is another song which depicts hard times, contemplates stealing to survive, and despairs of any possible solutions to the economic woes facing the family. Merle Haggard comes to the same conslusions in "A Working Man Can't Get Nowhere Today" (1977).

Conlee's version of "Nothing Behind You, Nothing In Sight" is one of the finest and clearest statements of how working men and women feel about their plight. He tells of how all week he sells his time to a company that is interested only in using his body and cares nothing for his mind, and of the lack of hope generated when the worker knows that all his tomorrows will be just alike, that there is nothing behind you and nothing in sight "when the worries have stolen the dreams from your night" (1982). He describes the plight of a woman who works in the home from "daylight to midnight" with no monetary rewards, but astutely observes that "what she needs most is some time all her own." Another Conlee hit, "Working Man" (1985), echoes the same themes. He describes a working man who must adapt to a supervisor on an assembly line who is usually in a mood to disapprove of all his efforts. The worker notes that all the others on the line have worried faces just like his, and that they are "showing the wear and tear in their eyes." He suggests that the system itself makes it hard on a working man who makes a living any way he can while barely existing on the installment plan.

Conlee's songs leave little hope for improvement and offer no solutions, and McGuffey Lane's "Making a Living's Been Killing Me" (1982) also rejects the dream without satisfactorily resolving the dilemma. He is being underpaid for overtime work and the money he is paid cannot buy any peace of mind. The frustration is compounded when the foreman tells him that 300 more will be laid off in the near-future, when he will probably be waiting his turn in the unemployment line. Lane also introduces the element described earlier by Paycheck and others, that the people at the top of the ladder are becoming richer while those at the bottom pay the taxes and have less than they need to survive.

Perhaps the best known song in this genre, due to its exposure as the theme song for a movie and a television series, is Dolly Parton's "9 to 5." While the movie suggested that the song was about secretaries in corporate offices, the lyrics are equally applicable to other occupations. Parton reinforces the idea that the worker is barely surviving and that the employers are always taking but seldom giving. Unlike the man in Conlee's song, she suggests that they do use the worker's mind, but do not give them credit for what they produce and that this will "drive you crazy if you let it" (1980).

The lyrics of "9 to 5," like those cited earlier, attribute part of the blame to management ("They let you dream just to watch them shatter"); however, more fault is found with the system ("It's a rich man's game, no matter what they call it"). In general, the economic system is seen as being no more fair than the legal and political systems discussed earlier. Johnny Cash and his friends expressed no guilt or moral constraints when they decided to steal a Cadillac "One Piece At A Time," because the large and impersonal "G.M. wouldn't miss just one little piece" (1975). Furthermore, to sweeten his victory over the economic system, Cash's hero also delighted in the havoc created at the courthouse when it took the whole staff to type the 60-pound title to his newly acquired vehicle.

Contrary to the conclusions of investigators who have focused on the alleged work ethic, considerable resentment toward the system is expressed in these lyrics. In one song a man convicted of murder admits his failure in society and in his personal life, but proudly boasts, "I Never Picked Cotton" (Clark, 1970). McGuffey Lane's hero in "Making a Living's Been Killing Me" decides to quit his job and go "where it don't make a damn what the boss man says" and Johnny Paycheck's "Take This Job And Shove It" (1977) expresses a similar disdain for the degrading system and his superiors.

While Paycheck's protagonist suggests that his foreman is "a regular dog" and his line boss a "fool," he merely expressed his contempt verbally. Johnny Cash, in Jerry Chesnut's "Oney" (1972), however, tells of a man who is retiring after 29 years in a shop, and is looking forward to a little nonverbal expression more than he is to a new gold watch. The worker in this song notes that the manual labor has built his muscles, whereas Oney (the foreman) has gotten soft. When the whistle blows to end the worker's last day on the job, he plans to pay Oney back for all the nights of sleep he missed and will finally show Oney who is the real boss with a "right hand full of knuckles."

The lyrics cited above seem to suggest that contemporary country music does actively question, in the traditional populist spirit, the fairness of the economic system. Other songs go even further, questioning the underlying values of the American Dream itself. Loretta Lynn's "Success" (1962) discusses the damage done to a personal relationship by a husband's pursuit of the dream, and a related theme was also raised in the chorus of Hank Williams, Jr.'s "American Dream," where he questions whether we want or really need the dream because all it does is drive us crazy (1982).

CONCLUSIONS: "LONG HAIRED COUNTRY BOY"

An examination of those songs which received the widest attention and acceptance by the country music audience from 1960 through 1986 suggests that many of the stereotypes of the country music message should be revised. The most popular songs, when taken as a group, offer a message that contradicts previous studies.

The *songs of living* indicate that the protagonist in most country songs is an individual seeking maximum freedom from any system, whether it be social, political, or economic. While they may not advocate the overthrow of any institution or system, there is little evidence to indicate they plan to suffer the resulting pain quietly. The freedom they seek is that of individuals trying to get through life with few outside constraints on their personal freedom—a freedom only infrequently and grudgingly sacrificed even to a spouse or the immediate family. Outside of this close circle, there is little support for any type of formally recognized group or organization.

The fierce individualism portrayed may help to explain the lack of references to racial matters in the songs. Since the music is primarily one of personal relationships, there is seldom any comment on groups of individuals. Formal or informal clusters are seldom mentioned. The sorrow and joys highlighted are those applicable to any person regardless of race, creed, or color. There is no support for the claim of racism in commercially popular music and little, except that previously seen material, which even refers to race.

The lyrics offer little support for any law, whether the law is generally perceived as for the public good or not. The characters portrayed in the songs resent being told what to do by anyone. A few songs support our national government, some (especially the songs expressing regional preferences) find satisfaction with particular political environments, and a few will support a political or governmental unit if it is attacked by outside forces; however, the primary emphasis is once again on the individual's exasperation with constraints levied by those outside the primary group.

If there is group identification, it is found in economic class consciousness. Many of the country music people encounter economic problems. These range from those identified by Dolly Parton's "In the Good Old Days (When Times Were Bad)" (1968) and in Loretta Lynn's "Coal Miner's Daughter" (1970), which reflect on life in the past, to songs of the present which describe people working at menial and boring jobs in modern factories or going belly up on the farm. The important finding here is the emphasis on unsatisfactory working conditions and the fatalistic lack of faith in ever fulfilling the American Dream. It is in this area where we find the greatest interest in group identification—poor or hard-working folks. Poor-but-proud is a common theme, followed closely by poor-but-better. Several of the love songs contain the latter theme. A poor man, who lost a lover to a rich man, implies that he is probably a better sexual partner than the rich man in "The Door Is Always Open" (Dave and Sugar, 1976), and a woman who married a man for his money admits the poor man she deserted was a superior lover in "Satin Sheets" (Pruett, 1973).

Moreover, in the songs emphasizing living, the theme of a class or group taking advantage of the poor is prevalent. We have offered examples from the songs of Merle Haggard, Johnny Paycheck, John Conlee, and Johnny Cash in particular. The "us vs. them" tactic so popular with politicians also finds favor in these messages. They often mention that they cannot identify with others outside their group. For instance, "Rednecks, White Socks, and Blue Ribbon Beer" suggests that these people described in the song are a little too noisy and loud to "fit in with that white collar crowd" (Russell, 1973).

Whatever the cause of the economic hardship, the solution is most often an individual one. "Busted" contains a reference to stealing for a living, but most are like the man found in Haggard's "Workin' Man Blues" (1969a) who will keep his nose to the grindstone and drink a little beer with his friends on the weekend. Although Hank Williams, Jr., sings that "the union is against the workers working against their will" (1985) there is little support for organizing a union, for this would be the antithesis of individualism and represent the forfeiting of cherished freedoms. These lyric heroes would be just as unlikely to join the Chamber of Commerce, nor do they seem inclined to flock to the Klu Klux Klan or the local bass club, either.

These "AM Anarchists" are individuals, and they prefer it that way. They covet few other life-styles and will defend their way of life in some of the most fascinating verbal ways imaginable. They do not particularly care what others might think of the way they act, work, or spend their free time, and—perhaps ironically—they will go out of their way to tell the world how they feel. As Charlie Daniels said in "Long Haired Country Boy," they are asking for nothing they cannot get on their own and if that is unsatisfactory to you then just leave them alone (1980).

REFERENCES

Booth, W. C. (1974). *Modern dogma and the rhetoric of assent*. Chicago: University of Chicago Press.

Burke, K. (1969). *A rhetoric of motives*. Berkeley: University of California Press.

Carter, J. (1978, October 2). Country music month, October 1978. In *Weekly compilation of presidential documents, 14*(39), 1653.

Danto, A. C. (1986). *The philosophical disenfranchisement of art*. New York: Columbia University Press.

DiMaggio, P., Peterson, R. A., & Esco, J., Jr. (1972). Country Music: Ballad of the silent majority. In R. S. Denisoff & R. A. Peterson (Eds.), *The sounds of social change* (pp. 38–55). Chicago: Rand McNally.

Gaillard, F. (1974, May–June). Sour notes at the Grand Ole Opry. *Southern Voices*, pp. 49–50, 77.

Grizzard, L. (1984). *Kathy Sue Loudermilk, I love you*. New York: Warner Books.

Holsti, O. R. (1969). *Content analysis for the social sciences and humanities*. Reading, MA: Addison–Wesley.

Horstman, D. (1986). *Sing your heart out, country boy* (rev. ed.). Nashville, TN: Country Music Foundation Press.

Jellicorse, J. L. (1974, June). *Myths and values in southern white racist music*. Paper presented at the Conference on Rhetoric of the Contemporary South. Boone, NC.

King, F. (1974, July) Red necks, white socks, and Blue Ribbon fear. *Harper's*, pp. 30–31, 34.

Lund, J. (1972). Fundamentalism, racism, and political reaction in country music. In R. S. Denisoff & R. A. Peterson (Eds.), *The sounds of social change* (79–91). Chicago: Rand McNally.

Mano, D. K. (1974, January 18). Going country. *National Review*, 89–90.

Nixon, R. M. (1975, March 25). The Grand Ole Opry. In *Weekly Compilation of Presidential Documents, 10*(12), 333.

Rodgers, R. S. (1981). Images of rednecks in country music: The lyrical persona of a southern superman. *Journal of Regional Culture, 1,* 71–81.
Rogers, J. N. (1983). *The country music message.* Englewood Cliffs, NJ: Prentice–Hall.
Rogers, J. N., Rodgers, R. S., & Beasley–Rodgers, P. J. (1981, March). *The country music message: An analysis of the most popular songs from 1965 to 1980.* Paper presented at the meeting of the Popular Culture Association, Cincinnati.
Smith, S. A. (1985). *Myth, media, and the southern mind.* Fayetteville: University of Arkansas Press.
Truzzi, M. (1969). The 100% American songbag: Conservative folksongs in America. *Western Folklore, 28,* 27–38.

DISCOGRAPHY

Alabama. (1980). Forty hour week (for a living). [Single No. PB–14085]. RCA.
Anderson, Bill. (1961). Po' Folks. [Single No. 57038]. Decca.
Anderson, Bill. (1982). Laid Off. [Single No. 1011]. Southern Tracks.
Booth, Tony. (1970). Irma Jackson. [Single No. 14112]. MGM.
Cargill, Henson. (1967). Skip a rope. [Single No. 1041]. Monument.
Cash, Johnny. (1964). The ballad of Ira Hayes. [Single No. 43058]. Columbia.
Cash, Johnny. (1972). Oney. [Single No. 45660]. Columbia.
Cash, Johnny. (1975). One piece at a time. [Single No. 103321]. Columbia.
Clark, Roy. (1970). I never picked cotton. [Single No. 17349]. Dot.
Conlee, John. (1981). Busted. [Single No. 52008]. MCA.
Conlee, John. (1982). Nothing behind you, nothing in sight. [Single No. 52070]. MCA.
Conlee, John. (1985). Working man. [Single No. 52543]. MCA.
Daniels, Charlie. (1980). Long haired country boy. [Single No. 5084–5]. Epic.
Dave and Sugar. (1976). The door is always open. [Single No. 10625]. RCA.
Davis, Mac. (1982). The beer drinkin' song. [Single No. 23551]. Casablanca/Polygram.
Drake, Guy. (1969). Welfare Cadillac. [Single No. 1]. Royal American.
Goldsboro, Bobby. (1974) I believe the South is gonna rise again. [Single No. 422]. United Artists.
Haggard, Merle. (1968). Hungry eyes. [Single No. 2383]. Capitol.
Haggard, Merle. (1969a) Workin' man blues. [Single No. 2503]. Capitol.
Haggard, Merle. (1969b). Okie from Muskogee. [Single No. 2626]. Capitol.
Haggard, Merle. (1969c). The fightin' side of me. [Single No. 2719]. Capitol.
Haggard, Merle. (1973). If we make it through December. [Single No. 3746]. Capitol.
Haggard, Merle. (1977). A working man can't get nowhere today. [Single No. 4477]. Capitol.
Hall, Tom T. (1972). (Old dogs—children and) watermelon wine. [Single No. 73346]. Mercury.
Jennings, Waylon. (1984). America. [Single No. 13908]. RCA.

Lane, McGuffey. (1982). Making a living's been killing me. [Single No. 52070]. Atlantic.

Lynn, Loretta. (1962). Success. [Single No. 31384]. Decca.

Lynn, Loretta. (1970). Coal miner's daughter. [Single No. 32749]. Decca.

McCall, C. W. (1975) Convoy. [Single No. 14839]. MGM.

Parton, Dolly. (1968). In the good old days (when times were bad). [Single No. 9657]. RCA.

Parton, Dolly. (1980). 9 to 5. [Single No. PB–12133]. RCA.

Paycheck, Johnny. (1977). Take this job and shove it. [Single No. 50469]. Epic.

Paycheck, Johnny. (1978). Me and the I.R.S. [Single No. 50539]. Epic.

Pride, Charley. (1985). Down on the farm. [Single No. PB–14045]. RCA.

Pruett, Jeanne. (1973). Satin sheets. [Single No. 40015]. MCA.

Reed, Jerry. (1982). She got the goldmine (and I got the shaft). [Single No. PB–13268]. RCA.

Rogers, Kenny. (1969). Reuben James. [Single No. 0854]. Reprise.

Russell, Johnny. (1972). Catfish John. [Single No. 0810]. RCA.

Russell, Johnny. (1973). Rednecks, white socks, and Blue Ribbon beer. [Single No. 0021]. RCA.

Russell, Johnny. (1980). Song of the South. [Single No. 57038]. Mercury.

Tucker, Tanya. (1974). I believe the South is gonna rise again. [Single No. 10069]. Columbia.

Wheeler, Billy Edd. (1964). Ode to the little brown shack out back. [Single No. 617]. Kapp.

White, Tony Joe. (1969). Willie and Laura Mae Jones. In Black and White. [LP No. 18114]. Monument.

Williams, Hank, Jr. (1982). The American dream. [Single No. 7–69960–C]. Elektra.

Williams, Hank, Jr. (1985). I'm for love. [Single No. 7–29022]. Warner Bros.

11

The Working American's Elegy: The Rhetoric of Bruce Springsteen

Michael R. Hemphill and Larry David Smith
Speech Communication Department,
University of Arkansas at Little Rock

Every generation has had its music: the folk anthems of the Depression, the big band sounds of World War II, the jazz of the Eisenhower years, the radical compositions of the 1960s, the disco beat of the 1970s, and the urban-based rhythms of the 1980s. Yet, the most enduring musical form of the 20th century may be rock and roll. A product of the 1950s, rock and roll represents a unique blend of blues, folk music, and jazz that mirrors three decades of rapid and oftentimes overwhelming societal change.

The emotion-releasing beat of rock and roll music no doubt provides a source of entertainment for a variety of audiences. However, to limit rock and roll's impact to that of entertainment is to do a gross injustice to this form of artistic expression. Since Bill Haley and the Comets' "Rock Around the Clock" overscored the opening credits of the movie *The Blackboard Jungle,* rock and roll has been inexorably connected with the dreams and frustrations of people searching for a better life.

Though not concerned with rock and roll Burke (1973) discussed how public messages describe realities for audiences by interpreting the affairs of daily living. By suggesting that artistic efforts contain "medicine" or "equipment for living" (p. 303), Burke argued that these symbolic enactments present people with knowledge of life's situations through prescriptive proverbs or stories. Whether these stories are expressed through a speech, a news account, or the lyrics of a song, the tales that artists weave reflect qualities that audiences may use in the negotiation of their daily lives.

One artist whose rock and roll narratives have provided medicine for audiences around the globe is New Jersey's Bruce Springsteen. Humphries and Hunt (1986) claimed that Springsteen maintains a "commitment to the roots and traditional qualities of rock'n'roll" since he "is linked to the full vitality of that culture" (p. 7). These writers also observed that "Springsteen is a particularly American artist" as his music contains the "same qualities as Thomas Wolfe in writing, of John Ford and Martin Scorsese in the cinema, of Edward Hopper in painting and of Woody Guthrie and Robert Johnson in folk music" (p. 7).

Springsteen often sings of those whose lives are in despair, whose successes are few, and whose dreams are of a better day. In this regard he has been cast as a common person's poet in that his narratives articulate realities many would prefer to ignore (Simels, 1981). In doing so, Springsteen's work functions not unlike those of artists in literature, theater, and cinema, since his music not only entertains, but also provides knowledge of the social sphere of human existence.

It is this function of Springsteen's music that motivates this critical venture. Through Burke's "representative anecdote" (Burke, 1969, pp. 59–62) we seek to chart how these constructions of social reality provide audiences with knowledge of their political world. In pursuing this goal, we will first overview our theoretical perspective, consider Springsteen's qualities as a narrator, and conclude with an analysis of his music through an anecdote we call the *worker's elegy*.

SOCIOLOGICAL CRITICISM: AN OVERVIEW

Burke's (1973) sociological criticism rests on his notion of ritual drama which he described as the "culminating form" of the "situations and acts" of the "social sphere" of life (p. 103). To Burke, the activities of daily living appear in recurrent patterns; therefore, the various forms of ritual drama reflect the essential natures of those patterns. One symbolic form in which ritual drama appears is narrative. Through narrative people learn of life's roles via an identification with the contents of a given tale or set of stories.[1] In other words, Burke argued that narrative offers equipment for living through its

---

[1] For more on identification and the fundamental elements of Burkean methodology see Burke (1965, 1966) and Nichols (1983).

capacity to "size up situations" and present people with "strategies for handling them" (1973, pp. 296–304).

Central to this process is the narrative's structure, since it follows "discursively a pattern that people might follow in reality" (Brummett, 1984a, p. 164). Chatman's (1978) structuralist theory addressed this facet of a narrative. Chatman argued that the two basic components of a narrative are the story (i.e., the characters and events) and the discourse (i.e., the means by which the tale is expressed or communicated). Chatman claimed that "the story is the *what* in a narrative" whereas the discourse, or "manifestation," represents "the *how*" (pp. 19–22).

The distinction between story and discourse is important in an analysis of rock and roll music. For instance, Simels (1982) invoked Chatman's discourse dimension when he observed the impact of the "resolutely leaden" (p. 100) melodies employed by Springsteen in some of his songs. While the manifestations of expression used by Springsteen are certainly a topic of interest, that feature of his labors must be reserved for another moment. Our challenge involves an interpretation of the content of Springsteen's narratives as they offer constructions of social reality for his highly heterogeneous audience. For assistance, we turn to Burke's representative anecdote.

Brummett (1984a) stated that unlike the more word-specific pentadic or cluster argon methods, the anecdote is a macroscopic Burkean tool. Specifically, an anecdote constitutes "a lens, filter, or template through which the critic studies and reconstructs" the subject matter in a way that "follows a dramatic plot" (p. 163).

This technique requires us to abstract from a selected body of discourse a representative plot or story line. The critic may use this method in a synecdotal fashion by examining an individual piece of discourse such as a particular song. Our interest, however, is an artist's entire body of work. For this task Brummett (1984b) recommended his metaphorical approach, that is, "looking for an anecdote that underlies groups of discourses . . . something that ties the discourses together, a characteristic they all share" (p. 6). Brummett (1984b) continued by noting that "people rarely rely on a single discourse as equipment for living" in favor of contemplating "groups of discourse" (p. 6).

Here we interpret Springsteen's music through Brummett's metaphorical technique. Such a strategy allows for a macroscopic analysis of all of Springsteen's records which, in turn, provides for an interpretation of his narratives' development across time. But first, some insight into this rock and roll narrator's background is warranted.

SPRINGSTEEN: AN ANECDOTAL ANALYSIS

Springsteen as Narrator[2]

Bruce Springsteen was born in Freehold, N.J., in 1949. Humphries and Hunt (1986) described his early years as "pretty normal for someone from that background—unadventurous, unscholastic, his only escape being radio or TV" (p. 8). For Springsteen, rock and roll was his source for escape. He once said: "Rock'n'roll, man, it changed my life. It was . . . the voice of America, the real America coming to your home. It was the liberating thing, the way out of the pits" (p. 8).

Springsteen's career began when he joined the Castilles in 1965. Reflecting on his early rock and roll influences, Springsteen admitted: "Elvis was one of the first. Otis Redding, Sam Cooke, Wilson Pickett, the Beatles, Fats, Benny Goodman, and a lot of jazz guys. You can hear them all in there if you want" (Knight, 1974, p. 24). By the early 1970s Springsteen had played in a number of bands and developed a loyal following in the Northeast. He was signed to a recording contract by Columbia Records in 1972.

Springsteen's records are well suited to anecdotal analysis due to the continuity of themes presented in his narratives. Douglas (1985) called his music "perhaps the most extended coherent expression of urgency in rock annals" (p. 485). In this vein, McConnell (1983) argued that Springsteen represents a "legitimate American storyteller" as he expresses Walt Whitman's "dream of a truly democratic poetry" (p. 431).

Springsteen's music and performances do not appear to be mere posturing. Springsteen often relates his personal connection with the songs he sings in concert. He talks of where he was when he first heard a rock and roll classic and often details the experiences that motivated him to write a particular song (Marsh, 1981, 1987). In a sense, Springsteen turns a concert into an elaborate self-disclosure, using the music and stories of his past interchangeably.

It appears that this facet of Springsteen's songs, that is his attention to individual character development, facilitates the audience's ability to identify with the contents of his narratives. When a song develops a story about individual characters a listener is able to bridge the gap from general to specific, transferring the situations depicted in the song to his or her own construction of social reality. Perhaps a review of Springsteen's music will help us further substantiate this aspect of his work.

---

[2] Biographical information about Springsteen, unless otherwise noted, is taken from Humpheries and Hunt (1986), Marsh (1981), and Rockwell (1975).

The Music: A Chronological Overview[3]

Since 1973, Springsteen has released eight albums. His first, *Greetings from Asbury Park, N. J.*, "displayed Springsteen's passion for grandiose narratives filled with oddball characters and exotic place names" (Sweeting, 1985, pp. 21–22). The songs were excessive in their imagery and focused on how blue-collar kids coped with their less than ideal existence. Despite heavy promotional efforts by Columbia Records and uncharacteristic acclaim from critics—many of whom lauded Springsteen as the new Bob Dylan (Rockwell, 1975)—the album produced only marginal sales.

In part because of *Greetings'* poor sales, CBS did not seriously promote the second album, *The Wild, The Innocent, The E Street Shuffle*, and its sales suffered as well. While *Wild* lacked in production qualities, it did further demonstrate Springsteen's lyrical gift. Still emphasizing blue-collar youth, Springsteen used the second side of the album to develop a narrative involving characters that would appear in subsequent songs (Loder, 1984).

More than 2 years passed before Springsteen released his third album, *Born to Run*. The production qualities were improved and Springsteen achieved moderate success with the album's title track. The songs described the characters' growing frustrations with their lives as they dealt less with dreams of escape and more with escape itself.

Three years later, Springsteen released *Darkness on the Edge of Town*. The themes in *Darkness* were not decidedly different from those on the earlier albums, just more desperate. By now, Springsteen had established himself as one of the industry's top artists and became somewhat of a national celebrity when his photograph appeared on the covers of *Time* and *Newsweek* during the same week.

The River, a two-record set, followed in 1980. While some critics claimed that Springsteen was a "Johnny one-note" who constantly rehashed "overheated teen dreams" (Simels, 1978, p. 108), it is clear that the characters in *River* had grown older, wiser in the ways of the world, and more intense in their frustrations. The album produced Springsteen's biggest hit to that point, "Hungry Heart."

In 1982 Springsteen recorded a collection of songs intended as a demonstration tape for an upcoming studio album. These compositions were subsequently released in their original form on the album *Nebraska*. A rare departure from band-oriented rock and roll, this album was much more depressing than previous records since its char-

---

[3] Unless otherwise noted, the information concerning Springsteen's albums is taken from Marsh (1981, 1987).

acters were continually placed in "no-win" situations of extreme proportions.

Springsteen's *Born in the U.S.A.*, released in 1985, produced a number of hit singles including, "Dancing in the Dark," "I'm on Fire," "Born in the U.S.A.," "Hometown," and "Glory Days." The worldwide tour in support of the album drew more than 5 million fans and generated $200 million in revenue (Humphries & Hunt, 1986). In virtually every respect, *Born in the U.S.A.* represented the climax of Springsteen's professional career.

The most recent album to be released by Springsteen was a five-record compilation of live performances entitled *Bruce Springsteen and the E Street Band: Live 1975–1985*. The album included concert performances of many of the songs from the previous seven albums, cover versions of other artist's songs, and new compositions. Moreover, this album featured Springsteen's self-disclosures that elaborated on his feelings regarding his music and society's conditions.

Taken in its entirety, this body of discourse offers the critic a coherent expression of social reality for anecdotal analysis. In pursuit of this objective we now introduce the worker's elegy story line.

The Worker's Elegy

Holman (1980) described the elegy as emphasizing expressions of sorrow through three distinct strategies. The central character either: (a) "laments the unresponsiveness of his mistress;" (b) "bemoans his unhappy lot and seeks to remedy it;" or (c) "regrets the sorry state of the world" (p. 95).

Applied to Springsteen's music, this story form produces an anecdote that articulates the state of being a victim and its impact on the lives of the characters portrayed. In these songs it is rare for this condition to be self-inflicted. That is, the characters suffer from situations that they apparently had little, if any, part in generating. In essence, these stories stress how the system has not delivered on its promises of a better life, improving relationships, or dreams that were supposed to come true.

For example, of the characters in "Spirits in the Night," Marsh (1981) wrote:

> Often what seems from a distance to be improvement is, close up, much worse—even a trap. At Greasy Lake, Crazy Janey and her pals gain no permanent freedom; in the end, they must drive off to return to their drudgery. (p. 73)

The narrator's girlfriend in "Racing In The Street" sat on her father's porch, stared into the night, and hated being born. In "Jackson Cage" Springsteen described the confusion of wondering whether the effort of dreaming of a better world is really worth it. In "Dancing in the Dark," Springsteen's character awakened feeling the same way as when he went to bed, tired and bored with himself. Clearly, the characters within these songs are trapped in situations and offered little means of changing or improving it. Their efforts to change their lives are, at best, only fleetingly successful and, at worst, compound their frustrations through failure.

It is important to note that the characters of this story line are not restricted by class or occupation. The scenarios described in these songs may be relevant to a variety of people working to improve their conditions. For instance, a Wall Street banker may experience a sense of subjugation to the system and, as a result, feel as trapped as Springsteen's coal miner, textile worker, or unemployed steelworker. Herein lies the strength of the worker's elegy anecdote as it organizes a reality that provides discursive medicine on an individual basis and, in turn, offers a means of coping with those perceived conditions.

When we apply this story line to Springsteen's work we also observe a distinct development in the way in which the characters cope with their victimage. As these characters grow older their means of coping change. Initally, the youth on Springsteen's early albums *dream* about a promised land and opportunities to leave their urban desperation behind. The young adults of the next few albums experience a form of *reckoning* with society's inability to deliver this promised land. Finally, the adults of his later albums *lament* that the passage of time has not brought them any closer to their dream.

Through an identification with the contents of these stories the audience may obtain medicine that they use to cope with their own situations. Perhaps a closer examination of the three phases of the worker's elegy—dreaming, reckoning, and lamenting—may elucidate on the nature of the medicine offered through Springsteen's music.

Dreaming. Much of Springsteen's early work involved the New Jersey towns, highways, and boardwalks that were such an integral part of his youth. There is a grittiness contained in the imagery of these early songs that makes the listener less than comfortable with the scenes being depicted. If Greasy Lake is the adolescent retreat in "Spirits in the Night," from what must these adolescents be retreating? The characters, with names like Crazy Janey, Jimmy the Saint, and Little Dynamite, are clearly uncomfortable with their surroundings.

Nevertheless, Springsteen allowed his youthful characters to fantasize, at least temporarily, about an escape from the control of the system that restricted their social mobility. These characters dreamed of a promised land where they would have control of their own lives. Humphries and Hunt (1986) described these songs as conjuring "up the American Dream, where every man can be a king, and the only ceiling to ambition is the extent of your dreams" (p. 7).

Perhaps no song articulated the importance of dreaming better than the opening song on *Born to Run*, "Thunder Road." The narrator, pleading with his girlfriend to go out riding in search of "the promised land," finished the song by exclaiming the town to be full of losers "and I'm pulling out of here to win." It was as if any other place held more promise for their futures.

Without question, Springsteen's version of the American Dream was distinct from that of most middle-class Americans. These characters never envisioned a college diploma that would lead to a job in corporate America. For example, in "Mary Queen of Arkansas," the narrator talked of a place "deep in Mexico" and longed just to "get a good job and start all over again clean." The narrator of "Rosalita" dreamed not of a house with a white picket fence, but of taking his girl to a cafe near San Diego "where they play guitars all night and day." Similarly, the victim in "For You" left home merely to "find a better reason than the one we were living for."

Notice how Springsteen's early characters used fantasy in their constructions of social reality. The narratives portrayed people dominated by society's institutions. Trapped in their neighborhoods, by their jobs, and by their parents' legacies, these characters are possessed by a unique form of anxiety. They are waiting for a chance to escape to a place where they have control over their lives.

Still, there is a certain amount of youthful optimism in the songs from the dreaming phase of the worker's elegy. The imagery of human cannonballs and the Flying Zambinis in "Wild Billy's Circus Song" takes on an almost dreamlike quality when seen from the eyes of the young boy tempted by the circus boss with the idea of joining the big top. In "Rosalita," Springsteen's main character exploded with pride when proclaiming hope to his girl in the form of a big record company advance that would carry them away from all the dread.

The fact that the characters perceived an opportunity for better times suggests a belief that the system would indeed relinquish control. As Mary Lou said in "Does This Bus Stop at 82nd Street?" when asked how she copes, "the dope's that there's still hope." While Springsteen constructed a social reality that placed his characters in a state of anxiety, he continued to offer hope to all who desired something better.

Reckoning. Though Springsteen allowed his characters to fantasize of a better life, they soon realized that their dreams would never come true. The social reality that permitted the dream to exist suddenly seemed incapable of providing the means of achieving that fantasy. Hence, Springsteen's characters live in a constant paradox of coping with a system that encourages, to the point of mandating, the improvement of one's condition, all the while cutting down every effort to do so. As Duncan (1986) stated, "Where there was once only hope, now there is also warning" (p. 52).

What happened to these characters may be nothing more than growing up and dreaming not of what *might be,* but recognizing what *is.* In other words, the people in these stories experienced a reckoning about the extent to which the system would allow their lives to be changed. The characters that appeared on Springsteen's later works seemed to have realized that "the line between survival and extinction is thin, like the line down the centre of a desert highway stretching away to nothing" (Sweeting, 1985, p. 40). In this respect, these songs represented a transition from the fantasy or dream of youth to the reckoning of early adulthood.

Such a transition is seen in "Fourth of July (Sandy)" with the narrator's growing disillusionment with the respite that the boardwalk once provided. The arcades, carnival rides, and fortune tellers lost their ability to provide an escape. Instead, dreams of a promised land slowly gave way to a realization that the system demands hard work. Marsh (1981) noted: "Faith, Springsteen seems to be saying, will get you so far, and not a step more. The rest is down to work and struggle, and you'd better not stop" (p. 256).

The irony is that many of these characters realized that their dreams, regardless of their individual struggles, would never come about. McConnell (1983) stated, "Springsteen understands, and articulates in song after song, the fact that the American quest for an infinitely expansive future is, in the end, a quest—or a compulsion—for failure" (p. 43). The kids who drove out to Greasy Lake in "Spirits in the Night" and dreamed of somewhere better are replaced in songs such as "The River" by men out of work, married too young, no longer concerned about the things that at one time seemed so important, and consumed with the feeling that a dream that doesn't come true is worse than a lie.

It is not surprising, then, that so many of these disillusioned characters grew tired of their struggle and sought relief outside of a social system that never delivered. These characters take to the streets in rebellion (e.g., The Rangers of "Jungleland"); or to their cars and motorcycles in aimless escape (e.g., the late-shift worker in "Open All Night"); or to crime (e.g., Ralph in "Johnny 99"). Sweeting (1985) observed these songs are "about a spiritual crisis in which man is left lost" since "he has nothing left to tie him into society anymore" (p. 60). Subsequently, the character was "isolated from the government . . . his job . . . his family . . . and . . . his friends" (p. 60).

In reviewing Springsteen's lyrics, Douglas (1985) wrote, "he asserts that the reality of American life for many of its inhabitants is economic and emotional depression" (p. 488). To that, we add spiritual depression as well. Before *Nebraska* was released, Springsteen commented

> After Watergate, America just died emotionally. . . . Nobody had any hope left. People were so horrified when they learned of the large-scale corruption in the land of the brave and the free that they stayed in their houses, scared and numb.
>
> (Humphries & Hunt, 1986, p. 53)

Perhaps nowhere is this condition of political victimage better articulated than on the *Nebraska* album. The haunting lyrics of these songs depicted an America that had turned its back on its people so severely that the only recourse was to fight back in the most violent of ways or give up entirely.

In "Nebraska," Springsteen painted perhaps his bleakest picture, the kids of Greasy Lake gone mad. In the title cut, the narrator and his girlfriend went on a murdering spree that left 10 people dead. There is no sorrow expressed in this song, only an admission that there is a meanness in the world that sometimes serves to hasten the inevitable subjugation to the system.

In "Johnny 99," Springsteen presented another victim of the dream unrealized. The main character, Ralph, robbed a store and shot the night clerk. At his sentencing, he argued that it was his unemployment, debts, and impending house foreclosure that placed the gun in his hands. In the end, Ralph pleaded for his execution rather than life in prison. In its most desperate form the reckoning produced a promised land that was no longer attainable by mere mortals.

Humphries and Hunt (1986) described the characters on *Nebraska* as "victims manipulated by faceless bureaucrats and political systems which are beyond their comprehension or control" (p. 53). As Springsteen argued: "It's a real simple story. You grow up, and they bury you" (Duncan, 1986, p. 51). It is this condition of reckoning that leads us to the final phase of the worker's elegy—the lament.

Lamenting. With the release of *Born in the U.S.A.* Springsteen introduced characters who have matured in their ability to cope with their lives. Gone are those who believed that the system would deliver them from their conditions. It is as if the lesson concerning the attainability of the American Dream had been painfully learned and accepted. In essence, these are individuals who have paid a price for security and family, and not received in kind.

For instance, in "Born in the U.S.A." the Vietnam veteran who lost his brother in the war sought help from the Veteran's Administration. The cruelly blunt reply from the public official conveyed there was no relief to be offered by the government.

In a similar vein, the narrator of "My Hometown" lamented not just the passing of a time when he drove around on his Daddy's lap, but his dying hometown where the jobs at the textile mill have gone forever. In the end, he contemplated moving to a different part of the country where jobs would be more plentiful. However, in "Seeds" the family moved to Houston only to find the promise of work as empty as the Texas oilfields.

Marsh (1981) argued that these characters "are the sort of people who are romanticized, depicted as the backbone of democracy, but almost never allowed to speak for themselves" (p. 218). Douglas (1985) maintained that "all of Springsteen's lyrics, several of them virtual anthems of the anger of protest and the hope for deliverance—suggest that America must come back and through for its abandoned" (p. 488). If John F. Kennedy inspired an age of asking what we could do for our country, Springsteen countered for those who never received anything in return.

Surprisingly, all is not lost on these characters. Instead of dreaming of deliverance, wallowing in the hopelessness of their current situation, and rebelling against society, the characters in Springsteen's latest songs often found solace in their relationships and their memories. Springsteen remarked how the "type of things that make people's lives heroic are a lot of times very small, little things" such as "things that happen in the kitchen" or "between a husband and a wife or between them and their kids" (Bream, 1986, p. 69). Springsteen concluded, "It's a grand experience, but it's not always grandiose" (p. 69).

Unlike the young husband in "The River" who watched his life's dreams evaporate and unlike the husband in "Hungry Heart" who abandoned his wife and child to escape the trap, the husband in "My Hometown" turned to his family to help cope with his dying dreams.

Correspondingly, in "Glory Days" one character laughed at her memories of youth to keep from crying about her unrealized ambitions.

One may wonder about the kind of medicine presented in this situation that grows more and more hopeless. While Springsteen's characters may have lamented their condition, they never gave up the dream. Herein lies our medicine. In talking about *Darkness on the Edge of Town,* Springsteen said:

> There's still hope, there's always hope. They throw dirt on you all your life, and some people get buried so deep in the dirt that they'll never get out. The album's about people who will never admit that they're buried that deep.
>
> (Marsh, 1981, p. 220)

In essence, Springsteen observed that the way to cope with our social reality is to continue to dream, even though the dream may never come true. Never, in any of his songs, do the characters realize dreams and wishes, and yet, never do they stop dreaming and wishing. Springsteen once said of the songs on *The River:*

> I finally got to the place where I realized I had paradoxes. . . . What happens to most people is when their first dream gets killed off, nothing ever takes its place. The important thing is to keep holding out for possibilities.
>
> (Humphries & Hunt, 1986, p. 44)

It is not surprising, then, Springsteen wrote in "Reason to Believe" that at the end of every hard day there is still some reason to dream that things will get better. Or, as in "Two Hearts," he wrote that once every man abandons his "childish dreams" he must "grow up to dream again."

As we have seen, the worker's elegy consists of three distinct phases. Taken separately, each phase weaves its own tale of hope, desperation, or acceptance. When considered in its entirety, this anecdote offers medicine regarding those conditions that constitute the ebb and flow of human relations.

CONCLUSION

In their interpretation of the political fantasies of Hollywood, Nimmo and Combs (1983) observed that American movies are "made by people who are part of their culture and the time they live in" (p. 105).

From that starting point they suggested that a movie represents a "cultural artifact" that "offers us insight into the immediate fantasies and enduring myths of the American people" (p. 106).

The authors claimed that art forms capture the audience's feelings about the present by "linking it in fantastic melodramas to the enduring myth of the American Dream" (p. 106). Nimmo and Combs concluded these constructions of "optimistic order or pessimistic disorder" (p. 106) reflect what is on the public's mind at a given point in time.

Here we have explored those cultural artifacts that are the musical narratives of Bruce Springsteen. Through Burke's sociological criticism we have endeavored to "assemble and codify this lore" (Burke, 1973, p. 301) via the Burkean method: the representative anecdote. Our objective corresponds with Nimmo and Combs's work in that we have observed how a popular art form such as Springsteen's music dramatizes our anxieties about the American Dream.

However, it appears the medicine presented in Springsteen's narratives often offers a confusing mixture of optimism and pessimism in that his tales stress the need for dreaming of a world that has been proven not to exist. Consequently, the worker's elegy ponders a situation predicated on a state of tragic victimage, all as it posits a never-say-die attitude. To Springsteen, even in a world of subjugation, the American Dream of individual prosperity remains an eternal bastion of hope.

Turning to methodology, our analysis also demonstrates the utility of anecdotal analysis. Not only does the representative anecdote serve as a means for synthesizing a large body of work, it also provides a strategy for evaluating that work's potential for providing medicine regarding life's situations.

However, no anecdotal analysis is definitive. Clearly, the eye of the beholder is at work in an effort such as this. For example, U. S. Senator Bill Bradley, columnist George Will, and President Ronald Reagan apparently viewed the song "Born in the U.S.A." as representing some kind of new patriotic movement sweeping the young people of America (Marsh, 1987). Sweeting (1985) argued, "if this is a eulogy for the glories of Reaganomics, you could have fooled thousands of Vietnam vets" (p. 6), which suggests the diversity of possible interpretations.

Our analysis argues that the worker's elegy constructs a political reality that is distinct from an image of government for all people. However, desperation, dreaming, and a desire to escape hopeless situations are not the sole province of the blue-collar worker. Perhaps this explains rock and roll's enduring impact on American society. It imposes no boundaries by providing medicine to anyone who chooses to listen and identify with its message. As Springsteen stated, rock and roll bands "will last as long as you look down into the audience and can see yourself, and your audience looks up at you and can see themselves—and as long as those reflections are human, realistic ones" (Loder, 1984, p. 70).

REFERENCES

Bream, J. (1986). Bruce Springsteen: Rock 'n' roll glory days! *Springsteen, 1*(1), 67–69.

Brummett, B. (1984a). Burke's representative anecodote as a method in media criticism. *Critical Studies in Mass Communication, 1*, 161–176.

Brummett, B. (1984b). The representative anecdote as a Burkean method applied to evangelical rhetoric. *The Southern Speech Communication Journal 50*, 1–23.

Burke, K. (1965). *Permanence and change.* Indianapolis: Bobbs–Merrill.

Burke, K. (1966). *Language as symbolic action.* Berkeley: University of California Press.

Burke, K. (1969). *A grammar of motives.* Berkeley: University of California Press.

Burke, K. (1973). *The philosophy of literary form.* Berkeley: University of California Press.

Chatman, S. (1978). *Story and discourse: Narrative structure in fiction and film.* Ithaca, NY: Cornell University Press.

Douglas, A. (1985, October). Bruce Springsteen and narrative rock: The art of extended urgency. *Dissent, 32*, 485–489.

Duncan, R. (1986). Lawdamercy, Springsteen saves! Testimony from the howling dog choir (or tramps like us, baby we're born again). *Springsteen, 1*(1), 50–59.

Holman, C. H. (1980). *A handbook to literature.* Indianapolis: Bobbs–Merrill.

Humphries, P., & Hunt, C. (1986). *Springsteen: Blinded by the light.* New York: Henry Holt.

Knight, P. (1974, September 12). Bruce Springsteen's lone star promendade. *Rolling Stone, 169*, No. 169, 24.

Loder, K. (1984, December 6). The Rolling Stone interview: Bruce Springsteen. *Rolling Stone*, 19–22, 70.

Marsh, D. (1981). *Born to run: The Bruce Springsteen story.* New York: Dell.

Marsh, D. (1987). *Glory days: Bruce Springsteen in the 1980's.* New York: Pantheon.

McConnell, F. (1983). A rock poet: From Fitzgerald to Springsteen. *Commonweal, 112*, 431–433.

Nichols, M. H. (1983). Kenneth Burke and the "New Rhetoric." In J. L. Golden, G. F. Berquist, & W. E. Coleman (Eds.), *The rhetoric of Western thought* (3rd ed.). Dubuque, IA: Kendall/Hunt.

Nimmo, D., & Combs, J. (1983). *Mediated political realities*. New York: Longman.

Rockwell, J. (1975, October 9). New Dylan from New Jersey? It might as well be Springsteen. *Rolling Stone, 197*.

Simels, S. (1978). Springsteen: A little too much darkness? *Stereo Review, 41*(2), 108.

Simels, S. (1981). Springsteen: The River. *Stereo Review, 46*(1), 102.

Simels, S. (1982). Bruce Springsteen. *Stereo Review, 46*(12), 100.

Sweeting, A. (1985). *Springsteen: Visions of America*. London: Holborn Group.

12

Rock Music and Cultural Theory in the German Democratic Republic

Edward Larkey
Department of Modern Languages and Linguistics,
University of Maryland Baltimore County

A discrepancy exists between the quantitative and qualitative international diffusion and reception of rock music from the United States and Great Britain on the one hand, and its theoretical reflection on the other. This holds true especially in the case of the rock music history of the German Democratic Republic (East Germany). From the outset, efforts of the cultural and political authorities in the GDR to draw up and carry out strategies for cultural development of the working class were consistently modified to accomodate the spontaneous popularity of the U.S., and later, Anglo-American rock music.

Rock music was not always considered a legitimate and acceptable form of youth cultural expression among leading cultural scientists and aestheticians in the GDR. Presently, however, a number of them propound a concept of rock music which employs industrially produced, electronic technology as a means of aesthetic-cultural production in the daily lives of East German youth. Rock music is thus expected to provide, in a spontaneous and collective manner, for an aesthetic-cultural intensification of young people's daily social experience and communication. GDR musicologist Peter Wicke's definition of popular music (Wicke, 1983, p. 3ff) would seem quite noncontroversial at first glance. He emphasizes its functional aspects in society, effecting its broad popularity among the masses of its youthful listeners in their daily activities.

Most historical treatments of popular music published in the GDR in the late sixties and seventies (Bachmann, 1967; Hofmann, 1971, 1973) concentrated largely on an ideological critique of the lyrics, the music structure comprising the melody, the harmony and the rhythm, or, the capitalist organizational structure of the music scene in the West. On the other hand, the same works refrained from critically reflecting the theoretical paradigms underlying domestic GDR popular music history. The resulting noncritical view of historical continuity promulgated in early GDR pop music historiography stands diametrically opposed to the reality of the sharp controversies surrounding the impact and response to Western popular music transmission into the country. Since one may assume that American audiences have not suffered from an overabundance of information on GDR popular music history, it appears useful to point out some interrelationships between rock music and cultural theory in the GDR.

The historical development of rock music in the GDR progressed through four distinct conceptual stages, in which it was viewed within the context of socialist-realist art, folk art, entertainment art, and mass or popular art and culture. These are not merely philosophical terms. Due to the close interrelationship between these concepts and practical policy decisions regarding youth culture, they represent conceptual paradigms of a much broader scope, governing the relationship of official cultural policies toward the foreign music on the one hand, and alternative culture and music strategies on the other. One of the basic dilemmas facing GDR popular music from the outset and a primary motivation for the continual search for viable alternatives was the politically interpreted, broad popularity of Anglo-American rock music, and a corresponding lack of comparable popularity for GDR music.

Official response to the rock'n'roll music spread into the country by the radio stations in the West in the fifties reflected a striking lack of understanding about the political and ideological nature of rock music and the objective conditions necessary for its production. This was especially true in the face of prevailing GDR cultural policies striving to build an autonomous socialist German culture in the eastern part of Germany, impervious to influences from the West. According to the views of GDR cultural ideologues (Abusch, 1957, pp. 12, 54–55), all forms of Western culture diverted attention from constructing the new society. The popular, highly visible, high output, industrially produced, standardized rock music was treated by Party leaders in the GDR as imperialist political propaganda, intentionally developed by the large record and media companies to subvert unwitting GDR youth.

Groups of youth in the larger urban centers met informally after work or school, calling themselves the "Presley Gang", the "42nd Street Gang", etc., cases which were pointed out as bad examples in the newspaper of the "Freie Deutsche Jugend", the GDR Party youth organization *Junge Welt* (September 21/22, 1957). These incidents perplexed Party officials, who were confronted with the dilemma that these very same youths under the supposedly "bad" indluence of these "gangs" were working remarkably well in the factories and at school (Ulbricht, 1958).

Nevertheless, as a result of the music's inherent rebelliousness, no rock'n'roll records were imported, jeans and so-called "conny-skirts" popularized in West German films and published articles were frowned upon, and bands were actively discouraged from playing rock'n'roll music. The music itself was denounced for not being genuine socialist-realist art, and it was accused of promoting frenetic over-excitement and decadence, and paving the way for moral and politically reactionary excesses (Eisler, 1958). Rock'n'roll dancing was considered tasteless, unartistic acrobatics, and termed "St. Vitus' dance" in official Party statements such as the above-mentioned.

All alternative strategies in the fifties avoided the question of industrializing cultural production and gearing it towards the cultural needs of youth, concentrating instead on improving merely "inner musical components" of the compositions. This approach oriented towards achieving a new national intonation gleaned from folk music, as well as retaining traditional harmonics derived from the European art music heritage. These alternative strategies sought to develop new melodies for reflecting the new and developing socialist life style emerging in the GDR (Czerny, 1959, p. 8). One short-lived result was a new dance step created in the city of Leipzig in 1959, whose Latin name of Lipsia was used to coin the name of the dance, the "Lipsi" (cf. Czerny, 1959).

A further significant effort to promote alternative forms of what was called "dance music" in the late fifties was a law enacted in 1958 requiring that 60% of the repertoire of GDR musical aggregations and radio and television broadcasts contain songs from socialist countries (Gerlach, 1984, p. 74). Forty percent of the repertoire was permitted from all other capitalist countries combined. This was not only designed to save royalties, but also had the political intention of popularizing GDR music.

Other forms of popular culture from the United States were only slightly less controversial in the early sixties. The Kingston Trio's "Tom Dooley", for example, was banned for inciting criminal activities among youth, and was attacked because of these alleged tendencies in the *Junge Welt* (November 26/27, 1960). The "Twist" was tolerated only after much debate and publicity attempting to modify and "humanize" its allegdly, non-artistic elements (Czerny, 1963, p. 6).

The broad-based, spontaneous popularity of the Beatles prompted a change in official attitudes toward youth-oriented British "beat" music of the sixties, reflected in its grudging acceptance by them as an industrially deformed, bastardized version of urban political folk music, such as the type prevalent in the thirties in the U.S. This was in reaction to the large numbers of GDR teenagers enthusiastically picking up the guitar, building instruments and amplifiers, and making music with any means at their disposal (cf. Leitner, 1983, p. 71). The groups called themselves the "Guitarmen", the "Butlers", the "Shatters", and other English names.

Official measures towards these groups initially supported their activities, aiming at overcoming their imitative aspects, such as English-sounding lyrics, long hair, and so forth. In 1963, a Beatles record was imported (AMIGA 850 040), and in 1964, the first youth radio program, "DT-64", was created to broadcast the new pop music on a regular basis. It will soon be expanded into a semi-autonomous radio station for youth within the GDR broadcasting network.

This early period of relative flexibility gave way to one of increased restrictions after the 1965 West European Tour of the Rolling Stones. At the time, similar rebelliousness was manifested among GDR youth during the rock'n'roll period. That appeared to prove to distrustful cultural politicians in the Party hierarchy that beat music provided the West with too much cultural and political influence, as was stated at the eleventh plenary session of the Central Committee of the SED in December of 1965 (Honecker, 1965, p. 69). Thereafter, long-haired youths were actively removed from schools and factories and taken to the barber shop, or shorn before entry into these institutions was permitted. Many groups heeded the urgings of Party officials to change their English names to Germanic ones, and English-like lyrics were censured. A number of other measures were decreed to limit the numbers of beat groups and their access to audiences in the mass media and at live concerts.

Officially-supported alternative strategies in the latter half of the sixties focussed on refurbishing and modernizing the conventional German "Schlager" (similar to the American "Top 40), particularly the music, but also the lyric content. Competitions were held on a yearly basis for amateur Schlager poets to try their hand at creating new lyrics. New lyrics were also the object of efforts to create a GDR political folk community among youth, modelled along the lines of the American "hootenany" movement of the sixties. Amateur GDR folk musicians used largely acoustic instruments and were active primarily through live performances. Not surprisingly, Bob Dylan seemed to exemplify the objectives of this strategy. Although these amateur political folk groups were originally intended to be forms of artistic and cultural self-expression for the musicians, they increasingly assumed the role of providing politically-oriented and acceptable entertainment for audiences at official gatherings of the youth organization. This development was criticized by Perry Friedman, one of the major promoters of the GDR "hootenany-movement", in an article appearing in *Junge Welt* (September 19, 1968), indicating that this was not the viable alternative to Western rock music sought after by GDR cultural strategists.

The seventies witnessed a thorough revision of official policies toward rock music, based on a concept of socialist entertainment art. (cf. Autorenkollektiv, 1979, pp. 432–426) This concept extended the scope of the political folk-community concept beyond purely political statements into other spheres of life. The entertainment notion led to a dramatic increase in the number of professional pop musicians licensed to play in front of live audiences, and to make records and radio productions. It also had the effect of targetting the areas of leisure and entertainment for technological and industrial development, as well as promoting increased diffusion of Western rock music in the GDR at levels previously considered politically and ideologically dangerous.

The state-run, government radio stations became the largest producers of the new youth popular music in the country, using programming derived from the hit parades of the West, emulating "Top 40" shows for pushing national GDR tunes (cf. Leitner, 1983, pp. 221ff.). Improvements in the mass media were directed toward maintaining media presence fo GDR pop music, while at the same time catering to the musical tastes of youth determined by the Anglo-American music, notwithstanding the 60:40 rule. Previously criticized Underground and Soul music of the sixties served as exemplary modes of collective youth cultural communication.

GDR cultural strategists sought to develop new forms of collective cultural communication during this phase, concentrating on popularizing GDR dance music in the increasing number of discotheques (cf. Mewis & Strulick, 1976, pp. 3–5). Alternative music stategies attempted to synthesize new forms of pop music and entertainment from the national and international scenes into a distinctly melodious, yet rhythmically stimulating, uniform, and characteristic national GDR pop music style, capable of replacing dependence on the music from the West (Mewis & Strulick, 1976.).

Experiences in the GDR with disco, new wave, and punk music, and, with break dancing as well within the framework of the entertainment concept, have exposed some of its inherent drawbacks. The large majority of GDR rock groups have had neither the technological nor financial resources to quantitatively or qualitatively compete with or creatively reproduce the newer disco music on the same scale as in the West (cf. Wicke, 1984, p. 4). Moreover, the popularity of the West German new wave and punk music among GDR youth challenged not only the prevailing notion of GDR entertainment, in both music aesthetics and in lyric content, society's goals were also challenged, much more intensely and concretely than ever before. In the GDR, such music was deemed detrimental to entertainment objectives of providing joy, diversion, and relaxation in the face of life's daily frustrations. Punk music and lyrics of such groups as "Virus X", "Namenlos" and others dealing with "unproductive" problems, such as the Ministry for State Security, the GDR rock scene, the deadening routine of office work, bans of the music, arrests of musicians, and police harrassment of the fans. In spite of this, GDR popular music has increasingly addressed specific problems of youth much more concretely than in the seventies, and has struggled to broaden its popularity and legitimacy among youth. One of the primary factors influencing this development has been the extensive production of tape cassettes made by the groups in basement studios.

Aggravating the problem of legitimacy and acceptability was the reliance on a highly centralized, institutionalized, hierarchically organized popular music industry. Further, a small number of highly qualified, privileged professional musicians capable of reproducing new sounds, but too isolated from the problems of the younger generation of youth born in the sixties controlled this industry.

Suggestions for improving these weaknesses have centered on the question of how to more effectively tap and support existing amateur groups who have a closer relationship to their audiences, but have relatively less access to the media, record production equipment, technology, and instruments to be able to adequately and quickly react to new international sound fashions. These discussions have sparked renewed interest by cultural politicians in developing regional and local ethnic elements in GDR popular music (cf. Hanke, 1982, p. 7). Other suggestions have focussed on sensitizing cultural politicians at local and regional levels to respond to, and support spontaneously emerging forms of amateur youth popular culture activities. This approach was elaborated in a round-table discussion of cultural scientists in 1984 (Gespraech ueber Probleme der Erforschung von Unterhaltungskunst, 1984, p. 1429), since politically motivated, aesthetic prejudices against mass culture from the West were seriously hampering efforts to promote a socialist youth culture in the GDR and to react in a flexible manner to Western influences.

The ongoing debate on how to improve socialist entertainment art has resulted in efforts by cultural theoreticians to define specific objectives of an industrially produced, socialist mass or popular culture in the GDR. The debate has provoked a shift in thinking as to how GDR rock music differentiates itself from that of the West and achieves comparable popularity. Peter Wicke, director of the Humboldt University's recently founded Center for Popular Music Research, and foremost theoretician on popular music and culture in the GDR, has argued that the popularity of rock music is not derived primarily from the structural components of the music (Wicke, 1979, p. 48ff). He believes that the social structure derived from the material conditions of production and reproduction in GDR society imparts meaning to the relatively arbitrary mix of sounds agglomerated into the aesthetic form of rock music. He postulates that the capitalist organization of popular culture thus produces a different context of meaning to the same sounds than does a socialist organizational structure.

Wicke, as well as other cultural scientists, have, since then, begun collecting and analyzing sociological and other data on how rock music in the GDR is functionally utilized in the daily lives of youth, somewhat along the lines of Frith's excellent study of rock music usage among British youth (cf. Frith, 1978). Official GDR perception of rock music has thus progressed from being a political threat in the fifties to that of a cultural challenge in the eighties. This change in attitude was accomplished against the background of developing the material conditions to objectively and subjectively absorb and respond to the foreign music.

Implications of this research have begun to filter into daily cultural policymaking decisions. The government has recently begun to address the question of how to ensure a continual supply of modern musical equipment on a mass scale. Previously cultivated informal business relationships with a number of private studios built up by professional musicians over the last decade have become codified into contractually determined prices for studio use. In addition, Western currency reserves of private citizens obtained from friends or relatives can now be siphoned into a special "intershop" foreign currency store for sophisticated electronic musical instruments in the Berlin district of Adlershof. Also, negotiations are underway with customs authorities to base the duties levied on imported musical instruments and studio electronics on the purchase price in the West, and not on much more expensive production prices in the GDR.

Other steps have been taken to expand musical outlets for East Germans. One such step was the recent authorization permitting 15 amateur rock and pop groups to become professional, representing a substantial increase in the number of professional musicians. In addition, a new radio program for showcasing newer tendencies on the periphery of the popular music continuum, such as avant-punk and fusion, has been created.

Finally, a major step in efforts to improve popular music in the GDR has been to reorganize the Committee for Entertainment Art from a largely advisory council of top artists into a body more nearly providing direct lines of communication accomodating the needs of artists, cultural policy planners, and audiences (cf. Neukonstituierung, 1985, pp. 57–61). All these measures taken together, then, indicate a significantly greater tolerance of officials toward the popular music of youth, as well as a notable willingness to accept a greater discrepancy between East German society's ideals of social and individual development on the one hand and the degree of actual personal fulfillment on the other.

Although Wicke has asserted that the cultural productivity of popular music consists of providing an avenue for cultural expression of youth daily experience, official criticism, and censure of Punk music indicate that such tolerance has yet to be fully achieved (Haase & Starr, 1985, pp. 75–77). Wicke and others have hypothesized that it will take some time for GDR economic conditions to progress to the point of being able to produce completely new forms and styles of entertainment activity, attaining comparable spontaneous popularity as those produced by the capitalist culture industries at the present (cf. Oehler, 1983, p. 239).

REFERENCE

Abusch, A. (1957). *Im ideologischen Kampf fuer eine sozialistische deutsche Kultur*. Berlin: Dietz.

Autorenkollektiv. (1979). *Musikgeschichte der Deutschen Demokratischen Republik*. Berlin: Verlag Neue Musik.

Bachmann, F. (1967). *Tanzmusik und Gesellschaft*. Leipzig: Zentralhaus-Publikation.

Czerny, P. (1959). Tanzmusik als Spiegel der Zeit. *Melodie und Rhythmus, 8,* 8ff.

Czerny, P. (1963). Wir und der Twist. *Melodie und Rhythmus, 1,* 6ff.

Eisler, G. (1958, October 18/19). Offene Worte. *Junge Welt.*

Fraeulein, Koennen Sie Lipsi Tanzen? (1959). *Melodie und Rhythmus, 6,* 2–4.

Friedman, P. (1968, September 19). Ohne Viel Schmus und Schablone. *Junge Welt.*

Frith, S. (1978). *The sociology of rock.* London: Constable.

Gati, C. (Ed.). (1974). *The politics of modernization in Eastern Europe.* New York: Praeger Publishers (Praeger Special Studies in International Politics and Government).

Gerlach, C. (1984). *Popmusik.* Berlin: VEB Lied der Zeit.

Gespraech ueber den Schlager. (1960, November 26/27). *Junge Welt.*

Gespraech ueber Probleme der Erforschung von Unterhaltungs-kunst. (1984). *Weimarer Beitraege, 30*(9), 1423–1445.

Haase, N., & Starr, T. (1985). Kommi-Punks: Punk rock behind the Iron Curtain in East Germany. *Whole Earth Review, 46,* 75–77.

Hanke, H. (1982, September). Unterhaltung in den 80er Jahren. *Informationen der Generaldirektion beim Komitee fuer Unterhaltungskunst, No. 5.*

Hofmann, H. P. (1971). *abc der Tanzmusik.* Berlin: VEB Lied der Zeit.

Hofmann, H. P. (1973). *Beat-rock-rhythm & blues-soul.* Berlin: VEB Lied der Zeit.

Honecker, E. (1965). *Bericht des Politbueros an die 11. Tagung des Zentralkomitees der SED.* Berlin: Dietz.

Hootenany: alle singen mit. (1966). *Melodie und Rhythmus, 8,* 6–8.

Leitner, O. (1983). *Rockszene DDR.* Reinbek: Rowohlt Taschenbuchverlag.

Mewis, A., & Strulick, C. (1976, May 3–5). Zu einigen Aspekten der Entwicklung der Beatmusik der DDR im Jahre 1975. *Informationen der Generaldirektion beim Komitee fuer Unterhaltungskunst, No. 3.*

Oehler, C. (1983). Zum Klassencharakter und zur ideologischen Bedeutung von Unterhaltungskunst in der internationalen Klassenauseinandersetzung. In Ministerium fuer Kultur (Ed.), *Praktische und theoretische Fragen der Entwicklung von Unterhaltung und Unterhaltungskunst in der DDR* (pp. 209–242). Berlin: Ministerium fuer Kultur.

Oeser. H. (1983). Perspektiven und Aufgaben. Die Entwicklung des kuenstlerischen Volksschaffens in den achtziger Jahren und die Aufgaben seiner Fachgebiete bei der Verwirklichung unserer kulturpolitischen Stategie. In Zentralhaus-Publikation (Ed.), *Aktuelle Probleme der kulturellen Massenarbeit* (Wissenschaftliche Beitraege No. 12, pp. 42–67). Leipzig: Zentralhaus-Publikation.

24.9.1984. Neukonstituierung des Komitees fuer Unterhaltungs-kunst der DDR. (1985). *Profil, 3,* 57–61. Leipzig: Zentralhauspublikation.

Ulbricht, W. (1958, August 2/3). Rede des Ersten Sekretaers des Zentralkomitees der SED. *Junge Welt.*

Wicke, P. (1979). *Popmusik—Studie der gesellschaftlichen Funktion einer Musikpraxis.* Unpublished Ph.D. Dissertation. Berlin: Humboldt-Universitaet.

Wicke, P. (1984, December). Populaere Musik und sozialistische Kultur. *Informationen der Generaldirektion beim Komitee fuer Unterhaltungskunst, 6.*

Wicke, P., & Ziegenruecker, W. (1985). *Rock, pop, jazz, folk: Handbuch der populaeren Musik.* Leipzig: Deutscher Verlag fuer Musik.

13

Intrepidity and Ideology in Eastern Bloc Chillers and Thrillers: A Case Study in System Legitimation

Steven M. Neuse
Department of Political Science,
University of Arkansas

INTRODUCTION

The juxtaposition of intrepidity and ideology is a seemingly unlikely pairing. Intrepidity brings to mind individual courage, resourcefulness, stalwart integrity, and flexible action. Ideology, on the other hand, is suggestive of systems of thought which all too often smother the human spirit or at the very least severely temper those infrequent attempts by human actors to be bold, resolute, valiant—or to act intrepidly. But it is just this pairing which forms the necessary basis for the modern thriller genre.[1] The thriller in all its varieties provides witness to the efforts of heroes to prevail in the face of the conspiracy of hostile ideological frameworks, sometimes those of the enemy

---

[1] I have taken a broad denotation of the genre which includes both crime and spy fiction. The thriller has its roots in an *empirical present* and thus, I generally exclude both science fiction and the more recently popular type characterized by horrific and/ or psychic machinations. It is a literature of mass appeal and is almost always structured in terms of the efforts of one or a few protagonists, usually acting in some degree of isolation, to avert the effects of a conspiracy. Palmer characterizes the "ideology" of the thriller in terms of "heroism/or competent individualism and conspiracy" (1979, p. 87).

without, sometimes the enemy within, sometimes both. The very requirements of the form itself, heroic action in response to challenge of unfriendly political thought systems, makes the thriller one of the most political of literary genres.

It is my contention that popular thriller fiction is clearly a political literature, one where "political ideas play a dominant role or . . . the political milieu is the dominant setting" (Howe, 1970, p. 19). I have argued that the medium, depending on the perspective of the author, can provide strong affirmation or devastating critique of the legitimacy of political systems in which the protagonist operates (Neuse, 1980, 1982). Along the way I have become increasingly aware that the genre is not just an Anglo-American venture. The Sjowall–Wahloo Inspector Beck series provides a telling Marxist critique of the modern Swedish welfare state. The crime and spy novels of West German Hans Helmut Kirst afford a damning commentary on the brutality of both Nazi and postwar industrial Germany. James McClure's South African police procedurals offer telling witness to degradation and moral emptiness of apartheid. The thriller has taken root in the third world too. One only need note Donald Yates' gathering of Latin American crime and detective stories or Esfandiary Fereidoun's hauntingly prescient novel 1959 of intrigue and assassination in Iran, *Day of Sacrifice.* [2]

I am fascinated most of all, however, by the unlikely and belated appearance of the genre in the Soviet Union and Eastern Europe. Long banned, spy and crime fiction has only recently emerged as a popular, officially sanctioned literary type. More than a dozen titles have been translated into English and an influential Soviet literary journal has lauded the achievements of a score or more of native thriller authors (Ilyina & Arkadi, 1975).

The essay which follows will trace the development of the genre in the Socialist bloc and will raise certain critical questions about the manner in which the form has been adapted to socialist reality. My objectives in developing the inquiry along these lines are twofold and will be addressed in subsequent sections. First, I am interested in understanding how a once-banned literary form became acceptable and even encouraged almost overnight.

My second objective, is to explain the seemingly improbable use of this particular literary form in a system in which fealty to collectivist ideology and the inerrant state is the norm. The seed of improbability

---

[2] Representative works of these and other cited authors are included in the *References.*

lies in my contention (undisputed by Western, and until recently, Marxist critics alike) that the thriller is a uniquely Western type whose form and substance is, in large measure, alien or antithetical to socialist statism. The typical Western thriller offers splendid witness to radical individualism, utilitarian action, and a healthy suspicion of institutional forces. Indeed, "the one political belief that the thriller could not accommodate is anti-individualism" (Palmer, 1979, p. 67). Furthermore, the terms of the battles in which the protagonist engages are such that "he can never participate fully in any community" (p. 83). Without a doubt, this is clearly an ideological statement which is difficult to square in societies in which the entrepreneurial spirit is disavowed and collective action so highly prized.

The Western thriller also adds a vigorous criticism of existing institutions and the ideologies which drive them. Indeed, it is the very conflict between hero and bureaucratic ineptness and torpor which quickens the form. The most profound of thriller writers (to include, for example, John LeCarré, Graham Greene, and Dashiell Hammett) suggest that the success of heroic effort is made problematical because conspiracy is not limited to one side or the other. Theirs is a radical assault, to use Mannheim's category, on the "total conception of ideology," a severe taking to task of the *Weltanschauung* of all parties to the struggle (Mannheim, 1936, pp. 56, 58). This is clear in LeCarré's statement that his spy novels reflect a reality which is unacceptable to both sides "that there is no victory and no virtue in the Cold War, only a condition of human illness and a political misery" (LeCarré, 1965, p. 6).

To be sure, not all Western thriller authors cut this wide a swath. In fact, most thrillers (those, for example of Ian Fleming, Helen MacIness, and Alistair MacLean) only take the "total conception of ideology" of the *enemy* to task. But even in the "traditional" thriller (to be distinguished from the "negative" thriller of LeCarré and others; see Neuse, 1982, p. 296) the plot is structured so that the hero often is frustrated in action because his own institutions are bedeviled by ineptness, paralysis of action, and the inability to discern the reality lying beyond bureaucratic or political perceptions. For the Western thriller writer, then, intrepid behavior forms the ideological basis for the drama and action which quickens the plot. Integrity inheres in the individual spirit, not in collective consciousness.

But, how does the socialist thriller resolve the tension between intrepidness and ideology or accommodate both dauntless individualism and collective solidarity? Is there room for any critical perspective on official institutions? These questions form the basis for this discussion of Eastern European and Soviet spy and crime fiction.[3]

THE SOVIET THRILLER—FROM PROSCRIPTION TO PROMOTION

The odyssey of the socialist thriller is a curious one. Until the late 1950s, indigenous examples were rare and all but a few Western titles were proscribed. Why is it the case that this form, perhaps the most popular of all in the West, did not take root in the East?

The most obvious reason was state censorship. The thriller, particularly the crime and detective variety, was perceived to be an inappropriate cultural form for socialist society. Some Marxist critics claimed that the detective novel was a "child of capitalism" (Kaemmel, 1983, p. 57), and that "police literature is a bourgeois literature" (Eisenstein, 1970, p. 29). The point of both critics was that the etiology and progression of the crime novel was peculiar to Western capitalism and in fact reflected elite efforts to legitimate the order necessary for advanced capitalist industrial society. Gramsci contended that Western crime literature gradually evolved from a "friend of the people" perspective (where often the criminal was a rogue hero battling established forces of injustice) to one where crime represented a distinct threat to proper social order and the authorities (official police or private detectives), the protectors of that order (Gramsci, 1970, p. 19).

The argument continued that the typical elements of crime fiction simply did not correspond to socialist reality. There was no place, for example, in collective societies for the private detective who clearly symbolized the entrepreneurial spirit and private property (Gubern, 1970, p. 11) or even worse "individualism against the state" (Kaemmel, 1983, p. 61).

A second Marxist claim was that the Western crime novel was in some sense a "manifestation of the neurosis of industrial society," (Gubern, 1970, p. 9) and that the fascination with crime reflected a morbid social disorder (Kaemmel, 1983, p. 57). To allow an indigenous literature of this sort in the East might well appear to be an admission of crisis, including the recognition that crime was rampant in socialist society.

A second reason for the long delay in the introduction of thriller

---

[3] The one caution I extend is that this study is based on an uncomfortably small sample of novels. The sample (perhaps I should say universe) includes all English translations and was derived from an exhaustive search utilizing several good bibliographies and university library OCLC facilities.

literature was summed up in Helbig's point that in the East the "mission of art is defined in terms of its popular *and* its partisan content" (1977, p. 797). The genre was long perceived to be nothing more than another Western manifestation of *trivial literatur* (p. 803) without aesthetic or social value (remember the quaint description of this form in Great Britain and the United States, "the entertainment"). This was precisely the gist of Kaemmel's critique of the Western detective novel. Not only was it ideologically offensive and culturally inappropriate, but it was useless and without purpose. He did note, however (writing originally in East Germany in 1962), that it might be possible in a socialist society to develop a

> Really modern criminal literature whose main purpose would then no longer be to pass the time and to titillate the nerves. It would have attained the function of transmitting knowledge, and thereby for the first time a serious literary function.
>
> (Kaemmel, 1983, p. 61)

A final reason for the late arrival of the thriller stems from the conflict between the requirements of the form itself and the imperatives of socialist literature, that is, the conflict between individualism and collectivism. My suspicion is that socialist writers simply may have had a difficult time for *technical* reasons (ideological and censorial considerations aside) in adapting the genre.

The dramatic change in attitude toward the thriller came sometime in the late 1950s, reflecting an official reassessment of the form's functional utility. One Soviet source notes that the socialist detective novel carries much greater "moral, social, and public weight" than its Western counterpart (Ilyina & Arkadi, 1975, p. 148). Michael Heller attributes the change to the post-Stalinist thaw. Police and spy literature was encouraged because it helped develop a positive image of the dreaded forces of order. The official goal of detective and spy fiction, according to Heller, is the creation of "the positive hero." Furthermore, the literature reinforces the notion that the Soviet Union is surrounded by enemies and that it is every citizen's duty to cooperate with official forces in bringing enemies of the state to ground (Heller, 1975, pp. 166–168). Sylvain Zegel contends that the acceptance of the crime novel also reflects grudging admission that socialism suffers some of the same defects, such as crime, as the West (1965, p. 309).

A final point regarding social utility relates to Helbig's observation of the practice of factualizing fiction in East German popular novels. Factualized fiction involves including purportedly true events (made plausible by the use of historical figures and events) in the body of the fiction and inviting the reader to accept such interpretations as fact. As I shall show later, the practice of "factualizing fiction" is utilized extensively by Soviet writers.

INDIVIDUALISM, IDEOLOGY, AND THE SYSTEM

On the surface, the socialist thriller is similar to its Western counterpart. The type runs the gamut from spies in enemy territory, to counterespionage, to murder, to crime in the streets. Heroism and diligent effort join to fight evil conspiracy of one sort or another. Detectives and secret agents abound and invariably manage to solve crimes and thwart enemy conspiracies.

Beyond form, however, there is a stark contrast between East and West. In the East, the role and image of the individual protagonist and his or her relationship to one's own system are cast in different terms and so too is the image of the conspiratorial forces which threaten the proper order. Little tension is generated between the categories of intrepidity and ideology. Heroes and operatives are invariably linked in cozy symbiotic relationships with omnicompetent and compassionate authorities who provide enlightened direction at every turn. There is an exaggerated effort to vilify the conspiracy or threat to the system with lengthy and tedious "interpretations of history." In general, then, the Eastern thriller is long on ideology and short on thrills while the Western variety tends to emphasize thrills over ideological preachment.

Having said this, I hasten to add that this brief description is appropriate to the Soviet (and one Bulgarian) works but not, interestingly, the Czechoslovakian and Polish representatives herein considered. The latter works, all published originally at home, are subtle or not so subtle debunkers of the state and its keepers of order. Intrepid action is more often the mark of the criminal, victim, or ordinary citizen. There is a real tension between intrepidity and ideology in these novels in that official institutions are unsparingly criticized. For purposes of contrast, I shall first consider the Soviet variety and then turn to the Czechoslovakian and Polish works.

The Soviet Thriller

The Soviet thriller seems clearly motivated by state interests. The genre provides an appropriate mechanism for bringing the Soviet reader beyond Stalinist terror to a sense of trust in official authority. What better groups to legitimize than the police, the secret police, and the spy? What better vehicle to raise the stature of official force and to create "the positive hero" than the thriller?

A review of the Soviet novel suggests three conclusions. First, they clearly take the shape and form of the Western thriller. Second, the genre is thoroughly functional, always seeming to reflect state purposes. Third, the Soviet thriller is a most tedious and moralistic political literature. Martin Cruz Smith, the author of *Gorky Park* notes: "Soviet detective stories are different. Imagine a murder mystery intending to reassure the reader that crime is not only rare but boring, that the authorities are in control and invariably victorious" (Smith, 1984, p. 9). The fundamental problem, then, is the failure to balance the intrepid and ideological dimensions. A balance which is crucial to successful execution: "Whether you think thrillers are first and foremost the incarnation of this ideology or the source of excitement is a matter of personal taste; objectively they are both, equally and simultaneously" (Palmer, 1979, p. 66). There is little tension or conflict in the Soviet thriller. Domestic crime is an aberration and the foreign enemy poses a transitory threat because it is rotten to the core and preordained to failure. The inevitability of this failure is developed in the novels through their interpretation of socialist intrepidity, the relationship of the protagonist to the system, and of the ultimate source of conspiracy, the external enemy.

In three of our novels, heroic Soviet spies are the center of attention, Semenov's *Seventeen Moments of Spring*, Kozhevnikov's *Shield and Sword*, and Ardamatsky's *Saturn Is Almost Invisible*. Two others feature fearless counterespionage agents, Gulyashki's *Zakhov Mission* (Bulgarian), and Ovalev's *Comrade Spy*. Five are domestic crime novels, Chernyonok's *Losing Bet*, Litvinoff's *Moscow Mystery*,[4] Nilin's *Comrade Venka*, Semenov's *Petrovka 38*, and Lipatov's *The Stoletov Dossier*.

Intrepidity. These novels differ markedly in their treatment of intrepid individualism. The three spy novels, Nilin's tale of crime detection in the early postrevolutionary period on the Soviet frontier and Lipatov's Siberian murder mystery feature protagonists who seemingly act as independent forces unfettered by bureaucratic direction. But intrepidity and heroism is heavily muted in the other novels, all of which have urban and domestic settings.

In the spy novels, all of which are set in Nazi Germany, the protagonists reflect total devotion to mission and almost superhuman capac-

---

[4] Ivy Litvinoff was the wife of a former Soviet minister of foreign relations and ambassador to the United States. It is the earliest publication by a *Soviet* citizen of a mystery novel that I have uncovered.

ities. Johann Weiss, the hero of *Shield and Sword*, penetrates the highest ranks of the Nazi state developing "An almost automatic capacity for cool, accurate, self-control. He could judge himself as though he were someone else looking on from outside. . . . He felt a peculiar kind of satisfaction when his power over this personality was complete" (Kozhevnikov, 1970, p. 25). Stirlitz, in *Seventeen Moments of Spring* also rises to highest levels of confidence in wartime Germany. His imposing presence even prompts the suspicious Gestapo leader Muller to say of him:

> He's a professional of the top class. . . . If he has been working against us, I'd hate to start even guessing at the extent of the damage he's caused to the Reich. An artist of that calibre is worth a thousand of our wretched soldiers.
>
> (Semenov, 1973, p. 230)

Weiss and Stirlitz's exploits are gargantuan. In addition to saving comdemned death camp inmates and rescuing Soviet agents from the Gestapo, they are instrumental in foiling German efforts to conclude a separate peace with the West. Stirlitz also is responsible for singlehandedly undoing the "Germans' very real chances of almost getting as far as actually making an atom bomb . . ." (Semenov, 1973, p. 224).

Saturn is Almost Invisible tells of the Soviet penetration of Admiral Canaris' Saturn project whose mission was to turn Soviet POWs and citizens behind German lines into German spies. A half-dozen Soviet working-class agents ("Rudin comes from several generations of workers. Kravtsov was still a shepherd boy seven years ago. . . . [Babakin's] 'academy' consists of working in a factory . . .") succeed in repatriating Russian turncoats, keeping Moscow apprised of Saturn project counterespionage activities, and ultimately in sabotaging the whole project and severely compromising Canaris and the Abwehr in Hitler's eyes (Ardamatsky, 1971, pp. 16, 246–247, 298).

Nilin casts his central character in a heroic mold, too. Venka, the young assistant district chief with the secret police campaigns with compassion against rebels and bandits on the Siberian frontier. He lambastes a colleague for unnecessary violence—"What a pig. Just who asked him to shoot a boy?" (1959, p. 12). He is a spartan who needs no rest when his comrades drop from exhaustion. Venka charms rebels into becoming collaborators by virtue of skillful interrogation "if you could even call it an interrogation" (Nilin, 1959, p. 25). He works alone much of the time in apprehending the worst of those who oppose the regime.

Without a doubt, intrepidity is central to these works. But how do the authors square such dauntless heroics with collectivist ideology? This question is particularly relevant when considering the way Soviet critics took John LeCarré to task about his novel, *The Looking Glass War.* In a 1966 review, *Moscow Literary Gazette* criticized LeCarré for *"elevating the spy to the rank of true hero of our age"* (Quoted in LeCarré 1966, p. 3; emphasis mine). It is ironic that all of the Soviet thriller protagonists assume far greater heroic proportions than any of LeCarré's characters.

One reason Soviet heroics is allowable stems from the protagonist's isolation. As long as the major character has only a tenuous link to his control, individual initiative and judgment is acceptable. And because the enemy is so utterly evil, the hero must rise above ordinary action to foil the darkness which threatens. And yet, heroism, or intrepidity, has its limits. Semenov reminds his readers that the agent is *nothing* without his center:

> When an agent is abroad and has lost touch with his central organization, he is unable to judge—at least with sufficient reliability—how important and effective is the work he happens to be engaged in. (1973, p. 150)

The intrepid spirit is always yoked with the guiding hand of an authority representing ultimate wisdom and direction. Intrepidity is a necessary condition for successful action. But intrepidity and proper authority form the necessary *and* sufficient conditions for ultimate success.

In the crime and counterespionage works, the structure of the situation tempers dauntless individualism and faceless functionaries prevail. Smith (1984, p. 9) notes, in reviewing *Losing Bet,* that the investigating officer "Senior Investigator Anton Birukov, has no past, no interest or emotions, almost no corporeal being. The other police are referred to as fellow 'operatives.' "

The same faceless quality characterizes the gaggle of detectives on the trail of a pair of murderous bank robbers in *Petrovka 38.* The only way Semenov simulates individualism is by featuring a stuttering detective and interjecting vignettes about the detectives' personal lives into the novel. In Ovalev's *Comrade Spy* and Litvinoff's *Moscow Mystery,* the detectives and counterespionage agents are nondescript. We only know that they are compassionate, fair, competent, and that ultimately they will prevail.

Only in *The Zakhov Mission* and *The Stoletov Dossier* do we find sparks of individualism. But even here, Zakhov, a modest archeologist, and Captain Proknorov are hardly heroic in stature. Zakhov plods around the Bulgarian countryside looking for a foreign agent. We find that he prefers potatoes to women (Gulyashki, 1969, p. 93) and that he is compassionate. Zakhov's only saving grace is that he is the only protagonist in this whole lot who tastes of the pleasures of the opposite sex. One can only assume that he had his fill of potatoes. Prokhorov, the militia detective charged with investigating a suspicious death in an isolated Siberian village, is pleasant but bland, too. He follows a tedious routine, questioning over and over virtually every acquaintance of the tractor driver Zhenya, who died after a mysterious fall from a logging train. The novel builds a case for heroism only for the fallen Zhenya, who sparked a revolt against his corrupt foreman, Gasilov. Near the close of the tale, Prokhorov, in reference to Zhenya, laments that "a hero of our time has died" (Lipatov, 1983, p. 436).

Thus there is little room for intrepidness in an effective bureaucracy. Officials are expected to exercise responsibility following the just procedures of the state. To acknowledge an intrepid spirit would be to admit of a flawed system. Only the lonely spy, operating far from control, can be independent, and, even then, he does so only at some risk to his mission.

One final point should be made regarding a typical characteristic of the Soviet protagonist. Almost without exception, they are imbued with a mawkish sense of compassion. In the midst of brutal crime and sordid circumstances, officialdom is consistently seen as kind and considerate. One of the suspects in *The Stoletov Dossier* asks Captain Prokhorov, "Why are they so patient and loyal, our dear old Soviet Militia? Are you the rule, or the exception that proves the rule?" (Lipatov, 1983, p. 213). Throughout *The Zakhov Mission,* Zakhov is presented as a person of great "gentleness and feeling" (Gulyashki, 1969, p. 132). The detectives in *Petrovka 38* watch assiduously after the well-being of the innocent teen-ager implicated in one of the bank robberies under investigation. Moreover, Detective, Rosykov "always treated thieves honorably, [and] was excessively polite" (Semenov, 1965, p. 164). The spies are equally compassionate. Weiss, Stirlitz, and the Saturn spies always have time, even under the most perilous circumstances, to rescue or care for beleaguered comrades and Germans who defect to the Soviet side. Clearly, the objective of such characterization is to emphasize that representatives of state order are an eminently decent sort: " 'Do you know what is on the Soviet Secret Service Badge? . . . A shield and a sword,' said Weiss, 'and it's our duty wherever we are to protect people with the shield.' " (Kozhevnikov, 1970, p. 271)

Systems of order: The enemy within? I mentioned earlier that the Western thriller writer has traditionally been critical of existing political institutions and ideologies, the enemy's and often his or her own. In the case of ideologues such as Howard "Watergate" Hunt, criticisms of "home base" are minimal (Vidal, 1973). But even in his novels the hero is compelled to operate outside the fuzziness and ineptness which bedevils the institutions of official order.

In the Soviet novels, however, none of the heroes, detective, spy or counterspy ever finds it necessary to go beyond or against the will of the agencies to which he or she is beholden. There is little tension or conflict between hero and handler. And none of these authors allowed their main characters to offer a thorough-going ideological critique of their *own* system in the style of LeCarré, Graham Greene, or the American hard-boiled detective tradition.

System affirmation is the overwhelming theme. There is nary an ambivalent character among these agents dedicated to upholding socialist order. Counterespionage agent Major Tkachev, after capturing an American spy in *Comrade Spy*, praises his subordinates: "They're good men. . . . He recalled reading in books from Western Europe and America, descriptions of people like himself and his men. They were always depicted as bloodthirsty and none too intelligent. It was ridiculous!" (Ovalev, 1965, p. 176).

And the bureaucratic apparatus which direct our socialist heroes are equally honorable. In *Seventeen Moments of Spring,* after Stirlitz derailed the secret Nazi–Western ally peace talks in Berne, his Soviet "contact informed him that Centre could not insist that he went back to Germany, realizing the . . . risk it might mean for him" (Semenov, 1973, p. 304). It is common, too, to extol the vigilance of the state. In *Comrade Spy,* the counterespionage forces come into action after the suspicious death (done in by an American spy) of a prominent academician who:

> Had long since been one of those scientists whose life and work are important enough to come within the purview of those agencies responsible for the safety of Soviet citizens. These agencies do not interfere in the work (not to mention the private lives) of such scientists. But they *are* responsible for safeguarding the special institutions and laboratories as well as the lives and security of the people who work there.
>
> (Ovalev, 1965, p. 68)

And most of all, official order follows the dictates of due process. In *Losing Bet,* the reader is reminded at least three times that the militia is faithful to the constraints of the law when it comes to interro-

gating suspects and conducting searches and seizures, and ultimately that "we have humane laws; we like to forgive" (Chernyonok,
1984, p. 156; see also pp. 155, 165, 234).

Even the theme of crime is turned that the system escapes culpa-
bility. Smith notes that the popularity of American detective fiction is
partly a function of the ubiquity of crime and corruption whereas in
the Soviet Union the same popularity stems from a fascination with
the rareness of criminal activity (p. 9). Thus, in Semenov, Chernyonok, and Litvinoff's works, crime is an aberration without social roots
or much consequence. Their villains operate in a splendid malicious
isolation. Moreover, their malefactors are stereotyped as "leeches,
not people . . . [who] . . . clamp on and suck your juices, growing fat
until the militia put the squeeze on them" (Chernyonok, 1984, p. 87).
In *Petrovka 38* the criminals are animal degenerates: One is named
Cheetah. Prokhor "moaned monotonously and frighteningly like an
injured dog" after being collared, another was told by Captain Kosta-
lya "but I'm a man, while you, you're an animal" (Semenov, 1965, p.
196) In both *Losing Bet* and *Moscow Mystery*, the culprits are seduced by the lure of capitalist greed. The murderer in *Moscow Mystery* turns out to be a counterrevolutionary member of the White Army
(Litvinoff, 1946, p. 266). In *Losing Bet*, the suspects include an artist
"culturally corrupted by the west," a Georgian capitalist, and a professional criminal influenced by Christianity. Thus, socialist society is
absolved: Crime is the progeny either of a random mutation of human into animal or of corrupting foreign ideologies.

It is important to note, however, that several novels do include critical themes. Semenov (in *Petrovka 38*) and Chernyonok highlight the
problem of alcoholism in the Soviet Union. In *The Stoletov Dossier*,
Prokhorov uncovers a corrupt system in which Gasilov, the logging
foreman, deliberately sets low production quotas so that "the plan is
always overfulfilled . . . [and] Gasilov gets an extremely high bonus
payment every month" (Lipatov, 1983, p. 218). The real hero is the
tractor driver Zhenya, who charged before he died that "to keep down
output means robbing the state" and attempted to lead his fellow
workers into a "strike in reverse," a heroic effort to produce beyond
the puny levels set by the bosses (Lipatov, 1983, pp. 374–375). Kozhevnikov and Arkamatsky levy not so subtle criticisms against Stalin
and Beria for not being prepared for the 1941 German invasion. Both
authors make the point that intelligence sources within Germany (including, of course, their protagonists) provided at great personal risk
ample warnings of German intentions, warnings which often were ignored or treated with scorn and skepticism at home (Kozhevnikov,
1970, p. 86; Ardamatsky, 1971, p. 8).

In all likelihood, these "criticisms" merely reflect officially approved concerns. Alcohol abuse and manipulation of production quotas have long been appropriate public topics. And questions regarding the lack of Soviet vigilance in 1939–1940 simply mirror revisionist criticisms of Stalinist errors and excesses.

In *Moscow Mystery* and *Comrade Venka* the reader sees a Soviet society in turmoil. Litvinoff reports of chaos in the streets of Moscow, the multitudes of homeless youth, and severe housing shortages. Nilin, too, writes of lawlessness on the eastern frontier. But these critiques are acceptable as historical statements which reflect how far Soviet society has progressed. Litvinoff notes in her introduction (published in 1946) how much things had changed since her 1926 novel. Even then progress was noticeable:

> The efforts of the state were by the year 1926 causing considerable depletion in the ranks of the flotsam and jetsam of Russian towns, those orphans of the storm, the children set adrift a few years before by famine and civil war.
>
> (Litvinoff, 1946, p. 82)

One of Nilin's characters affirms that "under communism a lot will happen. But first we have to catch all the bandits and fix things so that there won't be any more crookedness and speculation" (1959, p. 61). Thus, in the beginning, crime was present, but only as a function of a prerevolutionary malaise. In the end, communism prevails.

Conspiracy: The enemy without. Each of the Soviet thrillers is fraught with ideological overkill regarding the enemies of socialism. The conspiratorial forces are perfidious, venal, and cowardly. And the reader is reminded constantly of the need for eternal vigilance against these implacable foes. The most virulent anti-Western critique is found in the spy novels; all are set during World War II. This particular venue affords the opportunity to enlighten the Russian people about the Western conspiracy and to set the historical record straight.

Three themes highlight the moral bankruptcy of the West (especially Germany) and the conspiracy against socialism. First, almost without fail, Germans are portrayed as cowardly and depraved, especially officers of the *Wermacht*. Weiss's commander, Major Steinlitz, in one scene accuses his troops of cowardly behavior and then demands for himself "an escort of more than a dozen military vehicles" through an area where partisans *might* be lurking (Kozhevnikov, 1970, p. 63). The novels are laced with reports of German brutality and perfidy, few of which are necessary for plot development.

Nazi leaders are nothing but a pack of conniving and paranoid thieves, all trying to solidify their own positions in increasing desperation. The top echelon, including Himmler, Bormann, Schellenberg, and Goering, has little interest in pursuing affairs of state. They are much more interested in frenetically shipping personal (or Reich) assets out of the country or in jockeying for position following the imminent surrender. Page after tedious page records the smallest details of these intrigues.

To be sure, Reich leaders were often venal and grossly self-serving. But these novels, in their haste to propagandize, come across as grossly exaggerated caricature or comic opera parody. Again, these grotesque characterizations serve well to foster a desired anti-German vigilance.

The second theme is the Western attempt to conclude a separate peace with Germany to allow the allies to concentrate on the eastern front. In both *Sword and Shield* and *Seventeen Moments of Spring* the plot centers around Weiss and Stirlitz's heroic efforts to foil this pact. Here we see an excellent example of "factualizing fiction." The text of *Seventeen Moments of Spring* is rife with "factual" memoranda to and from Reich officials about the negotiations. There is even a transcript of a conversation between German negotiator Karl Wolff and Allen Dulles. The novels trade heavily on plausibility: Dulles was in Switzerland during World War II and several Reich leaders did put out feelers about "peace without Hitler" later in the war. They extrapolate, however, to the unsubstantiated conclusion that the Allies deliberately tried to conclude such a peace.

In *Seventeen Moments of Spring* Stirlitz foils the secret talks by exposing the fact that the one person the West would not negotiate with, Heinrich Himmler, was the moving force behind the talks. The novel ends with a "Personal and Secret [Reply] from Premier J. V. Stalin to the President Mr. F. Roosevelt" which scolds the Anglo-American alliance for not having the Russians "present at the meeting with the Germans in Switzerland," and asserts that "the Russians would never have denied the Americans and British the right to attend such a meeting" (Semenov, 1973, p. 302). In the end, the Soviet reader is left with claims that are hard to deny, particularly in a system where the historical record is difficult to check.

The third theme is the continuing Western threat. Weiss warns his superiors that:

> The allies have sent a complete army of agents to Germany [to study] the mood of the German people, the strength of the opposition. . . . Dulles is concerned to keep the Wermacht strong, even in defeat, so that it can crush the revolutionary movement in the country.
>
> (Kozhevnikov, 1970, p. 318)

Saturn is Almost Invisible concludes with the capture in Moscow long after the end of the war of a German spy who was once second in command of the Saturn project (Ardamatsky, 1971, p. 320). Thus, Germany is an abiding enemy and eternal vigilance is the order of the day. Still, the perfidy of America is not neglected. Ovalev reminds his readers in *Comrade Spy* that the American agent is "a man sent by that same gang of humanity-haters who were ready to transform whole world into a proving ground for atomic bombs" (1965, p. 176).

Assessment. In the Soviet thriller intrepidness is often appropriate to achieve the ends of the state. But, intrepid individualism is out of place where legitimate institutions are in place. Soviet peace keepers are able and compassionate in foiling the nefarious efforts of spies or domestic criminals. Socialism is unassailable—the enemies of socialism are implacable. The objective of these novels is to reinforce the notion that there is no tension between individual freedom or intrepidness and state ideology. The only tension which exists is between the protagonist *and* his authority, against their common enemy. But even this tension is weak because the socialist system is perfect and that of the enemy so depraved that there is no question of the final outcome. Thus, the form of the thriller lingers but the spirit does not. The genre perhaps serves its legitimating function, but it does not join intrepidity and ideology in such a manner to pose questions about paradoxical relationships between human will and institutional demands.

Thrillers in Dissent

The works of Czechoslovakian author Josef Skvorecky and Polish writers Jerzy Andrzejewski, Stanislaw Lem, and Leopold Tyrmand provide a stark contrast to the leaden Soviet plots. The backdrop for action for these authors is criminal activity. Each of these novels has a protagonist who operates in some relation to an official institutional and ideological order. But intrepid spirit is more the domain of ordinary individuals than the official forces and socialist order is not immune from question or even ridicule.

The intrepid spirit. The clearest manifestation of the intrepid spirit is the ex-hoodlum Nowak, "the man with the white eyes." In the novel of that name, Tyrmand portrays a postwar Warsaw dominated and paralyzed by organized crime. The police are unable to control a mounting crime wave and only the terrifying vigilante Nowak can save the day. With a few ordinary citizens, Nowak fights crime and foils an archcriminal's plot to sell thousands of forged tickets to a World Cup soccer match. Even the police are in awe of this just avenger, "a romantic and highly colored tale of a new Zorro, supposed to be the exterminator of evil and violence and the mysterious 'terror' of Warsaw's gangs" (Tyrmand, 1959, p. 129). Nowak is tested when the mob and police alike attempt to eliminate him. In the end, however, the criminal ring is broken, Nowak is vindicated, and official authority is ridiculed for its ineptness.

In *Miss Silver's Past,* intrepidness takes an unusual twist. The murderess, Miss Silver, is the real hero, along with the thoroughly lecherous publishing house editor, Leden, who plays detective. The plot centers around Leden's attempts to seduce the mysterious Miss Silver, who continuously rejects him and cozies up to his boss, Comrade Prochazka, the opportunistic and pompous head of a state publishing house. Eventually Prochazka drowns at a company picnic. Leden determines that Miss Silver killed him because Prochazka had spurned her Jewish sister after the Communist takeover in 1948. Skvorecky makes a strong statement here about the conflict between individualism and the state. The law has no claim on a criminal when his or her crime against the state is honorable and just. No tears are to be shed for the likes of Prochazka, an unprincipled bureaucratic hack:

> In the years 1930 to 1938 [he] was enlisted in the service of the Masaryk ideology; in the years 1939 to 1945 in the service of our Lord Jesus Christ; in the years 1945 to the present in the services of the philosophy of Marx, Engels, and Lenin; until the Twentieth Party Congress, also in the Service of Stalin.
>
> (Skvorecky, 1974, p. 61)

And Leden's individual spirit is lauded too: The rogue, who in his quest for Miss Silver shamelessly casts aside his own mistress, refuses to turn her over to state authority. Justice must go before official order.

Stanislaw Lem, known for his science fiction, has written two crime novels, *The Investigation* and *Chain of Chance,* which offer subtle but powerful critiques of the pretensions of *any* official order, capitalist or socialist. For Lem there are cosmic forces, inexplicable and random, which always frustrate human institutions and the rational ideology which drives them. *The Investigation* (1974), set in London, involves the investigation of a series of mysterious body snatchings (and later reappearances). The nondescript Lt. Gregory fails to solve the "crimes" (indeed, he never determines if there was any crime at all) and is reduced in the end to admitting the possibility of miraculous "Lazarus" type movements or nonhuman interventions. *Chain of Chance* is the tale of a private investigator retracing the steps of a dozen middle-aged men who became insane and either died or were driven to suicide after vacationing at an Italian spa. The protagonist searches in vain for a criminal but only after he too is nearly driven to suicide does he discover that the mysterious deaths were precipitated by the random concatenation of certain factors, factors shared by all the victims: "A person would die if he used the hormone ointment [for baldness], took Ritalin and mineral baths, and ate the Neapolitan-style sugar-roasted almonds" (Lem, 1975, p. 172).

Ashes and Diamonds tells of an unsuccessful attempt by anti-Communist partisans to murder an important Communist leader after the Soviet "liberation" of Poland in 1945. While this novel is less the traditional crime thriller than the others, nevertheless, the acts are criminal and there is a theme of intrepidity throughout. For Andrzejewski, intrepidness, whether that of the assassin or of official authority, is flawed. The assassin-designate is a highly complex person, heroic but ambivalent. So too is Staniewicz's target, a courageous Communist leader, who defers to the Christian piety of many of his fellow citizens and yet defends the new order. Andrzejewski's treatment of his characters closely parallels LeCarré's characterizations of major figures in his novels such as George Smiley and Alex Leamas in terms of an honorable but flawed heroism.

For the most part, there is a different witness to the intrepid spirit than in the Soviet works. Intrepidity is not often linked with official order. Quite the contrary, intrepid action in search of justice sometimes must be exercised outside formal structures of order or even in opposition to the law.

Ideological Critique. In contrast to Soviet thrillers, these novels are anything but system affirming. From Skvorecky's satiric/critique to Andrzejewski's subtle ambivalence there is a marked divergence from the Soviet affirmation of certitude and well-oiled and effective bureaucratic keepers of order.

Skvorecky highlights the absurdity of rule by philistines attentive only to party line. In the introduction to *Miss Silver's Past*, banned in Czechoslovakia in 1967, then published in 1969 and then banned again, he confides that he tried to make the novel "look like light literature, like an entertainment. . . . to make it a melodrama, a debased genre, so that it would escape the attention of the man with the rubber stamp" (1974, p. xvi). For him, the novel is not antisocialist, but only a protest, "against the private ownership of esthetics by a handful of hacks in the top echelons of a dictatorship's bureaucracy" (p. xvi). Leden reports endless editorial debates over whether

God should be capitalized in a new book or the dilemma of how to handle the religious overtones in *Uncle Tom's Cabin*. In the latter case, Prochazka assigned it to a translator "who adapted the work in such a masterful fashion that Uncle Tom talked like a trade-unionist and all references to the non-existent deity were eliminated." (Skvorecky, 1974, pp. 40–41) In combination, the exposé of bureaucratic inanity and the affirmation of the appropriateness of Miss Silver's felony provide a telling denial that all's well in the socialist paradise.

Ashes and Diamonds and *The Man with the White Eyes*, are telling criticisms of socialist order. Kalicki, an old guard Socialist in *Ashes and Diamonds*, says to his friend, the Communist Szcyuka, "I'm worried where you're taking Poland. . . . Russian imperialism and Russian aggression are the same" (Andrzejewski, 1965, chap. 6). In *The Man with the White Eyes*, socialist order is constantly debunked. A merchant seeking protection from street violence asks Meyernos, the archcriminal "what protection can the police give us, compared with you sir? Just look how feeble they are!" (Tyrmand, 1959, p. 113). Later at a police press conference, two reporters are overheard talking about the official police spokesman:

'Who's he?'

'Never heard of him,' said the other. 'He'll start off with a quotation from Lenin, see if he doesn't.'

'Then he'll wreck the whole thing.' said the first. 'As soon as he starts jawing about imperialists, I'm leaving!'

(Tyrmand, 1959, p. 258)

Indeed, many of the criminals are bureaucrats: Meyernos directs a state cooperative, and his partner in the soccer ticket scam, is a greedy functionary in the Ministry of Physical Culture.

But both novels, and Lem's, too, offer even more telling criticisms of socialist (or indeed, of any) order. They all witness to a certain ineradicable disorder in society beyond the control of any official force. Lem's novels, with their inexplicable events and random deaths, testify to a more cosmic disorder. Tyrmand and Andrzejewski's tales of street crime and political resistance testify to the more palpable social disorder which plagues even socialist regimes. The message is clear that social and political control is always tenuous, even in systems with pretensions of closure, and that no order, even socialist, can stay the tide of chaos. *The Chain of Chance* concludes with the assertion that "we now live in such a dense world of random chance, in a molecular and chaotic gas whose 'improbabilities' are amazing only to the individual human atoms" (Lem, 1975, p. 179).

Clearly, there is a remarkable difference between Soviet thrillers and those of Eastern Europe. To be sure, these novels comprise but a small sample of the total genre. However, the study has included virtually everything published in English. Certainly, there are Czechoslovakian and Polish thriller writers who are just as "system-affirming" as the Soviet and Bulgarian authors discussed above. I doubt, however, that anything like *Miss Silver's Past* or *The Man with the White Eyes* has been published in the Soviet Union.

Even considering the small sample, it hardly seems coincidental that the Soviet and Czechoslovakian–Polish novels are so different. In "The Tragedy of Central Europe," Czechoslovakian expatriate Milan Kundera helps explain this difference. Kundera argues that for the Eastern European, at least Hungarians, Czechoslovakians, and Poles, "the word Europe does not represent a phenomenon of geographic but a spiritual notion synonymous with the word 'West'" (1984), p. 33). These nations, in the East, but *European*, have little affinity with the Soviet Union and have striven mightily since 1945 to convince the West of that reality.

Thus, in part, we may be able to account for the marked differences in genres by appeal to Kundera's point. Czech and Polish works are more open and critical because theirs is a Western art. Not only is the intrepid spirit (an intrepidness not tied slavishly to proper authority) in evidence, but there is a true irreverence toward official structures of order. And we are full circle back to a Western literature where intrepidness and ideology are compatible and manage to coexist in healthy tension.

CONCLUSION

Thus, the Eastern thriller is also a political literature. The Soviet example contributes to system stability. The Eastern European variety is a clear example of artistic protest. This research suggests several new directions of inquiry. There is a substantial number of emigré thrillers, including works by East German Uwe Johnson (1963), Czechosolvakian Egon Hostovsky, (1952), Yugoslavian Igor Sentjurc (1959), and the Russians Nikolai Narokov (1958) and Victor Serge (1951). Their perspectives on intrepidity and ideology, radical individualism and statism, are similar to the Czechoslovakian and Polish works and well worth examining in a comparative context.

I am fascinated, too, by the development of two different forms of the popular thriller in the United States. On one hand, it would be instructive to compare the Soviet thriller with those of Martin Cruz Smith (*Gorky Park,* 1981) and Anthony Olcott (*Murder at the Red October,* 1982, and *May Day at Magadan,* 1983), Americans who also write Soviet crime novels. The realism of these works provides interesting contrast with the narrowness of the Soviet writings—particularly in reflecting on domestic crime and the forces of order in socialist systems. The other comparison is between the Soviet thriller and a new strain of American political fiction typified by Arnaud de Borchgrave and Robert Moss's works, *The Spike* (1980) and *Monimbo* (1983). In this new and very conservative fiction there is a clear effort at "factualizing fiction." In effect, these American works engage in the same kind of ideological overkill as the Soviets. This may prove an interesting and perhaps ominous development for the genre which at its very best strives to balance its thrills with ideological preachment.

REFERENCES

Andrzejewski, J. (1965). *Ashes and diamonds.* New York: Penguin Books.

Ardamatsky, V. (1971). *Saturn is almost invisible.* Moscow: Progress Publishers.

de Borchgrave, A., & Moss, R. (1980). *The spike.* New York: Avon.

de Borchgrave, A., & Moss, R. (1983). *Monimbo.* New York: Avon.

Chernyonok, M. (1984). *Losing bet.* New York: Dial Press/Doubleday.

Eisenstein, S. M. (1970). El genero policiaco. In R. Gubern (Ed.), *La novela criminal.* Barcelona: Tusqueta Editor.

Esfandiary, F. (1959). *Day of sacrifice.* New York: McDowell.

Gramsci, A. (1970). Sul romanzo poliziesco. In R. Gubern (Ed.), La novela criminal. Barcelona: Tusqueta Editor.

Gubern, R. (1970). Prologo. In R. Gubern (Ed.), *La novela criminal.* Barcelona: Tusqueta Editor.

Gulyashki, A. (1969). *The Zakhov Mission.* Garden City, NY: Doubleday.

Helbig, L. F. (1977, Fall). The myth of the 'other' America in East German popular consciousness. *Journal of Popular Culture, 10.*

Heller, M. (1975, Winter/Spring). Stalin and the detectives. *Survey, 21.*

Hostovsky, E. (1952). *Missing.* New York: Viking Press.

Howe, I. (1970). *Politics and the novel.* New York: Avon.

Ilyina, N., & Arkadi, A. (1975). Detective novels: A game and life. *Soviet Literature, 323.* Vol. 3

Johnson, U. (1963). *Speculations about Jakob.* New York: Grove Press.

Kaemmel, E. (1983). Literature under the table: The detective novel and its social mission. In G. W. Most & W. W. Stone (Eds.), *The poetics of murder.* New York: Harcourt Brace Jovanovich.

Kirst, H. H. (1964). *The night of the generals.* New York: Harper & Row.

Kirst, H. H. (1967). *Brothers in arms.* New York: Harper & Row.

Kozhevnikov, V. (1970). *Shield and sword: The amazing career of a Soviet agent in the Nazi secret service.* London: Macgibbon & Kee.

Kundera, M. (1984, April 26). The tragedy of Central Europe. *New York Review of Books, 31.*

LeCarré, J. (1966, May). To Russia with greeting: An open letter to the Moscow Literary Gazette. *Encounter, 26.*

Lem, S. (1974). *The investigation.* New York: Seabury.

Lem, S. (1975). *The chain of chance.* New York: Harcourt Brace Jovanovich.

Lipatov, V. (1983). *The Stoletov dossier.* Moscow: Raduga.

Litvinoff, I. (1946). *Moscow mystery.* New York: Howard–McCann.

Mannheim, K. (1936). *Ideology and utopia.* New York: Harcourt, Brace and World.

McClure, J. (1972). *The steam pig.* New York: Harper & Row.

McClure, J. (1976). *The snake.* New York: Harper & Row.

Narokov, N. (1958). *The chains of fear.* Chicago: Henry Regnery.

Neuse, S. M. (1980, January). Teaching political science with chillers and thrillers. *Teaching Political Science, 7.*

Neuse, S. M. (1982, Autumn). Bureaucratic malaise in the modern spy novel: Deighton, Greene, and LeCarre. *Public Administration, 60.*

Nilin, P. (1959). *Comrade Venka.* New York: Marzani & Munsell.

Olcott, A. (1982). *Murder at the Red October.* New York: Bantam.

Olcott, A. (1983). *May Day at Magadan.* New York: Bantam.

Ovalev, L. (1965). *Comrade spy.* New York: Avon.

Palmer, J. (1979). *Thrillers: Genesis and structure of a popular genre.* New York: St. Martin's.

Semenov, J. (1965). *Petrovka 38.* New York: Stein & Day.

Semenov, J. (1973). *Seventeen moments of spring.* Moscow: Progress Publishers.

Sentjurc, I. (1959). *Prayer for an assassin.* Garden City, NY: Doubleday.

Serge, V. (1951). *The case of Comrade Tulayev.* New York: Doubleday.

Sjowall, M., & Wahloo, P. (1965). *Roseanna.* New York: Random House.

Sjowall, M., & Wahloo, P. (1976). *The terrorists.* New York: Random House.

Skvorecy, J. (1974). *Miss Silver's past.* New York: Grove Press.

Smith, M. C. (1981). *Gorky Park.* New York: Random House.

Smith, M. C. (1984, May 6). Whodunit in Novosibirsk. *New York Times Book Review.*

Tyrmand, L. (1959). *The man with the white eyes.* New York: Knopf.

Vidal, G. (1973, December 13). The art and arts of E. Howard Hunt. *New York Review of Books, 20.*

Yates, D. (Ed.). (1972). *Latin blood: The best crime and detective stories of South America.* New York: Herder & Herder.

Zegel, S. (1965, May). Whodunit–Soviet Style. *Atlas, 9.*

14

The Kennedy Story in Folklore and Tabloids: Intertextuality in Political Communication

S. Elizabeth Bird

FOLKLORE AND MASS MEDIA

Folklore, the orally transmitted traditions of any given group of people, has rarely been considered by communications scholars, remaining the province of anthropologists and specialized folklorists. Yet the transmission and maintenance of folk traditions are clearly complex communication processes which are important in constituting the world-view of any culture. According to Bascom (1954), in a classic statement, folklore serves to educate, to validate culture, to maintain conformity, and to serve as an outlet for wish fulfillment.

Through folklore, such as tales, jokes, legends, and rumor, a culture reaffirms its values and offers answers to perplexing questions. Rodgers (1985), one of the few communications scholars to look closely at folklore as communication, offers an explanation for the importance of "urban legends"—the usually apochryphal tales that circulate orally about phantom hitchhikers, cats in microwaves, celebrities in unusual situations, and so on. Drawing on the work of Brunvand (1981) and others, Rodgers explains the importance of such legends in constituting and reconstituting a culture's world-view, which often appears unscientific, distrustful of government and technology, and reliant on sterotypical views of gender and different ethnic groups. Brunvand's study of urban legends points out that although the tales are told as entertainment, they depend on a degree of plausibility and authentication, confirming and revitalizing existing fears and stereotypes by articulating these in narrative form. The legends will continue to circulate in different, ever-changing variants as long as there is a reason to tell them. Almost all make some overt or implicit point; a lesson is learned in the telling.

Rodgers argues for the importance of analyzing oral tradition as popular communication, pointing out that folklore is a thriving process in contemporary, urban communities. Rodgers's work is unusual in bringing folklore into the realm of communication study. In general there has been virtually no contact between folklorists, with their emphasis on oral transmission, and media scholars, with theirs on mediated transmission. Increasingly, folklorists are having to look at media, but the approach is usually to identify folkloric motifs that appear in the media—folklore in literature, in television, and so on. Several researchers, such as Brunvand (1981) and Hobbs (1978), have shown how newspapers sometimes pass on urban legends, but the idea seems to be that this is somehow accidental, that newspapers are primarily concerned with "facts," but sometimes they get duped.

Thus Degh and Vazsonyi point out, "there is no doubt that media draws heavily on folklore and vice versa," (1973, p. 36), but they go on to distinguish between "genuine folk tradition" and the media contribution to it. Even those folklorists who study urban cultures will often ignore the fact that these contemporary "folk" are surrounded by messages from many sources other than face-to-face contact. For the sake of disciplinary convenience they continue to separate genres and sources in a way that misrepresents the actual cultural context.

Meanwhile, media researchers have viewed newspapers and other media as active transmitters that act upon passive consumers, in a one-way transmission process. The result has been a tradition in American media research that emphasizes effect rather than process, and the discovery of the uniqueness of media messages rather than their cultural context (Kepplinger, 1979). With both disciplines defending the uniqueness of oral versus media communication processes, there has been little opportunity for dialogue. Donald Allport Bird (1976) was one of the first to question this state of affairs, challenging folklorists to take a broader view of media:

> Folklore and mass communications share common frameworks of defined situations, structure, function, and tradition. Communication—whether folkloric or mass—frequently takes place through media and contains verbal and non-verbal expressive forms and common symbols that are often ritualistic and ceremonial. Mass communication in itself

in itself is a social, cultural phenomenon worthy of study by the folklorist. (pp. 285–286)

The crucial point here is the assertion that mass communication
in itself is worthy of study—not just the way folkloric themes sometimes filter into the media, but the process of the media message
itself, taking into account the interaction of the consumer in receiving
and interpreting the message.

In this study, I draw together some of the approaches of folklore
and media research to show that oral transmission and media transmission may not be as distinct in kind as the interdisciplinary barriers
would suggest. In addition, I suggest that scholars of political communication could enrich their understanding of audience's political
world-view by acknowledging the role of both oral communication
and nonmainstream media in representing that world-view.

The case study chosen is an examination of the image of President
John F. Kennedy in weekly "supermarket tabloid" newspapers, such
as the National Enquirer, Globe, Star, and others, which have an estimated combined circulation of around 12 million to 15 million copies
weekly (McDonald, 1984). This shows how that image draws on orally
transmitted "legends," but also how media accounts themselves
work like urban legends in restructuring diffuse beliefs, uncertainties,
and stereotypes in narrative form. The image of Kennedy can be seen
to derive from many sources, oral and mediated; to divide these into
entirely different processes, worthy of study by entirely different spe-
cialists, is artificial and unproductive. People contruct a view of reality
from all the culturally embedded messages they encounter, whether
these are oral, written, or electronic. Furthermore, the media themselves, as part of culture, develop their themes and tell their stories
in ways that are not unlike the process of oral transmission.

KENNEDY AND THE TABLOIDS

Several folklorists have pointed out the way supermarket tabloids
have picked up folkloristic stories, including Kennedy legends.
Blaustein (undated) has looked in a more general sense at the way
the National Enquirer restates the folk theme of "rags-to-riches" by
constantly retelling it through specific stories. His approach is, I believe, more fruitful than simply pointing out appearances of clearly
identifiable urban legends in print. Rather, we look for some kind of
cumulative themes that emerge from the papers over time.

These themes are clear, and have been listed by a writer who has made a living in the tabloid market (Holden, 1979). They include celebrity gossip, rags-to-riches stories, self-improvement through diet and exercise (often with an almost magical component), government waste and "conspiracies," occult and paranormal phenomena, and the handicapped overcoming terrible odds.

Tabloid interest in John F. Kennedy is consistent with several of these themes, and tabloid personnel say that he is still a guaranteed attraction on their covers.[1] The Kennedys seem to have a special status among political figures; folk traditions quite rarely grow around politics and politicians. Shortlived "joke cycles" frequently arise around political events (Preston, 1985), and some politicians, such as Abraham Lincoln and Winston Churchill, live on in anecdotes, usually about their endearing foibles (Barrick, 1976). A few politicians, such as Gary Hart, have briefly become the subject of both joke cycles and tabloid attention (*National Enquirer*, 1987). Kennedy, however, is unique in modern times in being the center of folk and popular traditions that still circulate 25 years after his death.

Kennedy's role as a tabloid hero only began to emerge after his death. Just as there is relatively little lasting political folklore, tabloids generally ignore conventional politics (although they are not apolitical, as we shall see). It was clearly Kennedy's developing status as a popular hero rather than as a president as such that turned him into a tabloid staple. During Kennedy's life, he was just another politician, and thus generally of little interest. Just before the 1960 New Hampshire primary, the *National Enquirer*, in a brief, soon-to-be dropped "political" column, reported that Kennedy's biggest drawback as a presidential candidate was "the vagueness of his popularity with the voters" (*National Enquirer*, 1960a), while in April of that year it commented: "He fears that his youthful appearance will cost him a good deal of support" (1960b, p. 10). Even the assassination itself was ignored in 1963 by the *National Enquirer*, which presumably was not anticipating the growth of a "legend."

However, not long after Kennedy's death, and especially following doubts raised by the Warren Commission findings, the legend was under way:

> Suddenly, the dead Kennedy became what he had been for relatively few in life—the hope for the future, the promise of advancement for the underdog, the notion of grace and magic, the hero, the Prince of youth . . . it was also the age-old horror of the slaying of the priest-king, which Kennedy had not been until he fell.
>
> (Edwards, 1984, p. 413)

---

[1] Series of interviews with staff of the *National Examiner*, February, 1986.

The legend seemed to spring up in printed and oral contexts simultaneously. Popular printed stories defining the image began to appear almost immediately after the assassination. In 1964, for instance, Warden and Childs of New York issued a 25-cent comic book, "The Illustrated Story of John F. Kennedy, Champion of Freedom" (Anonymous 1964). The picture book promised the "story of a great American family, whose history began in poverty and whose story was climaxed by reaching the highest office in the land." The booklet chronicles Kennedy's war heroism, his great work for peace, and finally the assassination, closing with the funeral and a rendering of the famous John Kennedy Jr. salute. "His mother now stepped forward and to forever bless the memory of her beloved husband, lit the Eternal Flame which shall burn forever by his grave." Kennedy also quickly became the hero of dozens of *corridos,* the orally composed ballads of Mexican-Americans (Dickey, 1978).

While the corridos primarily celebrated Kennedy as a peacemaker and respecter of ethnic rights, the oral legends and tabloids focused on three themes that have little to do directly with his politics. These themes have changed and developed in the years since the assassination, but an examination of available tabloid stories from the 1960s to 1980s show that they have remained quite consistent.[2] Perhaps the most striking is the "Kennedy-is-alive" story.

This legend is still circulating orally, and was first documented in the folklore literature in the late 1960s. De Caro and Oring (1969) detail tales collected from oral tradition that describe Kennedy as alive in a "vegetable-like state" in Athens, and the marriage of Jacqueline Kennedy to Aristotle Onassis as a carefully arranged fake, with sources often offering psychic Jeane Dixon as authority for the story. Rosenberg (1976) gives oral variants in which Kennedy is in Parkland Hospital in Dallas or at Camp David.

Rosenberg also discusses the circulation of the story, attributed to Truman Capote, in the Milwaukee *Metro-News* and the *National Informer,* a now-defunct Chicago-based tabloid, again including an explanation for Jacqueline Kennedy's marriage. Baker (1976) offers a variant reported in the *National Tattler* in 1971: Kennedy on a Greek

---

[2] Tabloid back issues are virtually impossible to obtain. Pre-1983 stories are part of a large collection of Kennedy memorabilia owned by Mrs. Mary Ferrell of Dallas. I do not claim to have had access to all tabloid stories. Remaining texts cited appeared in several weekly tabloids from July, 1983, through 1984. Some stories were obtained in the form of photocopies from publishers' offices; in these cases, page references are unavailable.

island owned by Onassis. His widow is supposed to have married Onassis only so she can visit the island without suspicion. The story also appeared in 1971 in the Montreal-based tabloid *Midnight* (which later became the *Globe*). In this story (1971b), the island is identified as Skorpios. The elaborate story includes photographs supposedly taken by a British tourist, and quotes "six unshakable eyewitnesses." The "witnesses" reported that Kennedy was "helpless like a baby. His body was wasted away." In addition, "The entire back of his head was a scarred mass. It had been operated on several times. There was a metal plate under the skin to protect the brain where the bone was broken away." Accordingly to a former staff member of that publication, the story and photographs were fabricated and staged, and were prompted by the widely known legends circulating orally at the time.[3] In another issue, (1971a), *Midnight* claimed that the story had recently appeared in the British *Sunday Express,* the Italian *Oggi,* and the Belgian *Zondag Nieuws.*

The most recent printed version appeared in the *National Examiner* (1983a). In this variant, Kennedy is being kept closely guarded at a retreat in the Swiss Alps. He has regained some of his mental functions, and on good days he has the ablities of an 11-year-old. The story is reminiscent both of urban legends and of mainstream news accounts in its attention to detail and insistence on attribution to reliable sources. In this case the authority is a Swedish psychic, Sven Petersen, "who contributes to para-psychology newsletters around the world and is especially respected for his experiments in communication with the dead." Throughout the story his expertise is stressed: "a reputation as one of the world's most skilled mediums" and "a considerable reputation for accuracy and veracity." The story also quotes a Chandra Singh, "a political scientist at the University of Calcutta," who maintains that these circumstances would explain the many discrepancies in accounts of what happened to Kennedy after the shooting. In this version, it is pointed out that Jacqueline Kennedy was not party to the secret, a point that indicates the way she has been gradually cut out of the picture over the years as the JFK image assumed prominence.

The story, of course, rests on the assumption that *National Examiner* readers have a great deal of faith in psychics, an assumption that pervades all tabloid narratives and which also underlies other stories that have developed the "Kennedy-is-alive" theme. In these cases, Kennedy has been reincarnated, first in the form of a 7-year-old Ger-

---

[3] Interview with Mary Perpich, former staff writer for *Midnight,* August 6, 1985, Memphis, Tenn.

man boy (*Sun,* 1984). "Psychics have confirmed that they can communicate with the spirit of JFK through Klaus Zimmerman," the account claims, adding that a U. S. government official "shook his head in amazement" when he interviewed the boy. Again, the details: "He even recalls a 1962 conversation between little Caroline Kennedy and the ambassador of Niger." Psychics quoted in the account predict that Klaus will grow up to be a great leader who will reunite East and West Berlin—echoes of "Ich bin ein Berliner," perhaps.

A month later, a 10-year-old Indian girl is "hailed by scientists and religious leaders as incredible proof of reincarnation (*National Examiner,* 1984c). Chandra Murakajee, "a world-respected parapsychologist and professor of antiquities," is quoted as saying, "there is little doubt that Sharda lived before as President Kennedy." Like Klaus, she suffers headaches that are her recollections of the assassination. Incidentally, the Mexican-American corridos also develop the notion of Kennedy living on, although in a more symbolic way. Dickey (1978, p. 55) suggests that the corridos "seem to be similar to the many rumors for years after Kennedy's death that he was still alive." He also mentions the case of at least one female *curandera,* or healer, "who invokes Kennedy's spiritual power as well as the power of other 'folk saints' as beneficial forces to help with her cures" (p. 55).

As Rosenberg (1976) points out, the notions of a dead mythic hero (or villain) being alive and ready to return, or returning in the form of another person, are widespread heroic motifs. Tied closely to the idea of Kennedy's return is the theme of a conspiracy that killed him: perhaps he is dead, but it took almost superhuman powers to kill him, a motif also discussed by Rosenberg. This old motif was probably fueled further by the genuine controversy over the Warren Commission's conclusions, and the uncertainties surrounding responsibility for the murder. Ambiguity and unsatisfactorarily explained circumstances traditionally provide fertile ground for the growth of legend and rumor (Mullen, 1972). The circumstances surrounding the assassination thus provide the second main focus for tabloid coverage of Kennedy.

Speculation about responsibility for the murder has raged through the tabloids for years, with the consensus being that a conspiracy was involved. The *National Enquirer* (1975) went so far as to offer $100,000 for proof of a conspiracy, the reward to expire 1 year later. Although it seems never to have been claimed, the *Enquirer* and other tabloids continued to uncover answers. Thus the *National Tattler* (no longer published) reported in 1975 its discovery of a "conspiracy plot" that would show that the CIA, in league with other government intelligence agencies, was involved in the assassination

(1975b). Another reported affidavit would show a plot "among Communists, the CIA and the John Birch society" (p. 4). The story adds the Mafia to the conspiracy, finally claiming that Richard M. Nixon and Watergate figures Frank Sturgis and E. Howard Hunt may also have been involved. The web is tangled further by the suggestion that Lee Harvey Oswald's killer, Jack Ruby, may have been "infected with cancer cells" in order to kill him.

The now-defunct tabloid *Modern People,* (1975c) reported that Oswald was "programmed" to kill Kennedy in the Soviet Union on the auspicious date of April 1, 1961. The Soviets used "a hypnotic technique known as RHIC-Edom," (Radio-Hypnotic Intracerebral Control-Electronic Dissolution of Memory). This used a miniaturized radio receiver surgically implanted in the cerebral region, making Oswald a "robot killer" who would immediately forget his crime. The CIA then used Oswald for its own purposes. According to another story in *Modern People,* (1975b) Jack Ruby and Sirhan Sirhan, killer of Robert Kennedy, were programmed in the same way. The effect of the conspiracy was dramatic: "You'll learn that on Nov. 22, 1963, our government was overthrown—by a handful of men who hold enormous power, not only in this nation, but throughout the world" (*Modern People,* 1975a).

Several years later, the *Globe,* (1983a) reports that "he died because a Buddhist curse guided three independent assassination teams to Dallas on that fateful day, claim two top psychics and a veteran investigator." The curse was invoked in November, 1963, by a group of Buddhist monks who blamed Kennedy for the assassination of the president of Vietnam and his brother. The curse set in motion three forces opposing Kennedy—the Guardians, a clandestine group of international archconservatives; CIA elements who said he was a threat to national security; and the Mafia, whose feud with the Kennedys dated back to the 1920s. The *National Enquirer,* in a special issue commemorating the assassination (1983), throws a new group into the conspiracy. "Working with top experts on the assassination" (p. 30), it identifies the assassins as French terrorists who hated Kennedy because of his speeches supporting Algerian independence.

A mystical aspect is added to the conspiracy by the theme that Kennedy apparently knew he was doomed, but like Jesus and other heroes, "he calmly accepted that, and played the role fate had assigned him" (*Globe,* 1983a). Earlier, the *National Tattler,* (1973) had drawn parallels between the Kennedy assassination and that of Lincoln, claiming both Presidents had premonitions of doom. "He did it (went to Dallas) purposely to test God's power" (p. 17). In 1973 the *Tattler* reported that Kennedy "was aware of the whims of fate. It was almost as if he knew what lay ahead." In the same story, the *Tattler* gave extended treatment to an account by psychic Jeane Dixon of a vision of the future President she had experienced in 1952: "God had given down a prophecy. . . . He had ordained a tragedy that would bring the Eternal Flame to the hearts and minds of men. . . ." (p. 27). The narrative effect sought here, as throughout the tabloid treatment of Kennedy, is "resonance" Herrnstein Smith (1981, p. 225). The stories are intended to evoke in the reader a complex of responses and emotions associated with the cultural heritage of "doomed hero" conventions. The *Enquirer's* cover photograph for its 1983 special issue is clearly chosen for its resonant qualities, showing Kennedy kneeling, hands folded in prayer, eyes gazing heavenward. In the same issue, the Enquirer, following an established tabloid tradition, develops the mystique surrounding the assassination with "a long list of people associated with the J. F. K. slaying who have died mysteriously and often violently since then" (p. 35).

As a kind of subplot, the idea of a "Kennedy curse" developed soon after the death of Robert Kennedy in 1968. The *National Tattler* (1973) proclaims, "surely it could be nothing less than a curse—a classic, ancient, and demonic curse—that casts its shadow so darkly over the Kennedy family." In the same issue, it suggests that Edward Kennedy may be the one "who will hurl back the curse for ever" (p. 15). *Midnight* (1973) reports a prediction by astrologer Tassia Lutha that Jacqueline Kennedy will be the next victim, and the curse is still cited as a major factor in such tragedies as the death of David Kennedy (*National Enquirer*, 1984; *National Examiner*, 1984a; *Star*, 1984, pp. 16–17). A strange echo of the living Kennedy theme appears in a *National Examiner* (1984f) story that asks, "Was David Kennedy buried alive?".

A final main theme of the Kennedy story is JFK's prowess with women, an aspect that has grown to heroic proportions since his death. As Owen Jones writes, "A hero is a man whose deeds epitomize the masculine attributes most highly valued within a society," (1971, p. 341) and prowess with women is certainly one of these.

News of Kennedy's womanizing was suppressed by the media during his life (Gans, 1980, p. 484) and many mainstream media have continued to play it down, preferring to present Kennedy as a more sanitized hero. It appears that at least for several years after his death, even the tabloids preferred to present Kennedy as a virtuous husband and father, but more recently Kennedy's sexuality has become a major part of the legend. Even in more mainstream media this aspect of Kennedy's image has come more to the fore, in spite of the scruples of "responsible" writers (Hochschild 1984):

> We've heard all this before in the *National Enquirer* and elsewhere, but it says something about our culture that it can appear as well in a biography whose title declares it celebratory. This, then, is yet another of the roles Kennedy played: Don Juan. Accompanied by winks, it too has become part of the myth-verification that the hero of World War II and the Cuban missile crisis was, in the same macho terms, heroic in bed as well. (p. 56)

The development of tabloid treatment of Kennedy's reported liaison with Marilyn Monroe demonstrates the change in the treatment of his sexuality. *Midnight,* in a 1974 cover story, claims to reveal the contents of Kennedy's personal diary, in which he declares his love for Monroe. He is portrayed as a man torn between duty and the powers of a seductress: "He was a man who loved and adored his wife and loved his children, and yet he could not ignore Marilyn's beauty, that mysterious sensual look in her eyes. . . . It tortured him too with the thought that he should never have been unfaithful to Jackie in the first place, that he should never have succumbed to Marilyn's charms" (p. 17). Reporting that Kennedy "worked hard and loved passionately," the article appears to suggest that the affair, while wrong, was simply a symptom of his strong, noble character. After all, what red-blooded man could resist "the siren song of Marilyn Monroe?" (p. 17).

A little later, the *Star* (1976), reports on the "sizzling affair" between Kennedy and Judith Campbell Exner, describing him as "the world's most perfect lover—active, warm, considerate, and above all, tender" (p. 4). By this point, there is little mention of any guilt, and the pattern of Kennedy's apparently insatiable appetites is being established. By the 1980s, the tabloids had become tireless in their listing of the women Kennedy supposedly seduced, including Judy Garland, Veronica Lake, Angie Dickinson, and Gene Tierney. The various affairs described provide not only a vivid picture of the heroic male role ascribed to Kennedy but also of conventional images of female sexuality, from helpless innocent, through insatiable slut, to untouchable princess. Most of the affairs share a feature that raises Kennedy's prowess to a mystical level. By now, Kennedy is invariably the active partner; the women involved could not help themselves, but fell completely under his spell, while he remained always in control. They were conquests to him, but he was the love of their lives.

Thus, Veronica Lake "would have given up Hollywood in a flash for the chance to be his bride," while Gene Tierney "succumbed to J.F.K.'s charm and fell very much in love" (*Globe,* 1983a). Marielle Novotny was said to be an 18-year-old Soviet spy who was ordered to seduce Kennedy and obtain state secrets. "But the Russian scheme backfired when Novotny succumbed to J.F.K.'s charms and fell madly in love with him." According to her husband, "J.F.K. was her first and probably her only true love" (*Globe*, 1983a). Florinda Bolkan, a Brazilian actress, was said to be Kennedy's last lover. "He was handsome, young, rich, intelligent, and at the height of his power. He could have had any woman he wanted" (*Globe*, 1983). Bolkan is quoted: "We were so close in that short time before his death that I believe he has watched over me ever since. There was something strange, almost supernatural, in our meeting. . . . He was my first love, and my last."

By the 1980s, even Marilyn Monroe is no longer the siren, but merely a victim of her own lust. According to the *National Examiner*, Monroe had sexual relations with both John and Robert Kennedy, and was pregnant by Robert when she died (*National Examiner*, 1984b, 1984e). She was also used by the Soviet Union, who extracted "pillow talk" secrets from her through a spy who became her lover and eventually murdered her. She is protrayed as a woman who had numerous lovers, most of whom, like Kennedy, used her. She has become almost the mirror image of the heroic portrayal of Kennedy—a clear example of a double standard at work.

One woman, however, was apparently special—she who in the tabloids became a mythical princess comparable with Kennedy's prince, and who seems to represent the other side of Monroe's sad nymphomaniac. Both the *National Examiner* and the *Globe* report on the "secret romance" between JFK and Princess Grace of Monaco. Like others, "Grace fell almost immediately under the sway of the president" (*Globe*, 1983a). In recurring verbal formulas, Kennedy is compared with Prince Rainier: "Kennedy at the height of his power and glamor, was almost embarrassingly superior in every way to the paunchy Prince of a tiny country devoted to gambling and vacations." According to the *National Examiner*, "he was at the height of his power—the most powerful man in the world and one who had brought a message of hope and peace for all" (1983b).

According to the *Globe*, Kennedy traveled secretly to Nice to meet Grace seven times, although there was some question as to whether the relationship was sexual. The *National Examiner* is more specific: "Grace, of course, was too principled ever to launch into an affair with Kennedy, but who's to say if her heart was ever her own, or Rainier's, after this momentous meeting" (1983b). On Kennedy's part, "who could blame him if for an instant, it crossed his mind that she would have been the perfect wife to reign with him in Camelot" (1983b).

Kennedy's actual wife, Jacqueline, seems to have almost disappeared from recent tabloids, apart from occasional appearances in gossip roundups and as peripheral to stories about the other Kennedys. One rather odd exception is a story describing how JFK installed listening devices in his wife's brassieres so that he could hear her conversations with aides (National Examiner, 1984a). Kennedy's total control over women, including his own wife, seems to reach an absurd level in this account.

However, the image of Jacqueline Kennedy has not remained static, but went through several permutations before the tabloids decided to ignore her. These changes were directly related to, and effectively made necessary by the development of Kennedy's sexual image. Initially, she was the devoted, grieving widow, who would keep the Eternal Flame alive. Her marriage to Aristotle Onassis destroyed that image. While early stories (mentioned above) sought to explain the marriage as a cover for visits to her injured husband, several tabloids later engaged in vicious character assassination. In 1969, the National Tattler (1969a) accused Jacqueline of using "pep pills, energy shots and so-called speed treatments" while she was First Lady (p. 13). Later that year, the Tattler (1969b) claimed, "The true picture of Jacqueline Kennedy Onassis is beginning to emerge from the Camelot legend—like a slap in the face" (p. 24). Describing her as "selfish, demanding, materialistic and relatively unfeeling woman" (p. 24) the paper attributes this to the fact that she is "flat as a board," and "that, in itself, can have horrendous psychological effects on a woman" (p. 24) The National Tattler's coverage seemed to reflect readers' opinions, such as that of a letter writer from Indianapolis: "She never did like our country. She travelled outside it during her time as First Lady. She left our country for a rich Greek" (1970).

Taking up the theme, Midnight (1972) reports that in his diary, JFK wrote, "Jackie can be a real bitch," and that he had considered divorce. Later, Midnight (1975) called Jacqueline "the world's merriest widow," claiming that "the world is shocked at her behavior" (p. 2). The same year, the now-defunct National Insider (1975), in an article on JFK's love life, dismissed Jacqueline as a wronged wife, reporting that she held "nude parties with handsome bucks" while her husband was away (p. 3). The derisive tone of the accounts of Jacqueline's supposed excesses contrasts markedly with those of her husband's, in which JFK is described as "a hard-driving sex machine" (p. 11). White House secretaries "would tell me what they would give for only one night with that man" (p. 11).

It seems that once the picture of Kennedy as heroic lover began to become clearer it became necessary first to discredit his wife, justifying Kennedy's reported affairs, a task made easier by her unpopular marriage. Later, it became possible simply to ignore her.

IMPLICATIONS

From this summary of tabloid stories, we have a picture of Kennedy as a mythic hero, potent both politically and sexually. He can die only as a result of treachery and in the face of exceptional odds, and his charisma transcends death itself.

An important question that arises is whether the tabloid media create an image and then foist it upon their readership, as mass media effects research would tend to suggest, or, conversely, whether tabloids merely passively reflect the image of the world already held by their readers. The answer is, I believe, more complex than such simplistic models would suggest.

The image of Kennedy that emerges from the tabloids is not unique to them, but includes elements that appear both in oral tradition and in other mass media (see e.g., Epstein, 1975). In addition, specific stories about Kennedy are often resonant with association that goes beyond him as an individual. Rather than plucking the stories out of thin air, it appears that the tabloids pick up on their readers' (and others') existing ideas and beliefs, restating them in narrative form, performing much the same function as the teller of an urban legend. It is likely that some readers will then pass them on orally through conversation and gossip. This is not to say that reading a tabloid is identical with hearing an oral legend, but if with Herrnstein Smith we agree that narrative of all kings is a "social transaction" (1981, p. 228) involving frames of reference shared by teller and audience, we may see them as comparable processes.

Even more than newspapers, tabloids place much emphasis on reader response and involvement. The *National Enquirer* alone receives more than 1 million letters a year, and all the tabloids use letters to gauge audience interest. It seems unlikely that the tabloids themselves have to create a belief in reincarnation, psychics, and the like—only to rearticulate it. The readers then pass on these beliefs, probably not in the form of detailed urban legends, but in gossip and rumor. As Rosnow and Fine (1976) have pointed out, the media often act as brokers of such rumor, the audience and media existing in a symbiotic relationship.

Like traditional storytellers, journalists often work by taking general themes and structuring them into a coherent narrative, using established formulas. Like the purely oral storytellers described by Lord (1971) in his classic analysis of formulaic oral composition, journalists have to work quickly and efficiently, slotting new information into frameworks that are clearly understood by both teller and audience. These constructed narratives then fragment back into oral tradition, only to be restructured by another storyteller, in a continuing, cyclical process.

Lord notes the effect of themes that recur over and over in slightly different forms:

> This common stock of formulas gives the traditional songs a homogeneity which strikes the listener or reader as soon as he has heard or read more than one song, and creates the impression that all singers know all the same formulas.
>
> (Lord, 1971, p. 49)

News is often similar. Graber (1984) observes that "most stories are simply minor updates of previous news or new examples of old themes" (p. 61), while Rock (1981) comments: "The content may change, but the forms will be enduring. Much news is, in fact, ritual. It conveys an impression of endlessly repeated drama whose themes are familiar and well-understood" (p. 68).

Folkloric communication and mass communication are, therefore, not the entirely different processes that both folklorists and mass communications researchers have implied. Tabloid journalism is a particular type of highly stylized communication that tends to represent the world-view of certain parts of the population, a world-view that may rest on attribution to psychics and celebrities as well as to the more conventional "authorities." However, all journalism is the construction of reality, and as process it belongs on the same continuum with oral tradition. Journalism, particularly of the "human interest" kind, is by nature storytelling, a fact that has only recently been fully recognized in the communications literature. From this view, journalism is not merely the objective reporting of facts, but the construction of narratives that conform to the expectations of reader and writer (Barkin, 1984; Bird & Dardenne, 1988; Eason, 1981).

Cohen (1973) observed the interrelationship between oral and print communication when analyzing 19th-century ballad and newspaper stories of a murder, both of which "distorted facts to accommodate a shared pattern of storytelling" (p. 4). Her assumption was that "these formulae are shared also by large numbers of the reading and listening public who accept and preserve these narratives" (pp. 4–5).

Darnton (1975) argues that this relationship is also a contemporary one. Storytelling codes provide a technique that still guides the construction of many news stories, involving the "manipulation of standardized images, clichés, angles, slants, and scenarios, which will call forth a conventional response in the minds of editors and readers" (p. 189). Recalling his experience as a *New York Times* re-

porter, he describes the way journalists could obtain quotes for particular, standard stories:

> When I needed such quotes I used to make them up, as did some of
> the others . . . for we knew what the bereaved mother and the mourning
> father should have said, and possibly even heard them speak what was
> in our minds rather than in theirs. (p. 190)

This being said, it should also be stressed that writing or reading
newspapers is not the same as telling or listening to a story. The news
is obviously mediated not only through the journalist, but also
through the institutional stuctures of the newspaper and of society at
large. Thus Hall (1975), acknowledges the social transaction between
newspapers and readers, commenting, "successful communication
in this field depends to some degree on a process of mutual confir-
mation between those who produce and those who consume" (p. 22).
He cautions, however, that "at the same time, the producers hold a
powerful position *vis-à-vis* their audiences'. . . ." (p. 22) and thus will
tend to set the agenda. As Nord (1980) points out, formulaic popular
genres are a product not only (or primarily in his view) of mutually
understood frameworks. They are also a product of economic forces
that make formulaic potboilers easy and profitable to turn out.

Nevertheless, a purely economic view begs the question of where
the formulas came from in the first place, and the answer, reinforced
by the evidence of folklore and popular culture, is that they are not
imposed from above. Slater (1982) in one of the few specific studies
that compares media and folkloric communication, argues that media framings are in large part determined by an awareness on the
part of journalists of existing folk schemata. She quotes a writer of
the popular *literatura de cordel* in Brazil, which have some clear similarities to tabloids: "It does no good to write about a child who was
born with two heads if there is not already a rumor to the effect, if
people are not already talking about it in the streets" (p. 53).

Tabloid writers tend to write stories that pick up on tales and images of Kennedy that already exist, in turn helping to keep these alive
and circulating. Significantly, we may notice gradual changes in the
tabloid image of Kennedy over the years, changes that while refining
details, do not radically alter the basic thread of the legend. Similarly,
Brunvard (1986) notes that a defining characteristic of folklore is that
it exhibits both continuity in overall story and variation of individual
details as circumstances change.

Young (1981), while agreeing that both economic considerations
and maintenance of a dominant ideology are fundamental to the

functioning of modern mass media, argues that particularly those media that must sell to working-class audiences must to a great extent represent the culture of their audiences. As Carey (1975) writes, news may be seen not so much as information giving, but as ritual or play, as social values are defined and celebrated through the telling of stories that lay out cultural codes. Indeed, Bascom's (1954) functions of folklore (mentioned above) could just as accurately be applied to news. The power of media's "ideological effect" as discussed by Hall (1977) and others derives not from coercion and forcing audiences to consume a product they dislike, but from using familiar narrative structures to frame stories in ways that reinforce hegemony.

According to Cawelti's discussion of "artistic matrices," face-to-face oral transmission might belong to the "communal matrix," where "there is a lack of distance between its elements and the absence of mediating figures within the system" (1978, p. 296). Closely related to this is the "mythological matrix" which "resembles the communal model in that there is a high degree of identification between creator-performer and audience, and the genres are a communal possession rather than individual creations" (p. 298). Through this matrix, a culture's values and beliefs are dramatized in such media as news and other popular culture, but with the "mythmaker" retaining control over the product. A dialectical relationship exists between symbolic systems and society so that, as Geertz (1973) notes, these symbolic systems are both a model of and a model for society, both reflecting and re-presenting value systems. It is here that media such as tabloids are situated, as they pick up existing folk ideas, representing them as story, and helping to reinforce and reshape the folk world-view.

The folk world-view of tabloid readers is not always shared by the culture as a whole. In fact, tabloids may be an example of what Young (1981) calls "the accommodative culture" of the working class, a culture which, although accommodated within the dominant ideology, may be at odds with that ideology: "This is evident, for example, in the language of newspapers directed to the working class involving the distinctly non-bourgeois world of fate, luck, inequality and cynicism" (p. 41).

Tabloids emphasize the personal over the political, as well as the unexplained, the mystical, and conspiracy theories of government, which are all reflected in many aspects of the Kennedy myth. As such, they represent aspects of the folk world-view of their targeted audiences, just as mainstream newspapers, with their emphasis on official sources, scientific explanation and so on, represent the folk world-view of theirs (with a considerable overlap between the two, of course). Although much of the mystical view did permeate the "quality" press and other media, it dominated the tabloids, which dealt exclusively in his personality and charisma, responding to their primarily working-class readers (Perpich & Lehnert, 1984). We see clearly the "paradox of charisma," as Geertz (1983) has termed it. Although

> Charisma is rooted in the sense of being near to the heart of things . . . a sentiment that is felt most characteristically and continuously by those who in fact dominate social affairs . . . its most flamboyant expressions tend to appear among people at some distance from the center, indeed often enough at a rather enormous distance, who want to be closer. (pp. 143–144)

Through tabloids, readers may feel that they are indeed getting closer to "the heart of things." The tabloids are permeated with a feeling of distrust of government, an assumption that those who run the country are guilty of waste, mismanagement, and constant coverups, whether these are of UFO sightings, cars that will run without gas, or the Kennedy assassination. The appeal of Kennedy seems at least in part due to a perception of him as having been outside and above the establishment. That outsider status is reinforced by the proliferation of conspiracy theories that consistently link government agencies both to the assassination and the "coverup." Tabloids seem to offer their readers some answers, and perhaps some feeling of control and power. A *National Tattler* reader declared: "I have read several stories in Tattler about the no-fuel engine, the oil company rip-offs and the cover-up of the JFK assassination. . . . I am glad that someone is trying to inform the people about what is going on in this country. . . . Even the dumbest of us know that we are being duped by most of the big companies. And these companies are being assisted by the government. . . ." (*National Tattler* 1975b).

We can not assume from this analysis of tabloids that their millions of readers receive the bulk of their political information from the papers. As already mentioned, Kennedy is one of the few politicians even to appear in tabloids. However, this analysis of the Kennedy "legend" may be useful in showing some features of a view of the world that is rarely acknowledged—a view where personality, aura, and mysticism are more relevant than policies and other details. This world view is not confined to tabloids, but merely more visible in them. Graber (1984), in her study of political news processing, reported that the news most people remembered best was human interest stories that "served no work-life or civic-life purposes" (p. 86). Even in "straight" newspapers, Graber found that political coverage seemed to acknowledge reader's interest, stressing candidates' personal qualities over professional capabilities.

Of course, there is no neat cause-and-effect relationship such that only people who read "quality" papers hold "nonmystical" images of Kennedy, or that only tabloid readers have heard that Kennedy is alive. Most people are exposed to information from a myriad sources. The point is simply that in a world where mass media and oral transmission go hand-in-hand, people's perceptions derive from communication processes of all kinds. As Blaustein (undated) points out: "The folklorist is essentially a student of human communication. In contemporary American society, the folklorist must take account of the bewilderingly complex mesh of communication channels through which our culture is generated, transmitted and perpetuated" (p. 2).

Distinctions between communication channels and genres, important as they may be to folklorists and communication scholars, are not as relevant to the "folk" in constructing a particular view of the world. As Johnson (1983) writes, "texts are encountered promiscuously; they pour in on us from all directions in diverse, coexisting media, and differently-paced flows. In everyday life, textual materials are complex, multiple, overlapping, co-existent, juxta-posed, in a word, 'inter-textual'" (p. 41).

Journalism and folklore are not only related on the occasions when newspapers report an "urban legend" as fact. Media, particularly such media as tabloids, are not merely good sources of folklore. Rather, media and oral tradition are comparable, though not identical, communication processes, during which narratives are constructed from familiar themes that repeat themselves over time. People do not necessarily transmit folklore and attend to media in different ways and for different purposes—both are part of the complex way in which cultural "reality" is constructed. It is easy for students of political communication to assume that most people construct their political world-view primarily from the barrage of messages they receive from "mainstream" media. This study suggests that this world-view develops in more complex ways, and that some aspects of it have almost nothing to do with the view of reality constructed by, say, the *New York Times*. The "truth" about John F. Kennedy differs among people, but whatever that perceived truth or image might be, it is a dynamic one that is fed by many kinds of interdependent communication processes.

REFERENCES

Anonymous. (1964). *The illustrated story of John F. Kennedy, champion of freedom.* New York: Warden & Childs.

Baker, R. L. (1976). The influence of mass culture on modern legends. *Southern Folklore Quarterly, 40,* 367–376.

Barkin, S. M. (1984). The journalist as storyteller: An interdisciplary perspective. *American Journalism, 1*(2), 27–33.

Barrick, M. E. (1976). The migratory anecdote and the folk concept of fame. *Mid-South Folklore, 4,* 39–47.

Bascom, W. R. (1954). Four functions of folklore. *Journal of American Folklore, 67,* 333–349.

Bird, D. A. (1976). A theory for folklore in mass media: Traditional patterns in the mass media. *Southern Folklore Quarterly, 40,* 285–305.

Bird, S. E., & Dardenne, R. W. (1988). Myth, chronicle, and story: Exploring the narrative qualities of news. In J. W. Carey (Ed.), *Mass communication as culture: Myth and narrative in television and the press* (pp. 67–86). Newbury Park, CA: Sage.

Blaustein, R. (undated). *Horatio Alger is alive and well: The rags to riches syndrome and the reaffirmation of belief in the National Enquirer.* Unpublished manuscript, Indiana Folklore Archive.

Brunvand, J. H. (1981). *The vanishing hitchhiker.* New York: W. W. Norton.

Brunvand, J. H. (1986). *The study of American folklore.* New York: W. W. Norton.

Carey, J. (1975). A cultural approach to communication. *Communication, 2,* 1–22.

Cawelti, J. G. (1978). The concept of artistic matrices. *Communication Research, 5*(3), 283–305.

Cohen, A. (1973). Poor Pearl, Poor girl: The murdered girl stereotype in ballad and newspaper. *Publications of American Folklore Society Memoir Series, 58.* Austin, TX.

Darnton, R. (1975). Writing news and telling stories. *Daedalus, 104*(2), 175–194.

De Caro, F. A., & Oring, E. (1969). J. F. K. is alive: a modern legend. *Folklore Forum, 2*(2), 54–55.

Degh, L., & Vazsonyi, A. (1973). The dialectics of legend. *Indiana University Folklore Preprint Series, 1*(6).

Dickey, D. W. (1978). *The Kennedy corridos: A study of the ballads of a Mexican American hero.* University of Texas Center for Mexican American Studies. Austin, TX.

Eason, D. L. (1981). Telling stories and making sense. *Journal of Popular Culture, 15*(2), 125–129.

Edwards, O. D. (1984). Remembering the Kennedys. *Journal of American Studies, 18*(3), 405–423.

Epstein, E. J. (1975). History as fiction. In *Between fact and fiction: The problem of journalism.* New York: Vintage Books.

Gans, H. J. (1980). *Deciding what's news: A study of C.B.S. Evening*

News, N.B.C. Nightly News, Newsweek, and Time. New York: Vintage Books.

Geertz, C. (1973). *The interpretation of cultures.* New York: Basic Books.

Geertz, C. (1983). Centers, kings, and charisma: symbolics of power. In *Local knowledge: Further essays in interpretive anthropology.* New York: Basic Books.

Globe, The (1983a, November 29). Series of stories on John F. Kennedy, pp. 4–7.

Globe, The (1983b, December). I was J. F. K's last lover.

Graber, D. A. (1984). *Processing the news: How people tame the information tide.* New York: Longman.

Hall, S. (1975). Introduction. In A. C. H. Smith, *Paper voices: The popular press and social change 1935–1965.* London: Chatto & Windus.

Hall, S. (1977). Culture, the media and the ideological effect. In J. Curran, M. Gurevitch, & J. Woolacott (Eds.), *Mass communication and society* (pp. 315–348). London: Edward Arnold.

Herrnstein Smith, B. (1981). Narrative versions, narrative theories. In W. J. T Mitchell (Ed.), *On narrative* (pp. 209–232). Chicago: Chicago University Press.

Hobbs, S. (1978). The folktale as news. *Oral History, 6*(2), 74–86.

Hochschild, A. (1984, February/March). Would J. F. K. be a hero now? *Mother Jones,* 56–57.

Holden, L. (1979, July). The incredibly rich tabloid market. *Writer's Digest,* 19–22.

Johnson, R. (1983). *What is cultural studies anyway?* Birmingham University: Centre for Contemporary Cultural Studies General Series SP 74.

Kepplinger, H. M. (1979). Paradigm change in communication research. *Communication, 4*(2), 160–171.

Lord, A. B. (1971). *The singer of tales.* Cambridge, MA: Harvard University Press.

McDonald, D. M. (1984). *Supermarket tabloids.* Paper presented at 14th annual convention of the Popular Culture Association, Toronto.

Midnight. (1971a, August 30). JFK did not die in Dallas, pp. 10–12.

Midnight. (1971b, October 18). Photos show JFK alive on Skorpios, pp. 14–15.

Midnight. (1972, February 14). JFK's personal diary—and the intimate thoughts he revealed before he was shot, p. 16.

Midnight. (1973, December 3). Series of stories on Kennedy, pp. 3, 16.

Midnight. (1974, March 11). JFK's diary reveals truth about his love for Marilyn Monroe, p. 17.

Midnight. (1975, May 26). Jackie is world's merriest widow, p. 2.

Modern People. (1975a, June 29) CIA conspiracy, p. 10.

Modern People. (1975b, July 2). Oswald, Ruby and Sirhan all programmed.

Modern People. (1975c, August 3). Oswald was brainwashed.

Mullen, P. B. (1972). Modern legend and rumor theory. *Journal of the Folklore Institute, 9,* 95–109.

National Enquirer, The (1960a, January 15). Political Notebook, p. 15.

National Enquirer, The (1960b, April 3). Political Notebook, p. 10.

National Enquirer, The (1975, September 2). $100,000 offered for proof of conspiracy.

National Enquirer, The (1983, November 22). Special section on John F. Kennedy, pp. 30–35.

National Enquirer, The (1984, May 15). Special section on David Kennedy, pp. 30–35.

National Enquirer, The (1987, June 2). Donna Rice; What really happened, pp. 32–33.

National Examiner, The (1983a, July 26). J. F. K. is alive!, p. 23.

National Examiner, The (1983b, September 13). Grace and J. F. K.'s love secrets.

National Examiner, The (1984a, May 15). Kennedy curse: who's next?, p. 11.

National Examiner, The (1984b, July 3). Marilyn was pregnant with Kennedy baby, p. 1.

National Examiner, The (1984c, August 7). I lived before as J. F. K.

National Examiner, The (1984d, September 4). J. F. K. bugged Jackie's bra, p. 1.

National Examiner, The (1984e, October 23). Marilyn Monroe seduced J. F. K. and Bobby for reds, p. 35.

National Examiner, The (1984f, November 20). Was David Kennedy buried alive?, p. 27.

National Insider, The (1975, July 27). Jackie wasn't wronged wife, pp. 3, 10–11.

National Tattler, The (1969a, July 13). Jackie and drugs, p. 13.

National Tattler, The (1969b, November 16). Why ex-photographer Jackie dropped her peeping-tom ways, p. 24.

National Tattler, The (1970). Letters, p. 14.

National Tattler, The (1973, November 25). Special Section on Kennedy, pp. 13–15.

National Tattler, The (1975a, February 9). Correlation between Kennedy and Lincoln assassinations, p. 17.

National Tattler, The (1975b, June 1). Letters, p. 2.

National Tattler, The (1975c, September). Investigative special: Kennedy murder solved!,

Nord, D. P. (1980). An economic perspective on formula in popular culture. *Journal of American Culture, 3*, 17–31.

Owen Jones, M. (1971). (PC + CB) × SD (R + I + E) = Hero. *New York Folklore Quarterly, 27*, 243–260.

Perpich, M. J., & Lehnert, E. (1984). *An attitude segmentation study of supermarket tabloid readers.* Paper presented at 14th annual convention of the Popular Culture Association, Toronto.

Preston, M. J. (1975). A year of political jokes (June, 1973–June, 1974); or, the silent majority speaks out. *Western Folklore, 34*, 233–244.

Rock, P. (1981). News as eternal recurrence. In S. Cohen & J. Young (Eds.),

The manufacture of news: Social problems, deviance and the mass media (pp. 64–70). London: Constable.

Rodgers, R. S. (1985). *Popular legend and urban folklore as popular communication.* Paper presented in Popular Communication Interest Group, annual convention of International Communication Association, Honolulu.

Rosenberg, B. A. (1976). Kennedy in Camelot: The Arthurian legend in America. *Western Folklore, 25*(1), 52–59.

Rosnow, R. L., & Fine, G. A. (1976). *Rumor and gossip: The social psychology of hearsay.* New York: Elsevier.

Slater, C. (1982). The hairy leg strikes: The individual artist and the Brazilian literatura de cordel. *Journal of American Folklore, 95,* 51–89.

Star, The (1976, June 15) JFK's sizzling affair with Judith Exner, p. 4.

Star, The (1984, May 15). Guilt-ridden David Kennedy's anguish, pp. 16–17.

Sun, The (1984, July 3). Boy, 7, is reincarnation of J. F. K.

Young, J. (1981). Beyond the consensual paradigm: A critique of left functionalism in media theory. In S. Cohen & J. Young (Eds.), *The manufacture of news: Social problems, deviance and the mass media* (pp. 393–421). London: Constable.

Author Index

Subject Index